Delinquent Networks
Youth Co-offending in Stockholm

This book presents a study of co-offending relations among youths under twenty-one suspected of criminal offences in Stockholm during 1991–5. In total, the study includes just over 22,000 individuals suspected of around 29,000 offences.

Jerzy Sarnecki employs the method of network analysis which makes it possible to study the ties, social bonds, interactions, differential associations and connections that are central to many of the sociologically oriented theories on the aetiology of crime. Up to now, network analysis has been used only rarely in the criminological context.

The book discusses many aspects of Stockholm's delinquent networks such as the existence of delinquent gangs and a criminal underworld, the durability of delinquent relations, and the choice of co-offenders with respect to sex, age, residential location, ethnic background and earlier delinquent experience. It also considers the effects of societal intervention on criminal networks. This unique study will appeal to a wide audience.

JERZY SARNECKI is Professor and Head of Criminology at Stockholm University and has published widely on crime and delinquency. He is the author of *Byråkratins innersta väsen* (The Essence of Bureaucracy, 1985) and *Skolan och brottsligheten* (The School System and Crime, 1987) as well as many reports for the National Council for Crime Prevention Sweden. He also contributed to *Cross-National Research in Self-Reported Crime and Delinquency* (1989) edited by M. W. Klein, to *Crime and Criminology at the End of the Century* (1997) edited by E. Raska and J. Saarand and with H. von Hofer and H. Tham to *Minorities and Crime: Diversity and Similarity Across Europe and the United States* (1997) edited by I. Marshall.

Cambridge Studies in Criminology

Editors:
Alfred Blumstein, *Carnegie Mellon University*
David Farrington, *University of Cambridge*

This series publishes high quality research monographs of either theoretical or empirical emphasis in all areas of criminology, including measurements of offending, explanations of offending, police, courts, incapacitation, corrections, sentencing, deterrence, rehabilitation, and other related topics. It is intended to be both interdisciplinary and international in scope.

Also in the series:

Delinquent Networks
Youth Co-offending in Stockholm

Jerzy Sarnecki

Stockholm University, Department of Criminology

CAMBRIDGE
UNIVERSITY PRESS

PUBLISHED BY THE PRESS SYNDICATE OF THE UNIVERSITY OF CAMBRIDGE
The Pitt Building, Trumpington Street, Cambridge, United Kingdom

CAMBRIDGE UNIVERSITY PRESS
The Edinburgh Building, Cambridge CB2 2RU, UK
40 West 20th Street, New York, NY 10011–4211, USA
477 Williamstown Road, Port Melbourne, VIC 3207, Australia
Ruiz de Alarcón 13, 28014 Madrid, Spain
Dock House, The Waterfront, Cape Town 8001, South Africa

http://www.cambridge.org

First published 2001

Printed in the United Kingdom at the University Press, Cambridge

Typeface ITC New Baskerville 10/13 pt   *System* QuarkXPress™   [SE]

A catalogue record for this book is available from the British Library

Library of Congress Cataloguing in Publication data

Sarnecki, Jerzy, 1947–
    Delinquent networks: youth co-offending in Stockholm / by Jerzy Sarnecki.
        p.   cm. – (Cambridge studies in criminology)
    Includes bibliographical references and index.
    ISBN 0 521 80239 3
    1. Juvenile delinquents – Sweden – Stockholm.   2. Juvenile delinquents –
Social networks – Sweden – Stockholm.   I. Title.   II. Series.

HV9184.S86   S268   2001
364.36′09487′3 – dc21   00-068951

ISBN 0 521 80239 3 hardback

Contents

Figures

Tables

Acknowledgements

The research project upon which this book is based was financed by the Swedish Council for Research in the Humanities and Social Sciences (HSFR). Certain parts of the project were also financed with grants from the National Board of Institutional Care in Sweden (SiS) and the Crime Prevention Centre of the Local Authority in Stockholm.

The project has involved the collection of a considerable amount of data. This material has been used as the basis for a large number of smaller projects carried out under my supervision by both postgraduate and undergraduate students at the Criminology Department of Stockholm University. The results from these studies are presented in this book. In this connection, I would like to thank the following people: Tove Pettersson, who worked on those parts of the project which focus on football hooligans and the networks' ethnic composition; David Shannon, who wrote two dissertations on young people admitted to secure care facilities; Lotta Fondèn, who worked on a preliminary study associated with this project, based on register data from the Stockholm Police and interviews with people suspected of offences in Stockholm in 1990; Urzula Aksamit and Barbara Krzyzanoska, whose finals dissertation examined the recidivism of a group of young people suspected of offences in 1991 with a varying number of co-offenders; Ulrika Arnfors, whose finals dissertation examined geographical aspects of the choice of co-offenders; and Anna William-Olsson, who wrote a dissertation based on interviews with key informants from the police and social services and with young people about the 'Ängen gang', a group of youngsters on whom the media had focused a great deal of attention.

The enormous body of data, which forms the empirical basis for the project, was compiled by two colleagues at the Police Authority in the County of Stockholm, Peter Astalos and Ronny Widén.

I would also like to thank Professor James F. Short, Jr., Washington State University, Professor Malcolm W. Klein, University of Southern California, Professor David P. Farrington, Cambridge University, Professor Ove Frank, Stockholm University Sweden and my colleagues at the Department of Criminology at Stockholm University, Professor Henrik Tham, Dr Jonas Ring, Dr Felipe Estrada and Fil. Lic. Tove Pettersson for their valuable comments on this manuscript.

And thanks again to David Shannon, who translated the manuscript into English and made a number of valuable suggestions as to the content. As is always the case however, the responsibility for any errors of commission or omission lies squarely on the shoulders of the author.

Finally, I would like to say a warm thank-you to Jack Zilberstein who generously gave my family and me the use of his apartment on Australia's Gold Coast. It was in this apartment that the major part of this book was produced.

CHAPTER ONE

Social network analysis and criminology

1.1 Introduction

This study employs a network analytical approach to examine co-offending. The aim is to test whether a network perspective can provide new approaches and fresh insights into the character of juvenile crime in a metropolitan area.

The most fundamental difference between traditional social science and research which employs a network perspective is that network analysis stipulates the existence of observable relationships among the objects under study. Over the past few decades, social network analysis has become an increasingly common approach within the social sciences in general.[1] It is still employed only rarely in criminological studies,[2] however, despite the fact that clear parallels exist between a network perspective and many aspects of criminological thought.

Many of the classics of criminological literature contained formulations consistent with the use of a social network perspective long before this approach became popular within social science. Shaw and McKay (1942), for example, in their *Juvenile Delinquency and Urban Areas* state that 'delinquent boys in these areas have contact not only with other delinquents who are their contemporaries but also with older offenders, who in turn had contact with delinquents preceding them, and so on . . . This contact means that the traditions of delinquency can be and are transmitted down through successive generations of boys, in much the same way that language and other social forms are transmitted' (Shaw and McKay 1942: 174).

It is well established that juvenile crime is to a large extent a group phenomenon. Young people often commit offences with members of their peer group (see for example Breckinridge and Abbot 1917; Shaw and McKay 1931, 1942; Sveri 1960; Short and Strodtbeck 1965; Klein and Crawford 1967; Gold 1970; Hood and Sparks 1970; Elliott, Huizinga and Ageton 1985; Sarnecki 1986; Short 1998a; Reiss and Farrington 1991).[3] We know too that delinquent juveniles often have friends who have themselves committed several offences.[4]

In an 'everyday' sense, social ties among criminally active young people are seen as a means whereby the young people in question exert an influence over one another to commit offences. Many parents express concern about the possibility that their teenagers may fall into 'bad company', for example.

In the scientific community too, the group-related characteristics of juvenile crime are often seen in causal terms. This is particularly true of learning and neutralisation theories such as those presented by Sutherland, Akers and Matza (Sutherland 1939; Matza 1964; Sutherland, Cressey and Luckenbill 1992; Akers 1998).

At the same time, we might also claim that all those theories which associate crime with a working class, or perhaps a more generally lower-class culture, or with different forms of subculture (e.g. Cohen 1955; Miller 1958; Cloward and Ohlin 1960; Ferrell and Sanders 1995) as well as the research tradition that has grown up around the American 'gang' (e.g. Thrasher 1927; Short and Strodtbeck 1965; Klein 1971, 1995), all stipulate the existence of a mechanism which both facilitates the spread of norms and values conducive to the commission of crime, and enables individuals to exert influence over one another. Even though the representatives of these traditions do not usually discuss how the process might operate in practice,[5] research of this kind requires an assumption about the existence of such a mechanism. Cohen, for instance, writes: 'The crucial condition for the emergence of new cultural forms is the existence, in effective interaction with one another, of a number of actors with similar problems of adjustment' (Cohen 1955: 59).

The most widespread view of the effect on crime of friendships among young people however is that having criminally active friends is *one of several factors* which increase the likelihood that an individual will commit offences.[6] The view expressed by Loeber and Farrington in this regard seems to be fairly typical. In summing up the most reliable predictors of serious and violent offending in youths aged between 12 and 14, they mention a 'lack of strong social ties, antisocial peers, non-serious delinquent acts, poor school attitude and performance and psychological conditions such as impulsivity' (Loeber and Farrington 1998: xxii). Associating with antisocial peers is also mentioned as being among the strongest predictors of serious and violent offending among those aged between 6 and 11 years.

Like any other social activity then, delinquency can be explained, at least in part, with reference to the relationships an individual establishes with others. And it is just this quality that makes the network perspective so potentially useful in the analysis of crime.

The following section takes up the question of why studies focusing on relationships between delinquent juveniles may be more relevant in the context of modern society than they were in the past. Following on from this general discussion, the basic principles of social network analysis are briefly introduced, and the relevance of the network approach for a number of the classical criminological perspectives is explained.

1.2 Changes in the social significance of the juvenile peer group

As has been mentioned, the central axiom of network analysis, namely that the propensity to commit criminal offences is affected by an individual's social relations, is compatible with most of the central criminological perspectives specified above. The social relations that constitute the principal focus for the current study are those existing between young delinquents and their peers. It is my contention that relations among youths and their peers are of considerably greater significance in the context of modern society than they have been before and, this being the case, it is important that such relations become the focus of serious research.

There is much to suggest that the changes witnessed by western society during this last century have increased the peer group's influence on the behaviour of young people, at the expense of the influence previously exerted by adults (Sarnecki 1997). The reasons underlying this change are to be sought in the social changes common to late industrial societies, which have led to the exclusion of young people from the labour force and the prolongation of their stay in the education system.

The introduction of compulsory education was in the first instance intended to compensate a shortfall in control which young people were experiencing at the time as a result of their new position in society (Bauman, 1992). This process then continued with the vigorous expansion of both school education (which in most western countries today lasts for at least twelve years) and other institutions such as the social services, the police, organised leisure-time activities for young people and so on. At the same time, the control over young people exerted by the family, the work environment and the neighbourhood has become less important. The type of formal social control exercised by authorities, however, has not been able to compensate for the reduced levels of informal control which resulted from the transition to new forms of production, urbanisation and so forth.

During the 1960s and 1970s this process was on the whole regarded as a positive development, since it was seen to have freed youth from the oppression of patriarchal society. Today the negative aspects of the process are more often those that receive the attention of social commentators, not least the low level of social control to which young people are exposed, and their lack of integration into mainstream society (Sarnecki 1997).

Many criminologists (e.g.; Clarke and Cornish 1983; von Hofer 1985; von Hofer and Tham 2000) feel that during the twentieth century the economic developments witnessed by the western world have increased opportunities for crime and thus led to an increase in the crime level itself. Such changes in the criminal opportunity structure cannot by themselves explain why the delinquency of young people has increased more than that of other age groups in most western countries, however. In my opinion (Sarnecki 1997) the remarkable increase in the delinquency of young people[7] seen in the West is related not only to the increase in criminal opportunities but also to the way that the vertical ties linking youths and adults have been weakened, whilst the horizontal ties linking young people to their peers have become stronger. Two visible results of this process have been the reduction in the control of youth exercised by parents and the emergence of the many so called 'youth cultures' so characteristic of the second half of the twentieth century. Young people today, excluded from the labour force and lacking the firm control exercised over earlier generations by adult society, have considerably more opportunity to participate in youth cultures which are often oppositional in terms of the mainstream culture.

There is thus good reason to believe that the altered position of young people in modern society has meant that they have to some extent been able to free themselves from the control (and probably also from the oppression) of the adult establishment, and have at the same time been given much more space in which to establish and develop relations with members of their peer group. This situation is described in the following somewhat uncompromising terms by Dishion et al: '. . . we have become a society where many children are essentially raised by peers' (1995: 821).

This is probably one of the macro-level factors underlying the observed increase in delinquency among youths in a large part of the western world. Against this background, I believe that micro-level studies of the social ties between young people are of particular interest for criminologists.

1.3 Network analysis and criminological theory

1.3.1 The network perspective

Since the network perspective remains relatively unknown within criminology, what follows is a short presentation of some of the concepts basic to this field of enquiry.

Stated simply, social network analysis looks at relations between social units (individuals or organisations), the patterns displayed by such relations and also at their implications (Wasserman and Faust 1994: 6). One of the most important tasks of network analysis is to attempt to explain, at least in part, the behaviour of the elements in a network by studying specific properties of the relations between these elements. Elements (in the context of this study, individuals) which are found to be close to one another (physically or socially) and which interact are generally assumed to affect one another's behaviour. It should be stressed, however, that 'face-to-face' encounters are not essential for this inter-individual influence to work, nor is it necessary that the interactions are *intended* to exert such influence (Marsden and Friedkin 1994).

Theories and empirical studies in this field appear to have developed in parallel and to some degree independently of one another in several different areas within social science. According to Borell and Johansson (1996) and Wasserman and Faust (1994) two different approaches are to be found behind the origins of the network perspective: the social-psychological and the anthropological.[8]

Barnes (1954) is widely held to be the first to have used the concept 'social network', but the research tradition in this area stretches back a good deal further than this. The network approach was first used in social-psychological research around the 1920s and 1930s, when the first sociograms were drawn up (Moreno 1934). Sociograms were used primarily to study relationships between individuals in a group, often a class of school children. The sociograms made it possible to see which of the pupils enjoyed the greatest popularity in a class, for example, and which of them were completely lacking in social contacts.

Sociometric techniques have also been used on occasion in the field of criminology (by among others Yablonsky 1962, Short and Strodtback 1965, Klein and Crawford 1967, and Sarnecki 1986). Klein and Crawford, for example, used this method to study how often the members of a thirty-strong Los Angeles gang had contact with one another in the space of a six-month period.

With time, analyses of this type were allowed to evolve thanks to the introduction of directed graphs (Cartwright and Harary 1956). Sociometric analyses could now differentiate among types of relation and the direction in which the relations went. Relations can thus be either reciprocal, such as when two individuals commit an offence together, or one-way, such as when one individual victimises another without provocation.

The introduction of directed graphs paved the way for the use of network analysis in epidemiological research, looking at different stages in the spread of disease. And it was soon realised that this type of scientific tool could be used to study much more than just the spread of illness. The method was also suitable for the study of the diffusion of different types of ideas and social behaviours. Coleman, Katz and Menzel (1957, 1966), for example, used this method to examine how attitudes to the use of new medicines are spread among doctors.[9] They found that informal networks were decisive, especially to begin with while there still existed a great deal of uncertainty as to the new medication's usefulness.

The other social-psychological approach that contributed to the development of network analysis originated during the 1930s and 1940s primarily at Harvard University, where different aspects of 'informal relations' in large systems were being studied (Scott 1991: 16). Among the research produced by this tradition, we find the classic study of the Hawthorn Western Electric Company in Chicago (Roethlisberger and Dickson 1934), which pointed to the significance of patterns of informal organisation in a workplace. For Scott, this was the first study to use the sociogram to describe 'actual relations observed in real situations' (Scott 1991: 18).

The anthropological tradition of network analysis has its origins in a group of researchers working at Manchester University during the 1950s. One of the names emerging from this tradition is Barnes (1954), referred to above, who produced the first scientific definition of the network concept in connection with his field study of a fishing community on a Norwegian island. Barnes describes the small Norwegian village in terms of the relations among the people living there. Each of the inhabitants in the village had contacts with a number of other people, who in turn had contacts with still others. One of the study's important discoveries was that the social networks found in the village had no obvious organisation and no clear leadership structure.

Another anthropologist active within this tradition was Bott (1955), who examined families in metropolitan areas and their contact networks. Bott's results showed that 'external networks' affected relationships within the family.

Mitchell (1969) was an important figure in the evolution of the anthropological network analytical tradition. Mitchell saw society as an enormous network of interpersonal relations. He felt that research should be focused on the study of the partial networks that together make up the complete societal network. The choice of which of these partial networks to study could be based either on individuals, whose personal (ego-centred) networks could then be examined, or on networks which served special functions, such as the relations within the extended family, between business contacts, friendship ties or other similar examples. In the present study, both of these options are employed. In some instances, the personal networks of actively delinquent individuals are examined, whilst at other times the focus shifts to complete networks comprising all directly or indirectly connected co-offenders.

Mitchell also introduced a number of concepts that are now commonplace in network analytical studies, and some of these will be used here. He made a distinction between two types of network characteristic:

> *morphological* characteristics, which refer to the patterning of relations in the network, such as *anchorage*, the person or persons who constitute the centre of a network, *reachability*, the extent to which an individual can be contacted by others in the network either by direct links, for example, or via mediating others, *density*, the number of links that are actually present in a network compared to the maximum possible number of links if all network members were maximally connected to one another and *range*, the number of persons to whom a certain individual is linked.
>
> *interactional* characteristics which refer to the nature of the relations, such as the *content* of the interactions (e.g. family, friendship or co-offending), the *direction* of the interaction (one-way or reciprocal), *durability* (how long the relation lasts) *intensity* and *frequency*.

The anthropological tradition within network analysis has focused much of its attention on personal (ego-centred) networks. One study using this approach is that of Granovetter (1974) which examines the ways in which educated men from a suburb of Boston find themselves jobs. The study shows that information relating to job opportunities is gleaned not in the first instance through close relations such as those with family and close friends, but rather through the considerably weaker ties formed in the course of one's working life. Another classic study of personal networks focused on women looking to obtain an illegal abortion (Lee 1969). In this instance it was found that women found abortionists through contacts with female friends of the same age. In order to find subjects for the study, Lees used similar techniques to those employed by the women to find an abortionist.[10]

Over the last few decades, the use of network analysis has spread to many other areas. This diffusion has been made possible by, amongst other things, the development of statistical methods with special relevance for the treatment of network data (see for example Frank 1991; Frank and Nowicki 1993; Wasserman and Faust 1994).

One area where the network approach is widely used today is in the treatment of individuals with various kinds of social and psychological disturbances. Network therapy is now an established form of treatment employed by both social workers and psychiatrists (e.g. Svedhem (ed.) 1985, and Svedhem 1991).

The network perspective is today firmly established within sociological, anthropological and economic thought. In sociological research, for example, the concept of social mechanisms (Hedström and Swedberg 1998) builds to a large extent on such social phenomena as diffusion and other factors affecting collective behaviour. Even though criminological thought seldom takes account of group behaviour, criminological theory does contain a number of perspectives that can be said to employ a network approach to the analysis of crime. These theoretical perspectives, as mentioned above, see the causes of crime as partially or completely associated with the individual's ties to different types of social network. The following sections discuss the network analytical aspects of a number of the classic criminological theories.

1.3.2 Differential association

Of the classic criminological theories, Sutherland's theory of differential association (Sutherland 1939 and 1947; Sutherland, Cressey and Luckenbill 1992) is perhaps the one that is closest to modern network analytical thought.

As we know, Sutherland is of the opinion that criminality, just like other forms of behaviour, is learned during interaction with other individuals, principally within primary groups. The learning process applies not only to the techniques necessary for the commission of offences but also to such aspects of offending as motivation, attitudes to crime, values and also to ways of rationalising what has happened. According to Sutherland, 'A person becomes delinquent because of an excess of definitions favourable to violation of law over definitions unfavourable to violation of law' (Sutherland, Cressey and Luckenbill 1992: 89). These definitions are learned primarily in the course of contacts with other individuals. In western society (Sutherland refers to the situation in America) one always has relations both to individuals who feel that legal norms should be adhered to unconditionally and to individuals who feel that non-compliance with such norms is more acceptable. It is this variety of relational content that Sutherland refers to as differential association. He writes: 'Differential associations may vary in frequency, duration, priority and intensity' (Sutherland, Cressey and Luckenbill 1992: 89).

These characteristics of Sutherland's conceptualisation of differential association correspond well with the interactional characteristics ascribed to the links between network members by Mitchell (1969), who wrote that such links can vary in durability, intensity and frequency.

As I have argued, we can assume that in modern western society, it is principally the peer group, made up of friends of the same age (and slightly older), that contains models for deviant or delinquent behaviour in young people. Seen from this perspective, membership in a network of delinquent youths should thus be seen as having considerable significance for whether or not a young person begins and continues to commit criminal offences (Sarnecki 1986).

Sutherland also wrote of 'definitions favourable to the violation of law'. If an individual's perception of the law as something that can be broken is stronger than the same individual's perception of the law as something to be obeyed then, according to Sutherland, this will result in the commission of crime (Sutherland 1947). Sutherland never goes any deeper into the question of how the learning of criminal/conformist behaviour takes place. For this reason Burgess and Akers (1966) integrated Sutherland's theory from 1947 with 'modern learning theory' (Akers 1998). Akers describes in some detail the processes which lead to the reinforcement of pro- and anti-social behaviours at the individual level. In the matter of the conditions in which the learning of antisocial behaviour takes place, Akers too sees different types of primary groups, and not least groups consisting of peers, as the central factors.

> The reinforcement can be nonsocial (as in the direct physiological effects of drugs or in unconditioned reinforcers such as food). But the theory posits that the principal behavioural effects come from interaction in or under the influence of those groups with which one is in differential association and which control sources and patterns of reinforcement, provide normative definitions, and expose one to behavioural models. The most important of these are primary groups such as peer and friendship groups and the family, but they also include work, school, church, and other membership and reference groups. (Akers 1998: 63)

The approach to the learning of criminal/conformist behaviour formulated in the above quotation is fully compatible with the modern network perspective. It should nonetheless be emphasised that the model is applicable not only to delinquency but to all forms of behaviour, of which criminality is but one. Methods used to study interactions between individuals and their networks are thus on the whole the same, regardless of whether it is a question of examining how membership in a 'professional' network affects doctors' choices in relation to new medicines (Coleman, Katz and Menzel 1957) or how young people choose to commit certain types of offence or to use certain types of drug.

Finally, it is worth mentioning that the term 'differential association' is today used even outside the field of criminology. Morris (1994: 27) for example talks of differential associations in connection with his description of the epidemiological spread of contagious disease. He makes the point that the methods of network analysis are particularly suited to this area of study.

1.3.3 Subcultures

Discussions touching on the significance of social networks in the aetiology of criminal behaviour highlight the issues of deviant subcultures and delinquent gangs. Criminological theory contains two different models for explaining the formation of deviant subcultures and gangs. The first explains these phenomena as the result of social disorganisation, the other in terms of strain.

Shaw and McKay (1942) saw the causes of crime in the social disorganisation prevalent in those parts of metropolitan areas populated by the poor, who often came from ethnic minorities. In these neighbourhoods, the predominant societal culture exerts only a weak influence and inhabitants choose a deviant rather than a conventional lifestyle relatively often. Such choices of lifestyle are often collective in nature. Young people, antagonistically disposed towards societal norms, and even their own parents, can thus find support for deviant lifestyles among their contemporaries. This sometimes leads to the formation of gangs. In turn, gangs evolve a delinquent tradition of their own which is then passed on to new recruits. Once a gang tradition has been established, it will often continue irrespective of any changes taking place in the neighbourhood. The tradition is thus passed on from one generation of juveniles to the next, or from one ethnic minority to another, as new groups come to predominate when the older inhabitants move away (Einstadter and Henry 1995: 133).

Shaw and McKay (1942) suggest that in such areas, a tradition of delinquent behaviour can evolve to become an established norm. Youngsters growing up in the area see a number of the older youths making a success of their delinquent lifestyle and use these as role models for their own behaviour. Alternative models for success are unlikely to be available in such areas.

Shaw and McKay's view of how such deviant cultures are passed on was influenced by an earlier version of Sutherland's (1939) theory of differential association (see above). They write:

> Of particular importance is the child's intimate association with predatory gangs or other forms of delinquent and criminal organisation. Through his contacts with these groups and by virtue of his participation in their activities he learns the techniques of stealing, becomes involved in binding relationships with his companions in delinquency, and acquires the attitudes appropriate to his position as a member of such groups. (Shaw and McKay 1942: 436)

This quotation contains a description of deviant subculture and delinquent gang formation of a kind that is relatively rare in the criminological literature.[11] Youths living in the same part of town form contacts with one another and find in this new group a means of sheltering from the disorganised values of their surroundings. The interactions within such networks involve the transference of norms, values and forms of behaviour. It is not unusual for these interactions to involve co-offending both in terms of individual acts and as a lifestyle for the members in the network. Coleman *et al.* (1957) maintain that networks are of considerable importance for the forms taken by behaviour where there is uncertainty as to the norms which apply. This could be relevant for juveniles living in 'zones of transition' as Shaw and McKay describe the poor, immigrant neighbourhoods where this process of neighbourhood impoverishment coincides with the maintenance of thriving subcultures.

The other model explaining the emergence of deviant subcultures is rooted in Merton's (1938) strain theory. This perspective sees subcultures as emerging as a result of the strain experienced by young members of the underclass[12] when they realise that their chances of achieving the kind of goals recognised by mainstream society are very limited. Cohen (1955), for example, suggests that as a result of strain, youths from the underclass reject the middle-class values that are predominant in society and acquire instead a set of oppositional and delinquent norms and values. Of the four ways of dealing with strain described by Merton,[13] Cohen appears to be most interested in the last – rebellion. For him, delinquent subcultures arise in reaction to the strain experienced by underclass youth. Such youths react to their 'status frustration' by turning the middle-class values on their head and becoming violent and destructive.

Miller (1958), too, felt that the culture of the underclass was for the most part divorced from the predominant middle-class culture. For Miller, the underclass culture is characterised by delinquency, violence, the glorification of physical strength and masculinity, bravery, risk-taking, excitement and sensation-seeking, as well as freedom from authority and so forth. According to Miller, the reason youths from the underclass commit criminal offences is to be found in their socialisation in an underclass value system, in terms of which such acts do not involve a deviation from norms. For Miller, this underclass culture is not limited to youth, but rather includes the whole of the underclass, even if it is among the young that it manifests itself most.

Cloward and Ohlin (1960) write of the 'conflict gang'. Unlike Cohen's gangs, however, the young people described by Cloward and Ohlin seem to be much more aware of the causes underlying their situation and are therefore much more purposeful in their struggles with the unjust societal structure which denies them the developmental opportunities they need. For Cloward and Ohlin, underclass youths react in a spirit of anger toward a society which so limits their chances of achieving established goals.

Agnew (1985), who revised Merton's strain theory, ascribes anger and frustration a central role in the causation of crime: 'Rather then being rationally directed, however, this anger is more the outbursts of youth frustrated by the constraints of a wide range of painful constraining situations from which they may wish to escape but are only able to *with peer support* through delinquent behaviour' (quoted in Einstadter and Henry 1995: 165, emphasis added).

In my opinion, this 'peer support' is the central factor in the context of transmission of delinquency. Strain may well have different effects depending on whether an individual is tied into a network comprising others in the same situation, has contacts of a different kind, or is socially isolated. It is likely that the 'rebellious' response described by Merton is much more probable if the anger resulting from social injustices can find a collective expression, with the individual finding support in a group of like-minded, contemporary peers. A more isolated individual might perhaps tend to choose other strategies to cope with strain, such as 'retreatism' for example. In addition, the individual's way of coping with strain may also be affected by the behavioural models that are available in his or her network. This last point is one which can be examined, at least in part, within the framework of the current project.

1.3.4 Neutralisation

The conception of a separate underclass culture has come in for a fair amount of criticism.[14] Sykes and Matza (1957) produced evidence suggesting that delinquent youths in fact embrace established, conventional norms to a considerable degree. They write that 'there is a good deal of evidence suggesting that many delinquents *do* experience a sense of guilt or shame . . .' (p. 665).

Sykes and Matza's argument is based on Sutherland's perspective, seeing delinquency as a behaviour that is learned in the course of a process of interaction. They write: 'Unfortunately, the specific content of what is learned – as opposed to the process by which it is learned – has received relatively little attention in either theory or research. Perhaps the single strongest school of thought on the nature of this content has centred on the idea of a delinquent subculture' (Sykes and Matza 1957: 664).

For Sykes and Matza, techniques which neutralise the effect of the existing system of norms are an important aspect of what youths learn in the course of their associations with models for deviant behaviour (or as one might put it today, in the context of their social networks). Thus young people learn ways in which delinquent acts and other breaches of the prevailing norm system, a norm system which they otherwise embrace, can be justified. Here too Sykes and Matza align themselves with Sutherland by seeing these neutralisation processes as central to what Sutherland calls 'definitions favourable to violation of law'. According to Sykes and Matza, then, an individual becomes deviant by learning techniques of neutralisation and not by learning attitudes, values and norms which contradict those of the prevailing mainstream culture.

Matza further develops his view of neutralisation as a mechanism central to the development of delinquency in his *Delinquency and Drift* (1964). Here he introduces the concept of 'drift', which we can see as a half-way house between the positivist, determinist view of delinquency as a result of pre-existing conditions and the classical 'rational choice' view of crime as the result of an individual's choosing between alternative ways of acting in a given situation. According to Matza, the young delinquent drifting towards crime is neither completely free to make his own choices nor entirely constrained by circumstances: 'Drift stands midway between freedom and control. Its basis is an area of the social structure in which control has been loosened, coupled with the abortiveness of adolescent endeavor to organize an autonomous subculture, and thus an independent source of control, around illegal action' (Matza 1964: 28).

The intimated dissolution of the bonds of social control tying the individual to mainstream society may well take place within groups of peers. Matza refers in this regard to a collective misunderstanding, which involves the mistaken belief that one's friends are accepting of a great deal more delinquency, substance abuse and so forth than they actually are. Matza's point is that it is youths with weak bonds to others who run the highest risk of being affected by this misunderstanding. He adds, however, that the desire for acceptance and status within the group (network) will limit the degree of honesty with which even those with a high degree of group involvement can discuss the acceptability or unacceptability of different types of behaviour (p. 56).

The desire to be accepted within the group usually weakens as the juveniles become older, but there are those, primarily men, who according to Matza are unable to establish a position for themselves in the labour market and who fail to establish relations with women of the same age. These individuals thus remain dependent on their contacts in the gang. These young adults maintain contact with the group which from Matza's point of view is 'Obviously . . . quite functional in the transmission of the subculture' (p. 56). At the same time, however, older youths cannot continue to associate with considerably younger juveniles indefinitely. This is seen by the young adults as humiliating in the context of their efforts to attain the status of 'grown men'.

1.3.5 Gangs

Descriptions of a specific type of criminal network, namely the gang, are widespread in the criminological literature. Thanks to comprehensive gang research, we know a considerable amount about the influence that active members of delinquent gangs have on one another. It should nonetheless be emphasised that gangs are not the only, and are not even the most common, form of crime-generative juvenile peer group (Klein and Crawford 1967; Morash 1983). Even if the definition of what constitutes a gang varies somewhat in the literature, it is quite obvious that the majority of group-related offences committed even in the metropolitan areas of North America are not carried out by gangs (Klein 1995, Short 1998b). In this context it might be useful to present the distinction made by Knox (1991) between gang-related crime and other group-related crime. The difference according to Knox is that the delinquency of gang members (often) takes place as a result of gang membership and is accepted and encouraged by the gang. This is not the case with offences committed by members in other forms of delinquent group (Knox 1991: 6). It should be noted, of course, that gang members also commit offences that are unrelated to their gang membership.

As I have already indicated, in spite (or perhaps because) of the comprehensive gang literature, academics active in this area have been unable to agree on a common definition of the gang concept (Thrasher 1927; Empey and Stafford 1991; Huff 1991, 1996; Klein 1995; Decker and Van Winkle 1996; Short 1996; Klein *et al.* 2001).

In a comment on Klein's (1995: 102–3) statement that variations in police definitions of gangs are confusing, Short writes:

> Unfortunately, definitions used by researchers are only slightly less so. It is no wonder that many who study youth collectivities do not use the term, choosing instead to study 'co-offending' (Reiss, 1986; Reiss and Farrington, 1991), 'bands of teenagers congregating on street corners' (Skogan, 1990), 'cliques' (Sullivan, 1989), 'unsupervised peer groups' (Sampson and Groves, 1989), 'peer groups' (McLeod, 1987), 'reference groups' (Sherif and Sherif, 1964), 'networks' of juveniles who violate the law (Sarnecki, 1986), or simply 'delinquent groups' (Warr, 1996). (Short 1998b: 15)

Some writers even suggest that a common definition will never be agreed and that its absence may well be productive for gang research. Horowitz (1991) writes: 'Agreement will likely never be achieved, and definitions often obscure problematic areas and may not encourage the development of new questions . . .' (p. 38).

Short and Horowitz thus contend both that there is a great deal of confusion surrounding the gang concept and that ironing out this confusion might in fact prove counter-productive. A review of the literature on American gangs nonetheless provides us with a number of elements which seem to crop up in the vast majority of definitions of the gang. Curry and Decker (1998) suggest that the following elements can be found in most of such definitions:

Gangs are groups of individuals.
Gangs have some form of symbol indicating gang membership (special items of clothing, tattoos, hand signals etc).
A specific form of communication[15] (which may be verbal or non-verbal – such as special words, hand signals or graffiti).
Durability (at least a year).
Territory (turf) which the gang defends. (This may be the area where the gang started its life, where most of the members live, or where members sell drugs, for example.)
Delinquency. (Gangs are deeply involved in criminal activity and see this as a feature of membership in the gang: pp. 2–6.)

Curry and Decker point out that it is sometimes easier to define who is a member of a gang than to define what a gang consists in: 'The most powerful measure of gang membership is self nomination. By this we mean that simply asking individuals whether or not they belong to a gang –

"claiming" in gang talk – is the best means of identifying who is a gang member' (p. 6).

Despite the lack of a generally accepted definition of the gang concept, a review of the modern American literature in this area (Hagedorn and Macon 1988; Sanchez-Jankowski 1991; Huff 1991, 1996; Knox 1991; Moore 1991; Padilla 1992; Klein 1995; Decker and Van Winkle 1996) gives the impression that the majority of gang researchers would agree on most of the points included by Curry and Decker in the description cited above of characteristics typical of gangs. The differences in the descriptions of gangs that can nonetheless be found in the work of these authors have mainly to do with the degree of organisation and the significance of drugs, primarily of drug sales, for the life of the gang. Certain of the gangs described in the literature (e.g. the 'Diamonds' studied by Padilla (1992), and the forty or so gangs from New York, Boston and Los Angeles studied by Sanchez-Janowski (1991), as well as some of the gangs in Huff's anthology, such as the Chinese gangs described by Ko-Lin Chin (1991)) seem to be more well-organised than others and to assign different roles to members on a much more rigid basis. This is probably a consequence of such gangs being more strictly focused on a certain type of crime (most often involving the distribution of drugs, but other forms of crime such as protection rackets, for example, are also found) and this focus demands a more rigid form of organisation.[16]

Over the last few years it has been pointed out that gangs are in no way a uniform phenomenon. Klein is of the opinion that there is a clear difference between what he calls 'street gangs' and prison or drug gangs, for example. For Klein, the concept of the 'juvenile, youth or delinquent gang' that was previously in common usage is no longer relevant, since gangs increasingly include individuals of twenty years of age or older (1995: 21). His *The American Street Gang. Its Nature, Prevalence and Control* excludes such delinquent groups as skinheads and motorcycle gangs from its analyses, a factor which Klein motivates in the following way: 'Street gangs seem aimless; skinheads and bikers are focused, always planning. Street gangs' members get into any and every kind of trouble. It's cafeteria-style crime – a little of this, a touch of that, two attempts at something else' (p. 22).

When Klein defines the characteristics which make a group classifiable as a street gang, he writes of:

> young people, who may range in age from 10 to 30 or occasionally older, whose cohesion is fostered in large part by their acceptance of or even commitment to delinquent or criminal involvement. They are principally but not exclusively male, principally but not exclusively minority in ethnicity or race, normally but not necessarily territorial, and highly versatile in their criminal offences. These

offences are not predominantly violent, but they are disproportionately violent when compared with the activities of other youth groups or individual persons . . . (p.75)

Klein's characterisation of street gangs is strikingly similar to the descriptions of gangs to be found in Thrasher's classic work on this phenomenon, *The Gang* (1927).[17] Even then, Thrasher saw the relationship between the emergence of gangs and the conditions in which young people, not unusually from ethnic minorities, are forced to live in a metropolitan area. For Thrasher the boys look for membership in this kind of group in order to experience 'the thrill and zest of participation in common interest, more especially in corporate action, in hunting, capture, conflict, flight and escape. Conflict with other gangs and the world about them furnishes the occasion for many of their exciting group activities' (p. 37).

Thrasher suggests that gangs grow out of spontaneously formed groups of young people when the bonds linking the members of the group to one another become strengthened as a result of conflict. This process consists of three stages. During the first stage, the group's boundaries are diffuse and its leadership unclear. Such gangs often survive for only a short time. Some gangs continue to evolve to the next stage, however, where membership boundaries and the leadership structure become more defined. This tends to be the result when the group is jointly subjected to some kind of threat. If, during the period which follows, the group members do not make the transition to a normal adult life as part of conventional society, the bonds between them can become further strengthened and the group's activity and the whole of its existence become focused on delinquency.

As with many later 'gang researchers', Thrasher felt that even though gang members commit many different kinds of offence, violent crimes play a central role in the life of the gang. This violence, both that which is directed at members of other groups, and that which members of other groups direct at the gang, works as a unifying factor and increases solidarity within the group. For Thrasher, however, gangs have no homogeneous structure but instead contain subgroups of members.

During the 1960s a number of studies were carried out in connection with ongoing crime-prevention programmes aimed at juvenile gang members (Short and Strodtbeck 1965; Spergel 1966; Klein 1971). In theoretical terms, these studies were on the whole underpinned by the subculture theories mentioned earlier in this chapter, that is, Cohen (1955), Cloward and Ohlin (1960) and Miller (1958). These studies give us the chance to better understand the group processes which take place in a gang and which lead to the gang culture being passed on. They can also give us some insight into the processes which lead to the correlation between underclass culture and resultant delinquent behaviour. Short and Strodtbeck, for example, focus on 'hypotheses relating to mechanisms by which norms and values associated with structural variation become translated into behaviours' (1965: 269).

These writers see the behaviour of criminally active gang members as a result of attempts to adapt to the conditions in which they live. For Short and Strodtbeck, participation in a delinquent peer group provides a feeling of belonging that to some degree compensates for all the failures these individuals have experienced 'in every strata of society and at every age' (Short and Strodtbeck 1965: 271). In turn, such failures result from the inability of the youngsters' parents, and of others in their social networks, to equip them with the social competence necessary to achieve any degree of success in conventional society. Seeking to compensate this shortfall by means of membership in a gang, however, often has devastating consequences. Membership in a group whose culture is predominantly that of the underclass and often also of ethnic minorities leads to a further worsening of social competence. In addition, membership in a gang where conflict with others is an important element (giving an individual status) means that these individuals are exposed to the risk of physical injury or even death as a result of violence.

In their study of gangs in Chicago, Short and Strodtbeck find that relations within these gangs are often short-lived and unstable. They suggest that this is due to the unstable conditions in which the gang members live, their lives being characterised by unemployment or by brief periods of employment, a lack of stability in family life, and unstable housing conditions.

Vulnerable youths thus look to gangs to satisfy a number of needs such as a need for shelter, identity, excitement, a sense of belonging, and status. The trouble is that gangs seldom satisfy these needs. Instead of finding shelter, gang members become even more exposed and vulnerable; instead of excitement, they find themselves spending day after day on a street corner. Groups are often very loosely formed, so the need for a sense of belonging is left unsatisfied, and within the group the individual often finds his social status being threatened (Short 1990).

It is clear that the youths who look to become gang members want to be part of a cohesive group. The fomentation of conflicts with other gangs and the frequent resort to violence are means of increasing group solidarity. According to a number of researchers (e.g. Klein 1995) cohesiveness is important both for a gang's durability and for its criminal activity. As was mentioned earlier, however, the level of cohesiveness shown by such delinquent groups seems to vary and remains a matter for debate.

Yablonsky (1962) lists a number of characteristics often ascribed to gangs by social workers and others. Among these are: an ascertainable number of members; the members are identifiable, that members have specified roles, that members agree on the rules of the gang, that there is clear leadership and so on. Yablonsky maintains that these characteristics are often missing from actively delinquent groups of young people. In his own work, he therefore chooses instead to speak of 'near groups'. If social workers (or detached workers) expect to find these characteristics in the gang, then this will contribute to increasing the gang's cohesiveness which may mean that such characteristics arise or are strengthened as a result of the workers' interest. Being seen by others as a unified group will have an effect on a group's cohesiveness. The perceptions of social workers, the police and the local press on such matters can easily become self-fulfilling prophecies (Klein 1995, cf. Merton 1968).

Klein (1995) states that the number of street gangs in the USA has increased dramatically over the last few decades. Gangs are no longer a purely metropolitan phenomenon. Klein sees the causes of this increase in the expansion of the urban underclass. He refers to Wilson (1987) who in his *The Truly Disadvantaged* argues that over the last few decades poor neighbourhoods in American cities have become further impoverished. This impoverishment is understood in part as a result of the reduction in the availability of unqualified industrial work, which provided the ghetto population's primary source of income. The simultaneous increase in service sector jobs has only partly eased the situation, since young men from the ghetto often lack the necessary qualifications (i.e. social competence) for such positions, which are often also extremely poorly paid.

In addition to the problem of unemployment, the poor metropolitan neighbourhoods have been further impoverished as a result of the way in which better-educated members of the minority groups that populate these areas (chiefly blacks and Latin-Americans) are now able to move away to middle-class neighbourhoods which were previously populated more or less exclusively by whites. As the middle class moves away, many institutions such as active churches, youth clubs, day-care centres etc., all of which are vital to the social life of the neighbourhood, also disappear. The school system also deteriorates (Wilson 1987).

Such a deterioration in the living conditions of people who reside in neighbourhoods that are increasingly ethnically segregated, correspondingly increases the pressure on family life, which in turn also suffers.

Relationships break down more easily if men are no longer able to provide for their families. The dissolution of social structure resulting from unemployment, broken families and the lack of social institutions means that the level of supervision of children becomes poor. This breakdown in social control paves the way for the formation of alternative bonds: to the gangs, for example.

It is not clear whether the gang phenomenon as described above is a purely American phenomenon or if it might also exist in metropolitan areas in Europe. Klein (1995) suggests that there is evidence for the existence of street gangs in at least some of the large European cities. He claims too that delinquent groups with at least some of the characteristics described above are also to be found in Sweden (p. 223). The question of whether this perception is verifiable on the basis of the network analyses carried out in Stockholm will be discussed later in this book.

Irrespective of whether street gangs of the American kind are to be found in Sweden or not, the individual and macro-level mechanisms which underpin the phenomenon are not in any crucial way unique to this one form of group-related juvenile crime. American gangs can be seen as a more cohesive form of the delinquent networks which I described in my study of delinquency in Borlänge (Sarnecki 1986, 1990a). Klein seems to share this opinion in the references to my study made in his own work (Klein 1995: 223).

1.3.6 Social bonding theory

A review of theories which explain delinquency either wholly or in part on the basis of relations between individuals would be incomplete if it did not refer to Hirschi's social-bonding theory (1969). This theory too is quite compatible with a network perspective. Hirschi's central idea is that the individual's propensity to commit offences is limited by the *bonds* linking him or her to conventional society. Hirschi introduces four elements constitutive of such bonds: attachment, commitment, involvement and belief. Of these, we might contend that attachment is the most important. Attachment refers to the ties linking an individual to parents and friends, and also to various institutions such as schools and societies.

According to Hirschi, however, the social bonds or, if you prefer, the links, which exist between an individual and his environment do not have a criminogenic effect but rather promote conformity. The stronger the social bonds, the less freedom an individual has to commit offences. For Hirschi, this relationship holds even for attachments to the peer group. In his *Causes of Delinquency* (1969), he notes the existence of relationships between juvenile offenders and delinquent peers, but he finds no way of dealing with this observation within the framework of his influential theory.[18]

A number of proponents of Hirschi's theory, however, have made the point that given the existence of a strong relationship between the delinquency of a certain individual and that of his or her peers, certain aspects of learning theory ought to be incorporated into control theory to explain this bond (Krohn and Massey 1980: 536; Box 1983: 178; Le Blanc and Caplan 1993: 287).

The causal process outlined by the authors mentioned above, once they have incorporated elements of learning theory into control theory, begins with family problems and a bad relationship between the child in question and parents and other adults at school. This in turn increases the likelihood that the child will *establish links with actively delinquent friends*. The establishment of such ties then affect the child's own delinquent activity (see also Johnson 1979: 61; Ring 1999).

It has also been noted that the relationship between the delinquent activity of peers and that of the individual seems to be particularly marked amongst highly delinquent individuals (Elliott, Huizinga and Ageton 1985: 38; Thornberry *et al.* 1991: 9).

The principal hypothesis in the current study thus corresponds with the view held by Hirschi's critics of the influence of the peer group on the individual. My own expectation (Sarnecki 1986) is that the existence of delinquent relations around an actor will influence that actor to higher levels of delinquency.

Hirschi contends further that relations between antisocial individuals are weaker than those between pro-social individuals. This contention will also be examined in the present study. Weak ties between individuals do not necessarily mean weak influence, however. In line with the network research described above (Granovetter 1974) even weak bonds can have an important impact on an individual's behaviour.

In a more general sense, Hirschi's social bonding theory is to be counted among those criminological theories whose tenets are consistent with the network perspective. A Hirschi-inspired network analysis would not in the first instance examine ties between delinquent peers, however. It would instead focus on ties to representatives of mainstream society, as do the majority of studies based on the network therapy approach.

1.3.7 Co-offending

One aspect of the group character of juvenile delinquency (and probably the most visible and easiest to research) is joint participation in crime, or co-offending. Reiss (1986, 1988), Reiss and Farrington (1991) and Warr (1996) suggest that relatively little research has focused on this phenomenon. Nor is co-offending taken into account in theories that aim to explain the aetiology of delinquency. Reiss and Farrington write that: 'With a few exceptions, causal theories do not take into account the fact that co-offending is an integral aspect of much criminal activity' (Farrington and Reiss 1991: 393).

At the same time, the fact that young people often commit offences in the company of peers has long been understood within the field of criminology. Shaw and McKay (1931) analysed material from the Cook County juvenile court in Chicago from the year 1928 and found that 82 per cent of the offences dealt with by the court in the course of the year were linked to two or more perpetrators.[19] As part of the study, Shaw and McKay also present a detailed description of the criminal career of one Sidney Blotzman, a boy whom they consider typical of the juvenile offenders brought before the court in question.

Sidney, who came from a poor family burdened with social problems, was first arrested for petty theft as an 8-year-old. His last crimes as recorded by Shaw and McKay were armed robbery and rape, committed at age 17.[20] In total, Sidney was registered in connection with thirteen crimes of which eleven were committed together with co-offenders. Shaw and McKay write that during this time, Sidney was involved in three different groups of young offenders, consisting of boys from the neighbourhoods where he lived. These groups were fairly large but in connection with the offences for which Sidney was registered, he never had more than three co-offenders. He thus committed offences with just a few members of the group at a time.

Shaw and McKay maintain that the character of Sidney's offences at different stages of his criminal career corresponded to the type of offences committed by others in the groups of which he was a member at these various points in time. When he committed the final, and most serious, offences he was part of a group that comprised some of the most dangerous criminals then to be found in Chicago.

In their description of the criminal offences committed by Sidney together with his (often somewhat older) co-offenders, Shaw and McKay identify a mechanism whereby proficiency in the commission of different types of offence is passed on from older to younger members in the criminally active group (Shaw and McKay 1931: 213). In other words, they identify what is clearly a learning process taking place in the group of juvenile delinquents.

A factor of central criminological concern in the matter of co-offending is the extent to which an individual's criminal activity is affected by his or her co-offenders. Two quite different scenarios are conceivable here. In one, the actors make rational choices about who they will choose to co-offend, on the basis of which people they feel they need to have with them in order successfully to commit a certain type of offence. (In an instance of this kind, a person's experience of a certain type of offence, technical proficiency, contact network, or personal characteristics may be decisive.) In the other scenario, it is in the nature of delinquency that it is influenced by the people with whom an individual happens to be at the time.

In the first scenario, delinquency is affected, at least to some degree, by whether or not an individual is able to find suitable co-offenders. Tremblay (1993), another who figures among those criminologists with an interest in co-offending, formulates this in the following way: 'In a variety of situations, the probability that a given violation will occur will partly depend on motivated offenders' ability to find "suitable" co-offenders' (Tremblay 1993: 17).

Tremblay reviews some of the co-offending literature to provide the basis for a discussion of whether the search for suitable co-offenders should be included 'as a distinct or additional component of the basic function specified by the routine activities theory provided by Cohen and Felson (1979)' (Tremblay 1993: 17). He concludes that it should be. At the same time he realises that this would involve the integration into routine activity theory of a number of other social scientific perspectives. Tremblay writes:

> A comprehensive understanding of the various suitability criteria that regulate the search for co-offenders and specific social conditions and settings that facilitate or inhibit the likelihood that such suitable co-offenders can be found may also provide the empirical basis upon which one could perhaps integrate, within an overall rational choice perspective, the routine activity crime opportunity theory, social network research, and Sutherland's cultural transmission tradition. (Tremblay 1993: 34)

The second scenario, wherein an individual's participation in crime in general, and in certain types of crime in particular, is influenced by the people the individual happens to be with at the time, involves seeing offending as unplanned and regarding the impulse to offend as arising spontaneously in the interactions of a group of individuals. The type of offence committed is thus not seen as predetermined by the composition of the group in question, but the offence is nonetheless, at least to some degree, the result of the group's composition and of the interaction among its members. This type of sequence of events seems to be more common among young people, and in connection with expressive crimes. My own studies in Borlänge (Sarnecki 1986) show that a significant proportion of the offences committed by juveniles were of precisely this character.

Irrespective of whether one chooses to work on the basis of one of the above-described extreme scenarios, or instead to see the commission of criminal offences and the choice of co-offenders as a process which contains elements from both models, it seems clear that co-offenders play an important role both in the matter of whether an offence is committed and for the character of the criminal activity engaged in.

Another question that has become topical in this context has to do with the extent to which older and more experienced delinquent youths recruit younger persons to participate in delinquent activities. There is support for such a possibility in a number of the empirical studies that focus on co-offending. Reiss and Farrington (1991) for example found that among the most criminally active individuals in the group of London youths they were studying, there were 'recruiters' who systematically committed offences with younger and less experienced co-offenders. In my own study of delinquent networks in Borlänge (Sarnecki 1986) I also found obvious signs of the networks' importance for the recruitment of new members.

On the basis of existing research, it is not always easy to stipulate just how contacts with other delinquents affect an individual's own delinquency. Reiss (1988) points out that researchers disagree as to the degree to which group membership is seen to influence an individual to begin committing offences. Among others, he cites West (1977) who asserts that it is unnecessary for a thief to belong to a group of thieves, for example, in order to learn how to steal. This kind of knowledge is readily available to more or less all young people.[21] Reiss, however, claims that access to a network of individuals with experience of more advanced criminality is necessary if an individual is to evolve into a professional thief.

His general approach to the significance of research on co-offending is that 'Understanding co-offending is central to understanding the aetiology of crime and effects of intervention strategies' (Reiss 1988: 117). He also writes that 'The use of network information may substantially increase the capacity to select high-rate offenders who account for the offending of others' (Reiss 1988: 150).

Reiss concludes his review of the present level of knowledge on co-offending (which for him is still rather deficient) by encouraging criminologists to look at offending from a network analytical perspective more frequently than they have done up to now. He writes: 'The artificial divorce of cohort from a changing environment and its reduction to a population of individuals unrelated in time and space restrict considerably what can be learned about individual (criminal) careers' (Reiss 1988: 166).

Short (1998b) expresses a similar view in his 1997 presidential address to the American Society of Criminology where he writes of the need for criminological research at the 'micro-level' and for criminologists to devote more attention to the contexts in which crimes occur. He remarks further on the failings of research which ignores the issue of the 'delinquency-producing process' (1998b: 17) and 'the interactional level' (p. 10).

1.4 Delinquent networks in Borlänge

The Borlänge study (Sarnecki 1982, 1983b, 1986, 1990) was the first criminological study to use network analytical methods to examine registered co-offending among crime suspects. This study covered all those juveniles suspected of offences in the Borlänge police district[22] during the period from 1975 to 1977 (575 individuals). These young people were then followed up in two stages, first in 1978–80 and then again in 1981–4. Individuals suspected of co-offending with these young people were also included in the follow-up.

Perhaps the most important result from the study consists in the fact that 45 per cent of all youths suspected of offences in Borlänge at some stage during the six-year study period could be linked together in a single large network. The members of this network accounted for the vast majority of all the offences for which juveniles were suspected in Borlänge.

In this large network it was possible to differentiate a number of groups (clusters) of youths in which the delinquent relations were significantly stronger than in the network as a whole. These groups showed some degree of continuity, presenting in similar constellations during several periods. In contrast, the rest of the youths suspected of offences in the town, to the extent that they appeared repeatedly, did so in continually new constellations of co-offenders.

The members of the three more long-lasting groups had committed more offences than the average for youths in the network as a whole. Generally speaking, it is true to say that the more central the position taken by an individual in the delinquent network, the higher the number of offences committed by that individual.

A smaller study was carried out to check the validity of the register data. A group of youths (twenty-nine individuals) included in the register study were interviewed about their relations with contemporary peers. Both the interview data and the register data were analysed using network analytical methods. A comparison between the results of the network analysis of the police data relating to the interviewees' co-offenders, and the information provided by the interviewees themselves regarding their friendships during the period in question, showed a high degree of correspondence. The youths included in the study seem often to have committed offences with the people they considered to be their best friends.

The results from the period 1980–4 show that a similar number of young people each year became known to the police in connection with offences, as was the case during each of the years from 1975 to 1979. The youths from these two periods had also committed roughly the same number of offences. When the members of the networks[23] formed during the later period were identified, it was found that many of the more criminally active of these had also been present in the more cohesive groups that were examined in the earlier period. Younger members of the networks identified during the earlier period had now become the most criminally active members of the new networks.

The conclusion drawn from these results, as has been mentioned above, was that network membership is significant for the youths' introduction to offending, and is especially significant for their continued offending. Once networks have become established in a geographical area, delinquency continues as new generations of juveniles become linked into the already existing structures. These new juveniles slowly 'advance' within the networks, taking over the more central positions from the older individuals who gradually leave the group. In their turn, the new central figures become responsible for the introduction of new generations of network members.

In this respect, results from the Borlänge study coincide with findings from American research examining how new gangs become established and how gangs, once they are established, continue their activities with a steady stream of new members (Klein 1995). At the same time, it is important to emphasise the fact that the networks (some of which are referred to in the study as 'gangs') examined in Borlänge seem to be somewhat less cohesive than many of their North American counterparts. The results from the interviews indicated that the youths questioned had no conception of themselves as belonging to a 'gang', a factor ranking among the most important signs that the phenomenon being studied is in fact a gang (see above).

1.5 Summary and conclusions

The review of literature contained in this chapter shows that most of the more influential theories on the causes of crime assume the exertion of some kind of influence among different actors. These influences are variously referred to as differential associations, social bonds, ties, interactions, learning, the transmission of cultures, subcultures or neutralisations, and so forth. All of these concepts have something in common in that they are difficult to study using traditional, quantitative social-scientific methodologies. Modern network analysis, such as is being employed increasingly frequently within the social sciences, constitutes an important breakthrough in this context.

Many of the theories presuppose the existence of some form of learning process which takes place among the members of the social networks in question. Sutherland's theory of differential association is based on the idea that individuals associate with one another and that the learning of both conformist and deviant behaviour takes place in the context of these associations. The associations with other individuals described by Sutherland are in practical terms nothing other than that which the terminology of network analysis refers to as 'ties'. Contacts with other delinquent individuals also play a central role in Matza's drift theory. And similarly, both strain and subculture theories assume that delinquent individuals are tied to one another socially and that different cultural elements are passed on in the networks of such individuals.

Hirschi's perspective is somewhat different. He does not see delinquent behaviour as learned, but rather suggests that certain individuals are freer to commit crimes by virtue of the fact that their bonds to established society are weak. But what do these social bonds consist in? Attachment at least involves ties to various people (primarily parents) and other societal institutions. What Hirschi does not include in his theory are the crime-generative influences which can be produced by bonds to contemporary peers, if those peers are themselves delinquent. On this point, however, control theory lacks empirical support, and a number of researchers feel that the theory needs supplementing with elements of social-learning theories. Hirschi contends further that the social attachment felt by young people with adjustment problems is often weak. Network-oriented research shows however that even weak ties can have an important impact on an individual's behaviour.

Making use of the network approach in the study of crime, and especially in the study of juvenile crime, is thus compatible with several different theoretical perspectives within criminology which are themselves based on a rather varied group of assumptions about the character of society and human nature and which are therefore often seen as incompatible. This means that the network-orientated researcher does not have to assume a definitive position in relation to these assumptions about the nature of man and society, and can content him or herself with the very general assumption that people influence one another's behaviour and that this influence is exerted by virtue of the fact that actors are tied in to different types of social network. As has been indicated above, I am of the opinion that the societal changes witnessed during this last century have led to a considerable increase in the peer group's significance for today's young people, as compared with their counterparts in earlier times. This constitutes the starting-point for the empirical component in this book.

Empirical research into how group processes affect juvenile delinquency has had the North American gangs as its primary focus. Even if the majority of crime in the USA is not committed by gangs, gang research has contributed with insights which in certain respects are also applicable to other groups. Studies with a more general focus on co-offending have been quite rare, although several writers have made the point that research into this kind of, as Short (1998b) put it, 'micro-level process' is needed in order to improve our understanding of the mechanisms which underlie juvenile crime. Research employing a network approach to study delinquency has been rarer still.

CHAPTER TWO

The aims and method of the study

2.1 The aims of the study

In the previous chapter, I have attempted to show that the network perspective is closely tied to criminological theory, even if it is seldom used in empirical criminological studies. What is interesting is that the network approach, in a methodological sense at least, is compatible with a number of different and often conflicting perspectives within criminological theory. The conclusion reached at the end of my (necessarily brief) discussion is that a study of juvenile offending in a metropolitan area which employs network methods may well contribute with new insights into this form of criminality. The network analyses employed in this study build primarily on the concept of co-offending.

The intention here is to use network methodology to examine the structure of co-offending and the formation of juvenile crime networks in a metropolitan area. The hope is that our understanding of juvenile crime will be improved when we examine not only the criminally active individuals themselves but also the relationships that exist among them.

In this context there is no reason to hide the fact that the organisation of the study is in large part governed by the possibilities and limitations associated with the need to gain access to relevant data.

2.1.1 Issues to be examined
The study will look at the following specific questions:

> What do the co-offending networks formed by youths in Stockholm look like? (A central network as was the case in Borlänge? A number of central groups? A more splintered structure?)

How stable are relations between co-offenders and how durable are the delinquent networks?

How do youths in Stockholm choose their co-offenders on the basis of sex, age, place of residence, offence type, and levels of criminal experience?

In which positions in the networks do we find the most experienced juvenile criminals, and where are youths with other serious social problems to be found?

How do societal interventions (such as placements in secure care facilities) affect the networks?

What kind of relationships are there between the types of social problem experienced by youths and the types of network they belong to?

What forms are taken by delinquent networks comprised of individuals who commit special kinds of group-related crime (football hooligans and extremist right- and left-wing groups)?

What role does ethnic background play in the choice of co-offenders and victims?

Does network analysis provide any support for the assertion that street gangs of the kind found in the USA are also to be found in Stockholm?

2.2 Method

The group character of juvenile crime is, as has been mentioned, something criminologists have long been aware of. The empirical study of this phenomenon is difficult, however. Warr writes: 'Group properties of delinquency are among the most difficult features of delinquency to measure or appraise. Ethnographic studies of delinquent groups face special difficulties in identifying and tracking group members, and survey research on groups requires true sociometric designs, where respondents report not only their own behaviour, but that of other group members as well. Such data are rare in sociology and even more so in criminology' (1996: 19).

Further difficulties can be added to those mentioned by Warr in the above quotation. Ethnographic studies of juvenile groups must of necessity be restricted to one group or a few, often fairly small, groups. This inevitably leads to problems of representativeness. There is nothing to say that the individuals studied are representative of the group, or that the groups studied are representative of other groups in the same area. Survey studies[1] are faced with the further problem that information is not forthcoming on reciprocal relations. Another problem is that one only collects data relating to the ego-centred network, and thus cannot study the indirect ties linking an individual to others. Data relating to the larger networks, including the indirect ties, are often important in network analysis. The information collected in surveys often relates only to how one of the parties to a relation feels about it. In the present study, these problems are avoided by using data from the police register.

The majority of the data for the study come from the centralised and computerised crime-reporting system operated by the Stockholm police (known by its abbreviation RAR). Data from other sources are also used, however, such data having primarily been generated in a number of other studies carried out in Stockholm at the same time as this one. Some of these studies were begun in collaboration with the network study, whilst others were independent of it, at least to begin with. These sources of data will be introduced in the parts of the text where the data they provided is referred to.

2.2.1 The elements of analysis

The empirical material on which a network analysis is based consists of two elements: objects, commonly referred to as *actors* (such as people or organisations or other social groupings) and relations among these objects. A relation may consist in the transference of material resources, or in business transactions, joint participation in social activities, psychological relationships, family ties, the spread of information, influence exerted to affect an attitude, or anything similar. A *link* exists between two actors when they interact with one another on a specific relation. Links may be symmetrical if the relations between A and B and between B and A are of the same character, or asymmetrical if these relations differ from one another[2] (Wasserman and Faust 1997).

For the purposes of the present study, the actors (in most cases at least[3]) are individuals suspected of offences by the police. Links are created by actors having jointly participated in criminal acts. Strictly speaking a crime is a legally defined act carried out by an actor. Such an act often creates a relation between the actor in question and others, however. These relations may take several different forms: relations between perpetrator and victim, relations between representatives of the justice system and perpetrators/victims, relations between co-offenders and so on. The primary focus of this study, as has been discussed at some length, will be relations between co-offenders.[4]

A *social network* comprises a limited number of actors and the relations among these actors (Wasserman and Faust 1997: 20). The networks studied here comprise various subgroups of the population of individuals aged twenty years or less who were registered by the police as suspects in the commission of offences in the city of Stockholm during the years from 1991 to 1995, their co-offenders, and the offences of which they are suspected.

The boundaries of the networks in this study are primarily time-based. The longer the time-frame covered by a specific analysis, the larger the networks examined. In certain contexts a six-month period is used (fig. 5.4), and in these cases the data are divided into ten such periods each covering either January to June or July to December of the year in question. These six-month periods are referred to in the text as spring 1991, autumn 1991, spring 1992, and so on. In other contexts a one-year period is used (figs. 5.1 and 5.2) but in most cases the analysis covers the whole of the study period, that is, the five years from 1991 to 1995 inclusive (see figs. 5.3, 7.1, 7.2, 8.1, 8.2, 10.1).

Within any specified time-frame, network size is limited by the fact that all the networks studied are examples of connected components. In the present context this means that an isolated actor with no links to others in a network is not considered a part of that network. Simply because two individuals are part of the same network does not in itself imply that they have committed offences together, however. They may well be connected indirectly via any number of intervening actors. A network is thus made up of all those actors who, within a specified time-frame, are linked to one another either directly or indirectly, together with all the links connecting these actors.

Thus in this study the network concept is used slightly differently from the way it is employed in research based strictly on graph theory. Each group of individuals who are linked together by known relationships (in most cases co-offending relations) are here conceptualised as *separate* networks. In graph theory such groups are referred to as connected components. The decision was taken not to employ the latter term here in an effort to make the text more accessible to the reader schooled primarily in criminology.

A computer program, *The Link Notebook. User's Guide* (1995) which translates information on the relationships between actors into graphic representations of these relationships, was employed to produce the networks for analysis.

The smallest networks consist of two actors connected by a link which signifies that they have co-offended on one or more occasions. The largest networks are comprised of a few thousand individuals.

In those cases where actors are not members of a network, that is, they have no known co-offenders; they will be referred to as *isolates*. It is important to note that an individual referred to as an isolate in the context of an analysis covering a specific period may well turn out to be linked into a network of co-offenders if the time-frame is extended, since it is quite possible that the individual in question will have committed offences with co-offenders at some other point during the five years of the study period.

The study begins from the assumption that in most cases co-offending involves actors exerting influence over one another. The influence of actors on one another within a criminal network can be either *direct* if the individuals are suspected of one or more joint offences, or *indirect* if the actors are linked into the same network but with no known direct contacts between them. Individuals in a network can thus influence one another even in the absence of direct contact between them (Marsden and Friedkin 1994: 4). The intensity of this indirect influence decreases as the *distance* and *reachability*[5] between two actors within a network (measured as the number of links separating them from one another and the number of alternative routes they can take to reach one another) increases.

Data referring to various characteristics of individuals are called *attribute data* in network analysis. A significant part of the analyses in this study are based on the examination of attribute data. In the process of such analyses, traditional statistical methods are employed, with tables and diagrams and in certain circumstances a measurement of central tendency and correlation/association.

2.2.2 Interpreting the results

It is important when working with police data to bear in mind that only a fraction of the actual amount of criminal activity is examined. In terms of the present study this means that where the data show two individuals linked together in the joint commission of a single offence, it may well be the case that these individuals have also co-offended 'invisibly' on several other occasions. Furthermore, the real networks of criminal relationships in Stockholm are very likely to be significantly larger and more dense (they are made up of more actors and contain more links per actor) than those presented here. It must be borne in mind that:

Actors whom these results show to be members of the same network are in reality probably involved in considerably more co-offending than is shown here.

Actors and networks that the data show to be unconnected may very well be linked to one another.

There are undoubtedly criminally active individuals not covered by the data that have co-offended with the young people included in this study.

Although individuals who are not linked in the data may in fact have co-offended, it seems reasonable to assume that the likelihood of two individuals having co-offended is higher if these individuals are indirectly connected (through membership of the same network) than if this is not the case. This is especially true for those individuals who lie relatively close to one another in a network.

Indirect connections between actors are thus interesting in two respects. They may involve the exertion of an indirect or mediated influence between actors, but at the same time they are indicative of an increased likelihood that the conditions necessary for the exertion of direct influence exist.

The extent to which the pattern of criminal ties present in the data can be deemed representative of ties not captured in the police register is largely dependent on the degree to which crimes cleared by the police constitute a random (representative) sample of the total number of crimes committed. If cleared crimes can be treated as a random sample of all crime, then the interpretation of results is rather less problematical than would otherwise be the case.

We can safely reject the possibility that the actors in our study represent a random sample of all criminally active youths in Stockholm and their co-offenders. There is good reason to assume, for example, that offences committed jointly by several individuals are cleared more often than those committed by individuals in isolation (Hindelang 1976: 122; Reiss 1988: 124 and 161). We must also take into account the fact that clear-up rates vary between different categories of offence and that having once been suspected of a crime the likelihood of again becoming a suspect is increased. Police practises, such as focusing attention on certain known delinquent individuals or groups, intensified policing of certain parts of the city and the like, also have an impact in this connection. At the same time it is safe to assume that the vast majority of Stockholm's most criminally active young people will have found their way into our data.

Notwithstanding the reservations mentioned above, the following discussion will assume that the picture of juvenile crime presented in the data is sufficiently representative of the unseen portion of crime as to allow for a certain amount of generalisation from our conclusions. We further assume that the process whereby suspects are registered by the police is not subject to substantial systematic errors and that the vast majority of those registered as suspects in the commission of offences have in fact committed these offences.[6]

In addition, when interpreting the results, we must bear in mind that the relationships between young co-offenders in reality involve a great deal more than simply the joint commission of criminal offences. Klein (1995), for example, makes the point that even the most criminally active street gangs

in the metropolitan areas of North America spend only a very minor proportion of their time in the planning and execution of criminal acts. Much more
time is spent simply 'hanging around' in one another's company doing
nothing in particular. On the basis of the initial results from the Borlänge
study (Sarnecki 1983b), I asserted that juvenile crime is to a large extent a
way of spending time in the company of friends of the same age. Committing
criminal offences is far from being the only possible pastime available to such
groups of friends, however, even if those friends are active criminals. If we
pay too much attention to the criminal ties linking delinquent youths, we
miss a large segment of the social networks of which these individuals are a
part (not least, to paraphrase Sutherland (1939), the contacts with models
of conformist behaviour). At the same time, the results from Borlänge show
that the most criminally active youths often commit offences with their best
friends and that the constitution of these individuals' circle of friends to a
large extent coincides with their circle of co-offenders.

2.3 Summary

This study constitutes an attempt to examine juvenile crime in a metropolitan area on the basis of a network perspective and with the help of network
methods. The study is of an exploratory nature, analysing a number of different aspects of co-offending and the networks that are formed when
youths are linked to one another on the basis of the suspicion that they have
committed offences together.

The study employs a number of concepts drawn from network analysis.
The most important are *actor*, which here refers to a suspected offender,
links, which arise when actors are suspected of the joint commission of
offences, and *networks*, which are formed as actors are linked to one another
on the basis of their co-offending. The size of networks is strongly affected
by the time period covered by a specific analysis, the longer the period, the
greater the probability that more actors will be linked to one another in a
network. Actors who at one stage appear only to commit offences by themselves can appear as part of a network if the period of analysis is extended.
Networks which appear as separate when viewed over a short period of time
can show themselves to be joined to one another with one or more links or
common actors as the time period is extended.

Studying the group characteristics of delinquency is difficult and
requires a special kind of data. Data on reported offences taken from the
police register make possible studies of this kind which do not have to limit
themselves to a few small groups of delinquent youths (as do ethnographic

studies) or to information from the one party in a reciprocal relation (survey studies).

Studying delinquency on the basis of register data does involve certain problems of its own. The information we have at our disposal in this study relates to only a small proportion of the total number of offences committed by the actors included in the study. Even if it is likely that we will have data relating to a large majority of the most delinquent individuals in Stockholm, we will be without data relating to many of the less actively delinquent actors who have committed offences but avoided discovery. In terms of the network analyses carried out here, this means that the number of links among the individuals included in the study will in reality have been significantly higher than the number shown in the data collected here, and also that the networks studied will in reality have been significantly larger and denser than those shown by our data. A good many indirect links among individuals will in reality have been direct, whilst the direct links will have been stronger (involving more offences) than is shown in our data.

Another problem presented by the data used in this study is that some (though probably only a little) of the information collected by the police will be wrong (the person suspected of the offence being in fact innocent). This means that our data will contain links which do not exist in reality. This problem is somewhat less serious than that relating to the fact that the majority of crimes are never cleared, however.

The fundamental assumption made in this study is that individuals who are linked to one another will exert a variety of forms of influence over one another. This influence may be direct, if the actors have taken part in the same offences, or indirect if they belong to the same network without being suspected in connection with the same offences. Their influence over one another is assumed to diminish with increases in their distance from one another within the network. As regards actors who lie close to one another in a network, it is more likely that these actors are in reality linked to one another but that the offences linking them together have not been cleared by the police.

The study is on the whole limited to links based on co-offending. There are however a number of other kinds of relation linking the actors examined here, and also linking these actors to other individuals, which may be of considerable importance for the actors' delinquency but which cannot be examined within the framework of the present study.

CHAPTER THREE

Actors and links

3.1 The data

The study includes all those individuals of age twenty or less who were suspected of one or more offences in the city of Stockholm during the years 1991 through 1995, and who were registered as such by the police; their co-offenders are also included, irrespective of age. The data drawn from the police register for this study include:

the personal identity numbers,[1] gender, age and postcode of the suspects
the date and kind of offences of which they are suspected
the personal identity number, gender, age and postcode of the co-offenders
the gender, age and postcode of the victims
a brief description of the offences in question

As was mentioned earlier, data from a number of other studies are also employed in the project and will be presented in more detail as and when they become relevant.

3.2 The actors

In total the study includes 22,091 individuals. Of these, 19,617 are persons of age 20 or younger who were suspected of offences in Stockholm during the study period. This group will be referred to as the study's principal population. The remaining 2,474 individuals (11 per cent of the total) were 21 years of age or older when they appeared in the data for the first time. They are included in the study because they were suspected of committing

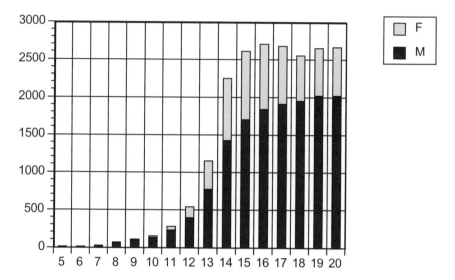

3.1 Distributions of gender and age in the principal population at the time of their first appearance as crime suspects between 1991 and 1995

offences jointly with individuals of 20 years of age or less. These older co-offenders have a median age of 26 years.

3.2.1 Age and gender

Of the 19,617 individuals included in the principal population, the youngest was 5 years old when he first became a suspect,[2] the oldest was 20 years old.[3] See figure 3.1.

It is interesting to note from figure 3.1 that the number of suspects in different age cohorts is relatively stable from one cohort to another for those cohorts aged between 15 and 20 years. It should also be noted that figure 3.1 is based on data relating to individuals and not data relating to offences. Some of the youths included in the study were suspected of more than one offence (see p. 41). If we instead examine the age distribution for the offenders from the principle population connected with each of the 33,896 offence participations[4] included in the study, however, the result is the same.

Females constitute around one-quarter of the suspects, although this proportion varies somewhat among different age groups. The proportion is largest among 14-year-olds (36 per cent). Girls account for 21 per cent of the youngest suspects, aged 11 or under, and 24 per cent of the 19- to 20-year-olds. The proportion of women found among the adult co-offenders is even lower (17 per cent).

3.2.2 The urban districts

A fairly large proportion of the postcode information from the police regis-ter is missing. We have postcodes for 14,336 individuals in total, which means that this data is missing for 35 per cent of the study population.[5]

The data that are available suggest that the majority of those included in the principle population (56 per cent) live in the city of Stockholm. Thirty-eight per cent are registered as living in other municipalities in the county of Stockholm, whilst only 7 per cent are registered as living outside the county.[6] In the majority of cases, then, young people suspected of offences in Stockholm come either from the city of Stockholm itself or from the neighbouring communities.

The pattern is more or less identical for the adult co-offenders (aged 21 or over). Fifty-seven per cent are registered as living in the city of Stockholm, 34 per cent in the county of Stockholm and 9 per cent elsewhere.

3.3 The links

In this study, the ties linking individuals together in the context of a crime are of two types. The first of these links individuals who commit offences jointly, the second links together a perpetrator with a victim. The study looks primarily at the first of these two types of link.

Crime is a complex concept, and its description will be approached here from a number of angles. I will be looking at delinquency both as a charac-teristic of the links which bind the individuals in the study together, for example, and as an attribute of the individuals themselves. When we reckon the number of crimes committed by an individual, the count corresponds to that described in the official statistics as 'offence participations'.

3.3.1 Offences and offence participations

The 22,091 actors included in the study were together suspected in connec-tion with 29,209 offences during the period from 1991 to 1995. If we instead sum the number of times the actors became 'suspects' we arrive at a total of 36,941 offence participations.[7] The number of offences will always be lower than the number of offence participations, since several actors can partici-pate in one and the same offence.

For the remainder of this study I will for the most part be describing delin-quency in terms of offence participations. One advantage with this approach is that it provides data at the level of the individual which can then be presented as an attribute of the actors studied. This form of presentation also provides a more correct picture of the significance of co-offending for

Table 3.1: *Offence participations among youths suspected of offences in Stockholm 1991–1995 and their suspected co-offenders, by offence category; per cent*

Offence category	%
Assault, attempted murder, murder	13.7
Sex offences	0.3
Mugging	2.9
Other crimes against the person	6.7
Shoplifting	23.4
Other thefts including burglary	18.2
Criminal damage	9.9
Other crimes against property	8.3
Crimes against police officers/public servants	7.0
Drug offences	3.4
Other offences	6,2
Total	100
N	36,941

the delinquency levels exhibited by the youths in this kind of study (Reiss 1988: 122).

3.3.2 Offence types
Table 3.1 shows how the 36,941 offence participations were spread over various offence categories. The table shows that property crimes dominate among the classified offences. Shoplifting is the most frequent offence category, accounting for almost one-quarter of the offence participations included in the study. We can also see that participation in violent offences is considerably less common than participation in crimes against property. Sex offences constitute the most rarely seen offence category (0.3 per cent), and drug offences were also relatively uncommon (3.4 per cent).

3.3.3 Reoffending
The overwhelming majority (74 per cent) of those included in the study were suspected of only one offence during the five-year period in question. Only 5,743 individuals (26 per cent) re-offended. Of these, 4,921 appear in two or more of the ten six-month study periods. Four individuals appear as suspects in all ten of these periods (See table 3.2). The low level of reoffending is in part the result of the way in which the data were collected for the study. Those individuals who pass their twenty-first birthday during the study

Table 3.2: *Youths suspected of offences in Stockholm 1991–1995 and their co-offenders by the number of six-month periods in which they appear in the data; cumulative per cent*

Number of periods	(cum.%)	N
10	0.0	4
9	0.1	21
8	0.3	58
7	0.6	122
6	1.2	260
5	3.3	516
4	4.4	971
3	8.6	1,905
2	22.3	4,921
1	100.0	22,091

period can appear thereafter only if they are suspected of committing offences jointly with others aged 20 or under.

3.3.4 Co-offending

Of the 22,091 individuals included in the study, 8825 (40 per cent) had no known co-offenders. These individuals appear in the study as isolates. The remaining 13,266 actors did have known co-offenders and were thus linked to other individuals. In total the study includes 25,207 such links. A link joins two individuals if they are suspected of having committed one or more offences together. These links are reciprocal if both actors are members of the principal population since joint participation in an offence indicates a reciprocal choice.[8] If one of the actors is not a member of the principal population (i.e. is 21 years of age or older) then the link will be unidirectional since the study only focuses on the choices made by members of the principal population.[9] For the data as a whole, we find an average of slightly more than 1.1 links per actor, but when the isolates are excluded this figure increases to 1.9 links per actor.

To calculate the average number of co-offenders per actor, we must multiply the number of links per actor by two. Thus for the data as a whole the actors were linked to an average of 2.3 co-offenders, and if we exclude the isolates this figure increases to 3.8.

The number of known co-offenders varies quite substantially among the individuals examined. Many of the young people studied (6,426 or

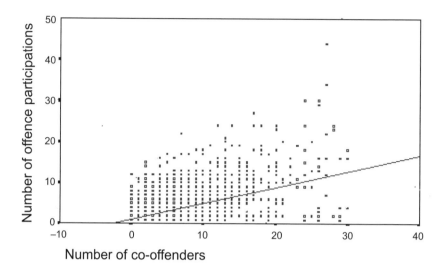

3.2 Correlation between number of offence participations and number of co-offenders (persons under 21) suspected of offences in Stockholm between 1991 and 1995

29 per cent) are linked to only a single known co-offender, whilst the individual with the highest number of known co-offenders is linked to 135 other actors.

There is a correlation between the number of co-offenders to whom an individual is linked and the number of offences for which the individual is suspected ($r = 0.24$). On average then, individuals with several links to other actors are more delinquent than those with fewer links. This relationship does not hold for actors with more than thirty co-offenders, however. These individuals have often committed relatively few offences, and the large number of co-offenders is the result of their having been arrested in connection with some kind of public-order offence (see chapters 7 and 8). There were a number of crimes of this kind registered during 1991 and 1992 in particular, and most of the actors who became suspects in connection with these did not find their way back into the police register during the remainder of the study period. When the 252 individuals (1 per cent of the study population) with thirty or more co-offenders are excluded, the correlation between the number of offences and the number of co-offenders becomes stronger ($r = 0.60$).

The linear relationship between the number of offences and the number of co-offenders is described by the equation: $y = 1.03 + 0.39x$, where y is the number of offences and x the number of co-offenders. The number of

Table 3.3: *Pairs of co-offenders among youths suspected of offences in Stockholm 1991–1995 and their co-offenders, after the number of six-month periods in which they appear in the data; cumulative frequencies*

Number of six-month periods	Pairs of co-offenders (cum.%)	N
6	0.0	2
5	0.0	8
4	0.0	18
3	0.4	94
2	2.5	658
1	100.0	25,207

offences for which an individual is suspected thus increases with an average of 0.39 for every additional co-offender.[10]

The finding that the more active delinquents tend to have more co-offenders corresponds with the results produced by Reiss in his review of the co-offending literature (1988: 133).

3.3.5 Longevity of co-offender relationships

As has been mentioned, the 22,091 actors in the study population are tied to one another with a total of 25,207 links. The vast majority of these links represent a single joint offence. Pairs or groups of actors suspected of co-offending together over a longer time-frame are extremely rare.

Table 3.3 shows that around 2.5 per cent of relationships between specific pairs of actors survive to outlive a single six-month period. Only two such relationships are sufficiently long-lived to appear in six of the ten six-month study periods. Information concerning the longevity of such relationships is limited in the same way as the data on reoffending, as a result of the sampling procedure. This does not seem to have affected the results to any great extent, however. For those individuals who turned 20 in 1995, and who were thus unaffected by the age limitation, 3.5 per cent of a total of 3,195 pairs of co-offenders appear in more than one of the six-month periods, whilst 0.7 per cent appear in three or more of these periods.[11]

These results agree with the findings produced by Reiss and Farrington (1991) in connection with their study of co-offending in a group of 400 or so working-class boys from London. Their results showed that co-offending relations rarely lasted more than a year. In his review of the co-offending literature, Reiss (1988: 131, 132) sees a pattern running through the few published studies focusing on this phenomenon, namely that co-offending relations are unstable and often subject to change.

3.3.6 Isolates and co-offenders

This study primarily addresses individuals who have committed offences (become suspects) together with others. Before we go any further in our examination of co-offending, however, we should note that 40 per cent of all the actors included in the study have no registered co-offenders. In the study's principal population this proportion reaches almost 44 per cent.[12] At the same time, only 29 per cent of the offence participations are associated with these isolates.

The word 'isolate' is thus used here to signify individuals who had no police-registered co-offenders during the study period. Given the low detection risk, it is probable that a good many of these individuals did indeed commit offences together with others during this period, but that these offences were not cleared by the police. They may also have co-offended prior to the beginning of the study period, after the conclusion of the study period, or outside of Stockholm (the study area).

Individuals with no known co-offenders – that is, isolates – differ from individuals who do have co-offenders in that they are on average suspected of fewer offence participations. The average number of offence participations per individual for isolates is 1.16 (SD 0.55) whilst for co-offenders it is 2.15 (SD 2.49). The vast majority of isolates, 88 per cent, were suspected of only a single offence during the five years of the study. The highest number of offence participations during the study period was twelve for the isolates and forty-four for the co-offenders. Of the isolates, 12 per cent were suspected of more than two offences, whilst for the co-offenders this figure was 66 per cent. These results correspond to both the findings produced by Hindenlang (1976: 121, 122), which show that lone offenders seldom commit many offences, and those from my own Borlänge study (Sarnecki 1986) which show that membership in a delinquent network was more or less a precondition for a long and intensive delinquent career.

There are also a number of significant differences between isolates and co-offenders in the matter of the types of offence committed, as we see in table 3.4. The overriding impression is that isolates are suspected of somewhat less serious offences than co-offenders. This is clearly visible when we examine the proportion of offences within the two groups that are made up of shoplifting offences. These constitute by far the most common offence committed by isolates, while they were significantly less common among the co-offenders. Instead of shoplifting, individuals with known co-offenders seemed to have devoted themselves more to other (more advanced) forms of theft, referred to in the table as 'other thefts including burglary'. This category consists primarily of different kinds of burglary and car thefts. The

Table 3.4: *Proportion of participations in various offence types for isolates and co-offenders suspected of offences in Stockholm 1991– 1995*

Offence category	Isolates	Co-offenders
Assault, attempted murder, murder	11.8	14.4
Sex offences	0.8	0.1
Mugging	0.3	3.9
Other crimes against the person	4.8	8.2
Shoplifting	38.7	17.5
Other thefts including burglary	5.1	23.2
Criminal damage	5.3	10.4
Other crimes against property	13.1	6.5
Crimes against police officers/public servants	4.2	8.1
Drug offences	1.3	4.2
Other offences	14.6	3.5
Total	100.0	100.0
N	10,565	26,376

more serious nature of the delinquency of the co-offenders also presents itself in the proportion of this group's crimes made up of mugging and drug offences. Isolates by contrast spent a bigger proportion of the time committing other property offences, among which frauds of a non-serious nature were the most common category. As regards crimes of violence, the differences between the two groups were fairly small.

Reiss and Farrington (1991) report that in their study of 411 London boys, co-offending was 'especially important for the offences of burglary and robbery' (p. 394), a finding that corresponds well with our own results.

Differences in the sex and age distributions of isolates and co-offenders were also examined. The proportion of girls was somewhat higher among the isolates – 31 per cent compared to 24 per cent among the co-offenders.

A comparison of the age distributions is somewhat more complicated, as several individuals appear repeatedly in the data at different ages. For the purposes of this comparison, we made the comparisons on the basis of individuals' ages (only including members of the principal population) when they first appeared in the material. No difference was found between isolates and co-offenders in this regard.

By contrast, Reiss and Farrington (1991: 372) found that among the London boys the proportion of individuals who committed (were convicted for) offences as isolates increased with age. The difference between our findings and those of Reiss and Farrington are a result of the use of different operationalisations of what constitutes an isolate. Whilst our calculations included those who committed no crimes in association with co-offenders, Reiss and Farrington examined each offence separately. Thus their results show that the young men studied tend more often to commit offences without co-offenders as they become older. A similar analysis of our own data produces similar, if rather weak, results. Of all the members of the principal population suspected of committing offences on their own, for example, 41 per cent are counted among its oldest group (from 18 to 20 years of age). The corresponding proportion among those suspected of offences with one or more co-offenders was 24 per cent.

It should thus be born in mind that those individuals treated in the study as co-offenders have often committed a number of the offences for which they are suspected as lone perpetrators. Of the 1,952 individuals whose criminal careers cover four or more of the ten six-month study periods, only 3 per cent were isolates (had no known co-offenders during any of these periods). At the same time, only 19 per cent had known co-offenders during each of the periods in which they were suspected of offences. This means that it is very common for an individual with a reasonably long criminal career to sometimes commit (be suspected of) offences alone and sometimes commit them together with co-offenders. Of these individuals, 81 per cent were suspected of offences with no known co-offenders in at least one of the periods during which they were themselves suspects. Once again these results coincide with the conclusions drawn by Reiss (1988: 151).[13]

3.3.7 The continuing criminal careers of individuals suspected of offences in spring 1991

This section examines the criminal careers of those who made their 'debut'[14] in registered delinquency either as isolates or with one or more co-offenders in the first six months of 1991. The choice of this period was made so as to allow for as long a follow-up period as possible. The data from this period includes a total of 3,118 individuals, 1,026 of whom were born between 1975 and 1981. In 1991 these young persons were between 10 and 16 years of age and could be followed up throughout the five years covered by the study, at which point the youngest had reached 14 or 15 years, and the eldest 20 to 21 years of age. Almost 48 per cent of these youths reoffended at some stage between the end of June 1991 and the end of December 1995.

There is a significant ($p < 0.0001$) but rather weak ($r = 0.18$) correlation between the number of known co-offenders linked to the youths in the first six months of 1991 and the number of offences committed by these youths

Table 3.5: *Reoffending frequency from autumn 1991 to autumn 1995 for youths born 1975–81 suspected of offences in Stockholm in spring 1991; by number of co-offenders in spring 1991*

Number of offences	Number of co-offenders 1991			
autumn 91–autumn 95	0	1	2	3 or more
0	58	52	42	38
1	17	18	10	13
2	7	8	13	7
3–6	11	16	20	21
7 or more	7	6	15	21
Total	100	100	100	100
N	509	254	129	134

during the period from the end of June 1991 to the end of December 1995. Those with more co-offenders in the first part of 1991 thus reoffended somewhat more often than those with fewer known co-offenders.

Table 3.5 shows that reoffending was lowest among individuals suspected of offences in spring 1991 either as isolates or with a single co-offender. Of the individuals suspected of offences as isolates in spring 1991, slightly more than 42 per cent reoffended during the remainder of the five-year study period according to our data, with a little under 7 per cent reoffending on seven or more occasions. The situation was fairly similar for those suspected in spring 1991 with a single co-offender. Here just under 48 per cent reoffended, whilst fewer than 6 per cent did so on seven or more occasions. For those suspected in the spring of 1991 with three or more suspected co-offenders, 62 per cent reoffended, 21 per cent on seven or more occasions.

The correlation between the number of co-offenders during the first six months of the study and the level of delinquency thereafter becomes somewhat stronger ($r = 0.24$) if those individuals under 13 years of age in spring 1991 are excluded. The correlation is more or less the same for girls and boys.

The individuals suspected of offences during the first six months of the study seldom remain isolates if they continue being registered for new offences. Of a total of 509 individuals aged from 10 to 16, who appeared with no co-offenders in the spring of 1991, 58 per cent did not reoffend to our knowledge. A little under 12 per cent continued to commit offences on their own (as far as we know) whilst the other 30 per cent were registered for new offences with one or more co-offenders.

There were sixty-two individuals among those with no known co-offenders in spring 1991 who were then suspected of seven or more offences. Of these, 86 per cent had five or more known co-offenders during the period from the end of June 1991 to the end of December 1995.

We can thus say that the usual career paths for individuals making their debut in our data as 'lone offenders' were either to stop offending altogether or to begin offending together with others. In those cases where the criminal career eventually became quite intensive, it usually included a relatively large number of co-offenders.

Aksamit and Krzyzanowska (1999) have profiled 14-year-olds from the principal population suspected of offences in 1991. The juveniles examined consisted of the following groups:

Group 1. Suspects without known co-offenders
Group 2. Suspects with one known co-offender
Group 3. Suspects with two known co-offenders
Group 4. Suspects with three or more co-offenders

Each of these groups consisted of fifty individuals chosen at random from their respective sub-populations.

The individuals in the four groups were followed up in the central police register of offenders (PBR) until March 1997. The advantages the PBR offender register has over the RAR offence report register is that the former contains information on all the offences committed by an individual that have led to an official response from the formal control apparatus, and on the form this response has taken, even when the offences are committed outside Stockholm. The disadvantage is that the PBR register only covers offences committed once the individual has turned 15 (the age of criminal responsibility). For the juveniles included in this part of the study, this means that their delinquency is recorded in the PBR register from some time during 1992.[15]

During the five years or so that the 14-year-old suspects from 1991 were followed up, the following proportions have reoffended according to the PBR offender register.

37 per cent of those with no known co-offenders
35 per cent of those with one known co-offender
62 per cent of those with two known co-offenders
58 per cent of those with three or more known co-offenders.

Thus 14-year-olds with two or more known co-offenders reoffended more often according to the PBR register than did their contemporaries suspected as lone offenders or together with a one other actor. Aksamit and Krzyzanowska's 1999 study also shows that among those who did reoffend, the ones with more co-offenders at age 14 were registered for more crimes and that this group also received sentences that were on average somewhat harsher.

In the study of 411 London males mentioned earlier, Reiss and Farrington (1991) state that the risk for recidivism was somewhat lower for individuals who committed offences alone. This result coincides with our own findings.

3.4 Summary and conclusions

The primary material used in the study consists of information from the RAR register of offences kept by the Stockholm police. The data taken from RAR provide the personal identity number of the suspects, their age, sex, postcode at time of registration, the type of offence for which they are suspected and the crime location. RAR also contains information on suspected co-offenders and on possible victims of the offences in question. Besides the RAR data, the study also includes a certain amount of data from a number of other, smaller studies.

The study includes all those aged 20 or under who were suspected of offences in Stockholm during the period from 1991 to 1995, and also their suspected co-offenders. In total, 22,091 actors are included in the study. Of these, 19,617 are persons aged 20 or less (the study's principal population). The remaining 2,474 are co-offenders aged 21 or over. The material showed it to be uncommon for juveniles to have adult co-offenders.

Very young individuals are uncommon in the study data. The largest group consists of actors aged between 15 and 20. Of those included in the data 27 per cent are females. The proportion of females was highest among 14-year-olds. The majority of the young people included in the study lived in the city of Stockholm (56 per cent). Very few individuals living outside the county of Stockholm found their way into the study data (7 per cent of the total).

Links between the individuals examined were formed by joint participation in criminal offences. The study covers a total of 29,209 offences. Since it was common for more than one individual to participate in an offence, the number of offence participations (36,941) exceeds the number of offences. The total number of links between co-offenders, on the other hand, was lower at 25,207.

Property crimes were the most common among the offences included in the study. Shoplifting made up the largest single offence category. Sex crimes and drug offences were fairly uncommon.

Of the individuals in the study (44 per cent of the principal population) 40 per cent had no known co-offenders during the five-year duration of the study. It was unusual, however, for individuals with a long and more intense criminal career to be isolates. On the other hand it was common for the more delinquent youths to commit offences both by themselves and together with co-offenders.

There is a significant, but rather weak, correlation between the number of known co-offenders and the number of offences committed during the study period. The higher the number of known co-offenders linked to a certain individual, the more delinquent that individual was found to be in terms of the number of offences committed.

The conclusion drawn is that some form of tie to a network of criminally active individuals is often important for a long criminal career which includes offences of a more serious kind. The actors who committed offences together with others in the early part of the study committed more offences and received harsher sentences than those whose 'debut' in delinquency was as an isolate or together with a single co-offender.

The results also show that it is very rare for the pairs of co-offenders that are formed during joint-offence participation to last longer than a single six-month period. It is thus contacts with delinquent individuals in general, and not contacts with a few specific actors, that is of importance for the continuation of a criminal career.

CHAPTER FOUR

The choice of co-offenders

The main point of departure for this book is the concept that individuals who commit offences together exert some form of influence over one another and that this influence has significance for their delinquency. It is thus of some interest to obtain more detailed information concerning the bases on which the choice of co-offenders is made and the criteria that affect which individuals commit offences together. In this chapter, the choices of co-offender made by the individuals included in the study will be examined in more detail.

Using the concept 'choice' is not entirely without problems in this context. The everyday use of the term implies that the individual in question is free to choose. Whilst such freedom does characterise a number of crime situations, it can be severely limited in others. It is not uncommon for a number of individuals to participate in the same delinquent act without any of them having made a conscious decision to act in concert with others. This may happen in the case of a public-order disturbance, for example, where an individual may decide to participate in the criminal act itself, whilst having no way of choosing which others are going to figure as co-offenders. The concept of choice, then, as it is used in this study with respect to co-offenders, is to be understood in a much wider sense than is the everyday use of this term.

The calculations presented below build on the data in their original condition, that is before they were subjected to the network analysis. They are primarily based on the 46,576 choices of co-offender made by members of the principal population during the years from 1991 to 1995. Each time an individual from the principal population made a choice of co-offender that was registered in RAR, a pair was formed. If the individual committed an

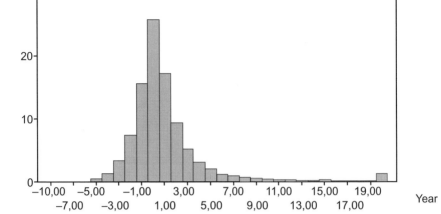

4.1 Distribution of age differences[a] between actors (persons under 21) and co-offenders suspected of offences in Stockholm between 1991 and 1995

[a] Age of co-offender minus age of actor at the time of the offence.

offence with several co-offenders simultaneously then pairs containing this individual are formed with each of the co-offenders present. This means that in connection with an offence where three individuals (A, B and C) are present, all of whom are members of the principal population, six pairs are formed: AB, BA, AC, CA, BC and CB.

If these individuals are then suspected of another joint offence, a further six pairs are formed, although this is only the case if all three individuals are still under 21 years of age. If one of the actors (C, for example) is 21 or over, then his choice of co-offenders is not counted. The pairs formed in this instance are thus: AB, BA, AC and BC.

4.1 Age and choice of co-offenders

On average, the co-offenders included in the study are 1.3 years (SD 4.5) older than the members of the principal population.[1] The fact that co-offenders are on average slightly older is to be expected, since individuals aged over 21 were included as co-offenders but were not a part of the principal population. In total, 29 per cent of co-offenders were younger than the actor in focus, 26 per cent were of the same age (born the same year), and 45 per cent were older.

Figure 4.1 shows that among the youths studied, there was a small group who were suspected of committing offences together with persons

THE CHOICE OF CO-OFFENDERS **53**

Table 4.1: *Proportion of suspected co-offenders of youths suspected of offences in Stockholm 1991–95 who were younger than, born the same year as, and older than the actors themselves. Pairs. Per cent*

Age	Younger	Same	Older	Sum	N
–10	23.5	18.7	57.8	100.0	403
11–14	14.7	35.5	49.8	100.0	6,038
15–17	23.1	28.0	48.9	100.0	21,874
18–20	38.0	21.9	40.1	100.0	18,261
Total	28.7	25.8	45.5	100.0	46,576

who were much older (twenty or more years) than themselves. In police circles we hear sometimes of older, more experienced criminals co-offending with much younger persons. Such cases seem to be rare, however. It is much more common for individuals who offend together to come from more or less the same age group. In 76 per cent of all the pairs studied, the age difference was two years or less. In those instances where youths have co-offended with adults, the older co-offenders are most often relatively young adults. This finding coincides with the results produced by Klein and Crawford (1967) in their study of gangs in Los Angeles, which show that young offenders rarely act together with older criminals. Reiss and Farrington (1991) and Warr (1996) have also made similar findings.

The average age difference between actors and their co-offenders is greatest (+4.0 years) for the youngest actors, aged 10 years or under (see appendix, table A1). Some of these children were suspected of offences with considerably older individuals.[2] For other age groups, the average age difference between actors and co-offenders is rather small and varies between +0.9 for 12- to 13-year-olds and their co-offenders, and +1.8 for the oldest individuals. There is a slight tendency for the age difference between actors and their co-offenders, and for the variance in the age of co-offenders, to increase as actors become older.

Table 4.1 presents the proportion of co-offenders that were younger than, the same age as, or older than the actors in focus. Table 4.1 shows that if we disregard the very young actors, there is a clear tendency for the proportion of co-offenders that are younger than the actors to increase as the actors become older, from around 15 per cent for actors aged from 11 to 14, to 38 per cent for the oldest actors. At the same time, the proportion of co-offenders of the same age as the actors falls from a little over 35 per cent for the 11- to 15-year-olds to just under 22 per cent for the oldest actors.

Table 4.2: *Proportion of boys and girls under 21 years of age suspected co-offending in Stockholm 1991–1995 together with individuals of the same or the opposite sex respectively. Pairs. Per cent*

| | Sex of co-offenders | | | |
Sex of actors	F	M	Total	N
F	56.3	43.7	100.0	7,301
M	6.2	93.8	100.0	39,098
Total	14.1	85.9	100.0	46,399

The proportion of co-offenders that are older than the actors does not present a similarly clear pattern, on the other hand. It seems to be lowest for the 18- to 20-year-olds and somewhat higher for the youngest actors, but the differences are small, and seem in part to be the result of random variations.

4.2 Sex and choice of co-offenders

Of the 46,399 pairs where data is available on the sex of both co-offenders, 79 per cent consisted of two males. In 9 per cent of the pairs both participants were females whilst the other 12 per cent consisted of one male and one female. Table 4.2 shows that boys chose boys as co-offenders in almost 94 per cent of cases. Girls also chose co-offenders of the same sex more often. Just over 56 per cent of the girls suspected of co-offending chose a female co-offender.

If we look at both the information relating to the co-offenders' sex and that relating to their age at the same time, a number of interesting points emerge. In the vast majority of cases, boys chose other boys as co-offenders irrespective of age. The proportion of males among the co-offenders of boys in the principal population varies between 92 per cent for actors aged from 18 to 19 and 98 per cent for 13-year-olds. There is a general but weak tendency for the proportion of male co-offenders to decline with increasing age, but as has been shown this proportion never falls below 92 per cent.

For the girls, on the other hand, the situation changed quite dramatically with increasing age (see table A2 in the appendix). Girls aged from 12 to 13 chose other girls as co-offenders almost as often as boys chose other boys (in 92 to 93 per cent of cases). The older girls, however, chose other girls to a decreasing extent. Seventeen-year-old girls chose other girls as co-offenders in 50 per cent of cases, whilst the oldest girls in the principal population (those who would turn 21 during the year in which they were suspected of the offences in question) had female co-offenders in only 28 per cent of cases.

The age differentials between pairs of co-offenders vary somewhat between groups of pairs with different gender compositions. The age difference between female co-offenders is 1.0 year (SD 4.6) and between male co-offenders 1.2 years (SD 4.1). When a female from the principal population is suspected of co-offending with a male, however, the age difference is on average 3.8 years (SD 5.9).[3] The male co-offenders chosen by the females included in the study were thus on average considerably older than the girls themselves and were also older than the co-offenders in pairs comprising individuals of the same sex. The variation in the age of those co-offending with girls from the principal population was also greater than the variation in age among the pairs comprising two individuals of the same sex.

4.3 Residential location and choice of co-offenders

This section examines how the youths chose their co-offenders from a geographical perspective. As was mentioned earlier, the data concerning the study population's residential location are somewhat less than perfect. Data concerning pairs is particularly sensitive to the problem of missing information, since the analysis demands that we have postcode data for both individuals in the pair. Sixty-four per cent of the pairs had to be coded as missing data because of these problems. Nonetheless, there is no reason to believe that the cases where complete postcode information was unavailable for one or both members of a pair should differ in some more systematic or significant way from those cases where such information was available

Before moving on to an analysis of the results concerning the relationship between residential location and choice of co-offenders, a few words are in order on the matter of the five-digit postcodes which form the basis for the analysis. The county of Stockholm[4] is divided into 2,676 postcode areas of which 1,400 are found inside the city limits of Stockholm.[5] These postcode areas are relatively small and often include a limited number of addresses. People with the same postcode can usually be assumed to be fairly close neighbours. The first three digits of the postcode relate to a somewhat larger area – often a suburb or large neighbourhood. There are eighty-four such areas in the county of Stockholm. The first two digits in combination refer to the nine postal wards into which the county of Stockholm is divided.[6] The first digit specifies different parts of the country, and all the postcodes in greater Stockholm begin with the number 1.

It should also be noted that certain aspects of the validity of the data on residential location used in the study are not entirely beyond question. The data are most often based on the place where an individual was last registered as residing, which presents problems since some young people, and particularly those aged from 18 to 20 who are highly delinquent, do not have a permanent address but rather live at different addresses on a more-or-less temporary basis, with friends, for example, or in residential care facilities. Thus while the data presented here will undoubtedly tell us something about a place to which an individual has some sort of tie, such as the parental home, it may in some cases be misleading with regard to the question of where the youth is usually to be found at that point in time.

If we look at the available information from the pairs we find:

14 per cent of co-offender choices link together individuals who are near neighbours (all five digits in the postcode were the same)

52 per cent of co-offender choices link individuals from the same part of town (first three postcode digits the same)

67 per cent of co-offender choices link together individuals resident in the same postcode ward within the county (first two digits of postcode the same)

95 per cent of co-offender choices link individuals living in the same county (first digit in postcode the same)

only 5 per cent of co-offender choices link two individuals who come from different counties.

These results correspond well with the findings presented by Reiss (1988) in his review of the co-offending literature, where he states that: 'Juvenile offenders commonly belong to territorially based groups and typically select their co-offenders from those groups or territory where they reside' (Reiss 1988: 138). We should not ignore, however, the fact that there are a considerable number of exceptions to this general principle.

Alsterholt's finals dissertation in criminology (1997) analyses choices of co-offender and crime location on the basis of a sample taken from the data of the network study for autumn 1995. Measuring the distance as the crow flies between the addresses of co-offenders, Alsterholt found that in about one-third of the choices of co-offender, the individuals in question lived more than 3 kilometres from one another (p. 27). She also found that the average distance between the places of residence of pairs of co-offenders was less than the average distance between the offenders' places of residence and the crime location. Alsterholt made another interesting finding: those who committed their offences alone did so at greater distance from their place of residence than did those who committed their offences with one or more co-offenders (p. 21).

As one might expect, the distance between the places of residence of co-offenders varied with the age of the actors in question. The younger the individual, the more often he/she seemed to choose co-offenders from the area immediately surrounding his/her own place of residence. Table A3 in the appendix shows that just over half of the youngest actors' (aged 10 or under) co-offenders had the same postcode as the actor in question. Co-offenders who did not live in the same part of the city were very rare in this age group (6 per cent). Table A3 also shows that the distance between the places of residence of co-offenders increases with the age of the actors. From ages 16 to 17, co-offenders with the same postcode become rather rare (about 10 per cent of the pairs).

Thus the choice of co-offenders from the same residential area became increasingly rare as the actors became older. It should be noted, however, that even in the oldest age group members of the principal population still chose their co-offenders either from among those living in their immediate neighbourhood, or at least in the same part of town, in about 30 per cent of cases.

As the proportion of co-offenders living close to one another decreased with increases in the actors' age, so the proportion of individuals choosing each other as co-offenders despite living in different parts of Stockholm, or even (in exceptional cases) where one half of the pair lived outside Stockholm, increased. In just over half of the pairs involving the oldest youths in the study, the individuals lived either in different parts of the county, or even further apart than this. Pairs containing individuals who lived outside Greater Stockholm were nonetheless rare even among the oldest actors, and did not exceed 14 per cent of the pairs studied even here.

Table A4 in the appendix presents the correspondence between residential addresses (postcodes) in relation to the choices of co-offender made by males and females respectively from the principal population. The table shows no great differences between the sexes in this respect.

4.4 Offence type and choice of co-offenders

If we are to understand the social mechanisms involved in the choice of co-offenders made by young people, it is important to know if such choices vary when youths commit different types of offence. The greater such variations show themselves to be, the higher the degree of rationality we can expect to find at the back of these choices (see Tremblay 1993).

In tables A5, A6 and A7 in the appendix, data on the choices of co-offenders made by the youths in the study are presented in relation to offence type, age, sex and residential address. The following is a presentation of the most important findings contained in these tables.

In general it is fair to say that the constitution of the pairs varies among different types of offence. The variations are rarely dramatic, but are nonetheless quite apparent and indicate a clear interaction between types of offence and the choice of co-offender. The following are a few examples:

Pairs suspected of shoplifting are made up of two girls more often than is true for other offence types (52 per cent of shoplifting pairs as against 9 per cent for all crime types). The average age difference between co-offenders in pairs suspected of this type of offence is relatively small (+0.7 years as against +1.3 years for all offence types). Individuals suspected of shoplifting also live close to their co-offenders more often than is the case for other offences (23 per cent have the same postcode and a further 48 per cent live in the same part of town). The general impression is that youths committing shoplifting offences do not expend a great deal of effort in looking for co-offenders for this type of offence. They find such co-offenders in all probability among those with whom they consort more generally, which, for the younger juveniles, who most often commit this type of offence, means individuals of the same age and the same sex who live in the same area. They will probably also go to the same school. (Juveniles, particularly younger juveniles, as a rule go to school with children of the same age from the same part of town as themselves.)

The choice of co-offenders in relation to vandalism in many ways follows a similar pattern to that outlined above in relation to shoplifting. Even here, actors choose co-offenders of more or less the same age who live near by. In the case of vandalism too then, it seems likely that choices of co-offenders are made from among those individuals with whom the actors spend their time more generally. What differentiates vandalism from shoplifting, however, is that it is nearly always boys that are suspected of this type of offence, with 87 per cent of the pairs suspected of vandalism offences being made up of two males.

The choice of co-offenders in relation to drug offences (in most cases the buying and selling of illicit substances) presents a different pattern. In most cases (80 per cent) the pairs are made up of two males. This proportion is the same as the average for all offence types taken together. The majority of co-offenders chosen by the actors examined were older than the actors themselves. The average age difference was considerable (+5.9 years). Furthermore, the co-offenders suspected together in relation to drug offences seldom lived near one another. In only 7 per cent of cases did both members of the pairs concerned have the same postcode, and in a further 19 per cent of cases, they lived in the same part of town. This is lower than the average. To get hold of drugs often requires the youths to extend their personal contact network to include individuals who are considerably older than themselves and who often live in other parts of the county of Stockholm. This is a more natural pattern for the actors suspected of drug offences than for those suspected of shoplifting or vandalism, since the drug-offence suspects are significantly older.

The choice of co-offenders in relation to public-order offences is in some ways similar to that of the choice in relation to drug offences. Here, too, co-offenders are often chosen from among individuals who live a long way from the actors' home address (30 per cent of the pairs contain a member who lives outside the county of Stockholm while only 13 per cent live in the same part of town or have the same postcode). The age difference between individuals in the pairs lies closer to the average for all offence types, however. Here too, the majority of the pairs consist exclusively of males.

To round off this discussion, a few words on differences between crimes against the person and property offences: predictably enough, pairs relating to crimes against the person more often consist of two males than is the case for property offences. The exception to this rule is the offence category 'other crimes against the person', which often consists of threats and where the proportion of females is reasonably high.

It also seems to be the case that co-offenders committing property offences are in general more often from the same area than co-offenders committing violent offences. Muggings are a case in point here: these are often committed by boys of the same age who nonetheless in most cases live a long way from one another.

The general picture is thus one where, even if the composition of the pairs as regards the suspects' age, sex and place of residence does not vary dramatically between different offence types, the differences that were observed follow a fairly logical pattern. For less advanced offences, the youths choose co-offenders from among the individuals they go around with on a regular basis. For certain types of offence which demand special characteristics in a co-offender (such as the purchase of drugs) or for offences which in some other way have a character of their own (public disorder in connection with a sporting event, for example) co-offenders are sought from outside this circle. These offences are such that they cannot be committed unless the actor finds a suitable co-offender. Tremblay's (1993) view of the choice of co-offenders as a behaviour which can be understood in terms of the 'rational choice' perspective is thus to some extent confirmed by our results.

4.5 Earlier delinquency and choice of co-offenders

Another important aspect of the process whereby influence is exerted between co-offenders concerns the relation between individuals whose levels of earlier delinquency, and thus whose levels of experience of offending, differ. Results from the Borlänge study (Sarnecki 1986) suggest that differences in the level of experience between 'teacher' and 'pupil' are rarely very large in co-offender relationships. The more experienced youths seldom commit offences together with juveniles who according to police data have no earlier experience of offending.[7] Reiss and Farrington (1991) also found that the London males included in their study tended to choose co-offenders whose level of delinquent experience was similar to their own. They also found a small group, however, who systematically committed offences together with younger and less experienced offenders. Reiss and Farrington considered this to be a group of recruiters, individuals who recruit new members into delinquent networks. Warr (1996: 33) maintains that most delinquent juvenile groups contain an individual who is identifiable by virtue of his being older and more experienced than the others.

This part of the study is based on choices of co-offender made by one member of the study's principal population of another member of the principal population during the last six months of 1995. The remaining nine six-month study periods, from spring 1991 to spring 1995, are used as the basis for information on the actors' level of delinquency prior to the point that constitutes the focus of the analysis. Individuals who are not members of the principal population (i.e. persons of 21 years of age or older) are excluded, since we have no data on their delinquency in cases where they have co-offended with other individuals aged 21 or over.[8]

Table 4.3 presents pairs consisting of members of the principal population who were suspected of offences in autumn 1995 grouped on the basis of the number of offences for which both individuals were suspected during the previous nine six-month study periods (from spring 1991 to spring 1995). It is striking that the more delinquent an individual, the more likely that his/her co-offenders during autumn 1995 would also present a high level of earlier delinquency.

At the same time, the table also shows that individuals with no earlier reg-

Table 4.3: *Choices of co-offenders made by individuals aged twenty years or less in Stockholm in autumn 1995, grouped on the basis of the number of registered offences for which members of the pairs have been suspected between spring 1991 and spring 1995. Pairs. Per cent*

Number of suspected offences – actors	Number of suspected offences – co-offenders				
	0	1–3	4–6	7 or more	All
0	60	45	27	25	48
1–3	32	37	34	36	34
4–6	4	10	20	20	10
7 or more	4	8	19	19	8
Total	100	100	100	100	100
N	1,944	1,431	396	386	4,157

istered delinquency are suspected of co-offending with individuals presenting all the different levels of previous delinquency contained in the table. Individuals with no known previous delinquency constitute almost half (48 per cent) of the actors studied. Sixty per cent of the individuals with no known previous delinquency were suspected during autumn 1995 of committing offences together with other individuals with no experience of delinquency. The remaining 40 per cent were suspected of offences together with individuals whose level of delinquent experience varied from one suspected offence during spring 1991 to spring 1995, to seven or more suspected offences during this period. (Of those with no known previous delinquent experience 4 per cent were suspected of co-offending with individuals earlier suspected in connection with seven or more offences.)

If we look at the other extreme group in the table, those who according to the police data were the most delinquent individuals, we see that in 25 per cent of the pairs containing one of these highly delinquent individuals, the other co-offender has no known earlier delinquency. In somewhat fewer, 19 per cent, of the pairs containing one of the most delinquent individuals, the other co-offender has an equally high level of previous delinquency.

The more experienced delinquents do thus seem to tend to choose co-offenders with a similar level of delinquency to their own. At the same time, however, we find that individuals previously unregistered in connection with offences, or who have only been suspected of a few offences, are often suspected of co-offending with individuals who are more, even much more, experienced delinquents than themselves.

4.5.1 The composition and delinquency of different types of pair

This section looks more closely at the choice of co-offenders in three different types of pair in the data from autumn 1995:

pairs where both actors had not previously been suspected of offences

pairs where one of the actors had not previously been suspected of offences while the other had previously been suspected of participation in four or more offences

pairs where both actors had previously been suspected of four or more offences

The aim here is to shed a little more light on the phenomena discussed in previous sections.

Table 4.4 shows that pairs consisting of individuals with no known previous delinquency, and those where one or both members have somewhat more delinquent experience, present a number of differences with respect to the pairs' background characteristics and also with respect to the offences of which the members of the pairs are suspected.

Pairs consisting of two individuals with no known previous delinquency were more often composed of girls than were pairs in the other two groups. The members of these pairs were younger, and they lived close to one another more often. The offences for which the members of these pairs were suspected were often less serious than those committed by the members of the other two pair types examined. Thus the members of these pairs were suspected of considerably more shoplifting offences and significantly fewer robberies and other theft offences than the members of the other pair types presented in table 4.4. The actors in these pairs were also on average somewhat less criminally active during autumn 1995 compared with the other two pair types.

The other extreme group, where both individuals in the pair had considerable delinquent experience, presented characteristics that were in many respects the opposite of those described above. The members were on average older, the proportion of pairs containing females was extremely small and it was rare for the members of the pairs to live close to one another. The common offence types committed by these pairs were considerably more serious, with a higher proportion of assaults, muggings and other types of theft among which a significant proportion consisted of various kinds of burglary. The members of these pairs also presented a somewhat higher level of registered delinquent activity during autumn 1995.

Perhaps the most interesting group of pairs is one where a member had

Table 4.4: *Comparison between pairs consisting of actors suspected of offences in Stockholm in autumn 1995. (1) Both actors with no known delinquent experience previously (spring 1991–spring 1995). (2) One actor with no known previous offences, the other suspected of four or more offences (spring 1991–spring 1995). (3) Both actors suspected of four or more offences (spring 1991–spring 1995)*

	(1) Neither suspected before	(2) One not suspected before, the other with four or more offences	(3) Both suspected of four or more previous offences
Number of pairs	1,169	203	301
Sex			
female/female %	31	2	1
female/male %	12	17	0
male/male %	57	81	99
Age			
Average age actors, years	15.8	17.4	18.1
Average age co-offender, years	17.3	18.1	19.1
Age difference, years	1.5	0.7	1.0
Postal address			
Same postcode %	19	2	8
First three digits the same %	58	36	34
First two digits the same %	80	56	45
First digit the same %	94	97	100
Offence participations			
Assault, attempted murder, murder %	9	11	18
Sex offences %	0	1	0
Mugging %	2	13	13
Other crimes against the person %	13	12	12
Shoplifting %	37	8	2
Other thefts including burglary %	9	26	44
Criminal damage %	11	13	5
Other crimes against property %	3	2	0
Drug offences %	2	9	3
Public-order offences %	0	1	3
Other offences %	14	4	0
Average number of offences per actor, autumn 1995	1.4	1.9	2.0

no know previous delinquency whilst the other was a relatively experienced delinquent. It is in this type of pair that one could imagine the schooling of new network members taking place. It must be noted, however, that this type of pair was relatively rare in the data. Of the total of 4,157 pairs comprising members of the principal population suspected of offences in autumn 1995, just under 5 per cent consisted of this type (pairs consisting of two individuals without previous delinquent experience constituted 28 per cent of the total, whilst pairs where both members had been suspected of four or more offences made up 7 per cent).

The background characteristics of the pairs which, according to the police data, consisted of one experienced and one inexperienced delinquent, were such that it was very rare for such pairs to be comprised of two girls. A relatively high proportion of these pairs (17 per cent) on the other hand were comprised of a boy and a girl. In all such pairs it was the boy who was the more experienced delinquent, and often also the older party. Otherwise the average age difference between the actors in this type of pair was rather small (0.7 years). It was uncommon for the members of this type of pair to live close to one another. There are very few cases where both members have the same postcode (only 2 per cent), and it was relatively uncommon for both members even to live in the same part of town.

The seriousness of the offences committed by this type of pair lies somewhere in between that of the other two pair types described. Members of these pairs were suspected of more assault offences than those in pairs with no previous delinquency, but of fewer than those in pairs consisting of two more experienced delinquents. The situation was similar for other theft offences, but the reverse for shoplifting offences. Here, the proportion of such offences committed by members of pairs with one experienced and one inexperienced delinquent was relatively low (8 per cent, compared with 37 per cent for pairs with two inexperienced members, and 2 per cent for pairs consisting of two experienced delinquents). The proportion of muggings was as high as in those pairs made up of two experienced delinquents.

Drug offences constitute an interesting exception here. Members of the pairs containing individuals with different levels of delinquent experience presented a higher proportion of such offences than did the other pair types. This was apparently due to the fact that some of the delinquency in these pairs consisted in youths with no prior delinquent experience seeking to buy drugs from considerably more experienced delinquents.

4.6 Summary and conclusions

This part of the study has examined how members of the principal population, that is, youths aged 20 or under suspected of offences in Stockholm between 1991 and 1995, chose their co-offenders. The data includes 46,576 choices of co-offender, each of which was treated as a separated pair for the purposes of this analysis.

The general tendency was for the young people in the principal population to choose co-offenders who were similar to themselves in terms of age, sex and place of residence. In terms of the similarities of sex and age shown by pairs of co-offenders, our results are similar to those presented by Reiss and Farrington (1991) from their study of co-offending among a group of London youths.

Of the pairs examined here, 76 per cent were made up of individuals of roughly the same age (plus or minus two years). Large age differences, of ten years or more between actors taking part in the same offence, were very rare, and hardly ever occurred where one of the individuals in the pair was less then 13 or 14 years old.

Similarly, it was very unusual for male actors to choose female co-offenders. Of all pairs, 89 per cent were single-sex pairs, the vast majority consisting of two males. Even if girls seem to prefer other girls as co-offenders, the proportion of girls choosing to commit offences with other females was lower than the proportion of boys choosing other males as co-offenders. The older girls chose males as co-offenders much more often than their younger counterparts. The male co-offenders chosen by girls were on average considerably older than the girls were themselves. The age differences in the single sex pairs, on the other hand, were relatively small.

Data relating to the place where the youths in the study lived could have been a lot better (the amount of missing data was considerable) and thus the results from this part of the analysis must be treated with caution. It seems clear, nonetheless, that the actors examined sometimes committed offences with individuals living in other parts of the county, or even with people registered as living in other parts of the country. It was much more common to choose co-offenders from among those who lived near by, however. In just over half the pairs examined, both suspects lived in the same part of town. In only one-third of cases did the co-offenders live more than 3 kilometres from each other. Unsurprisingly, the distance between co-offenders' places of residence increased with age. The participants in mixed sex pairs, on the other hand, did not tend to live very far apart.

The study lends some support to the position that the choice of co-offender is to some extent a rational process, steered by consideration of the offence type to be committed. The co-offenders chosen for less advanced forms of delinquency, such as shoplifting, seemed to come from among those that the individuals would spend time with more generally (i.e. individuals of the same age, same sex, and living in the same area). In the case of more advanced offences, however, or those which required specific qualities of a co-offender, the choices made were somewhat different. In certain instances the mechanism behind the choices was fairly self-evident. An individual wanting to buy drugs, for example, would be forced to seek out a dealer who would often be older than the individual in question and who might well live at some distance. There were other crimes, though, where the co-offenders chosen were often not contemporary neighbours or schoolmates living near by: burglary and mugging, for example.

Interpreting these results from a causal perspective is not without its problems. Sarnecki (1986) maintains that a large part of all juvenile offences are unplanned and spontaneous. Whether or not an offence is committed depends on the coincidence of a whole range factors, one of which may involve the other persons that an individual happens to find himself with at the time. It may well be the case that rather than actively seeking out a dealer in order to by drugs, for example, one happens to buy the drugs as a result of having chanced upon a person who can sell them.

The examination of the pairs consisting of those members of the principal population suspected of offences in the last six months of 1995 shows that youths who themselves present a high level of delinquency tend to choose as co-offenders other similarly delinquent individuals, while those with no known delinquent experience tend to choose others with no apparent prior delinquent experience.

When pairs comprising two actors with no known delinquent experience are compared with pairs where one or both actors has been suspected in connection with at least four offences, a number of characteristic differences present themselves. The members of the pairs with no delinquent experience were younger, were more often girls, more often lived close together and more often committed less serious offences. The pairs comprising two experienced delinquents consisted almost exclusively of boys, who were older, lived further apart from one another and whose delinquency was both more intense and made up of more serious offences.

Pairs comprising individuals presenting a large difference in their respective levels of delinquent experience were rare. A considerable proportion of them comprised an experienced male delinquent and an inexperienced and often younger female. The members of such pairs quite rarely lived close to one another. Their delinquency was in most respects not as advanced as in the pairs comprising two experienced delinquents, but was significantly more advanced than that of the pairs with no known previous delinquent involvement. The exceptions to this rule were mugging and drug offences. The proportion of mugging offences committed by these pairs was as large as the proportion committed by the experienced pairs, while in the case of drug offences it was common that the less experienced individual sought out someone with considerable delinquent experience in order to buy drugs.

If we accept that the learning of criminal behaviours takes place to a large extent in the networks examined, it would seem that a considerable amount of this learning occurs in contacts, not between individuals where one had a good deal of delinquent experience whilst the other was relatively inexperienced, but rather that the transference of information, norms, values and delinquent techniques takes place between individuals with similar levels of delinquent experience. It should be remembered, nonetheless, that in the larger networks where the majority of the more advanced and persistent delinquents are to be found (see chapter 5), the distance within the networks between these experienced delinquents and the younger more inexperienced youths is never particularly large. And as was pointed out earlier, influence between individuals in a network can also be exerted other than via direct, visible contacts.

CHAPTER FIVE

The network

From a network analytical perspective, networks comprise both actors and the links which tie these actors to one another.

5.1 Networks by six-month periods

Dividing the material into ten six-month periods creates 5,710 networks.[1] The largest of these comprises 151 individuals, and the smallest, of which there are 3,681, contain just a pair of actors (i.e. a dyad). The individuals in the study are spread over these networks in the following way:

14 per cent are linked into networks comprising six or more actors
20 per cent are linked into networks comprising three to five actors
26 per cent constitute the half of a pair of actors
40 per cent appear as isolates

The single largest networks in each six-month period contain between 23 and 151 actors. As mentioned above, several of these networks are distinctive in the sense that they are in essence comprised of individuals suspected in connection with a single joint offence. The largest network, for example (151 actors) is primarily the result of a single incident where a large group of young people occupied the offices of a newspaper.

5.2 The largest networks of 1995

If the time-frame is extended so that the networks depict the pattern of co-offending over the course of a whole year rather than six months, the networks produced become considerably larger. The two largest networks for the spring and autumn of 1995, for example, contain twenty-three and forty-five actors respectively. When the time-frame is extended to cover the whole of 1995, however, the largest network comprises 285 actors. In addition, we find a further seven large networks which comprise between twenty and thirty actors.

In network 1/1995 (figure 5.1) it is possible to pick out sixteen smaller clusters of actors, each of which is linked internally by one or more joint offences. These clusters include between five and twenty-two actors and between six and sixty-six links. The link density in these clusters is much greater than that of the network as a whole.

These different areas within the network are often linked to one another by means of a single individual having been suspected during the course of the year of committing offences with two, or occasionally even more, groups of young people. There are twenty or so such individuals and these occupy key positions in the network. It is the presence of such individuals in different groups of criminally active youths that creates different subgroups (clusters) in a large network.

The other seven networks (figure 5.2) are significantly smaller. An analysis of the clustering within these networks does not indicate the presence of several different clusters as was the case in network 1/1995. Here too though, specific actors can be identified who play an important part in pulling the networks together.

On average, the 451 actors in the networks presented in figures 5.1 and 5.2 are linked to 3.7 co-offenders each. The individuals linked to the most co-offenders are a 17-year-old boy with sixteen known co-offenders and a 19-year-old with nineteen known co-offenders during 1995. In general, we find that the larger networks are relatively sparsely linked, that is, the number of links present is relatively small in relation to the number of links that are theoretically possible given the number of actors.

In the smaller networks comprising from three to nineteen actors we find an average of 2.6 co-offenders per actor. The link density in these smaller networks is higher, however. This is due to the fact that these networks are in many cases the result of a single offence, committed jointly by a number of youths. In such cases, all the actors in the network are linked to all the others. If we look at all the individuals present in the material from 1995 we find an average of 2.1 co-offenders per actor.

The members of the larger networks are suspected of a variety of offence types. Once those suspected of only a very few offences are discounted we find no groups in the material that specialise in a specific type of crime. In figures 5.1 and 5.2, actors suspected of at least one violent offence, and links

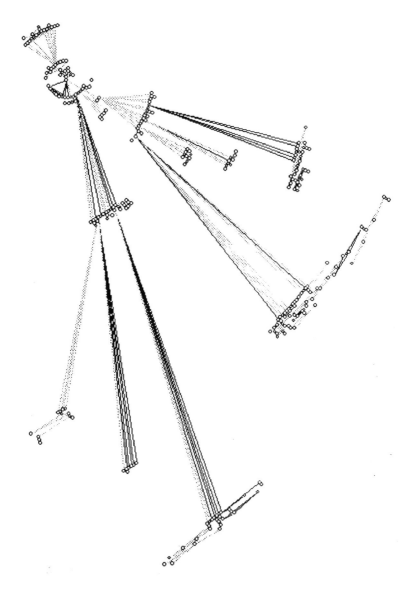

5.1 Youths suspected of offences in Stockholm in 1995 and their known co-offenders: the largest network. Links consisting of violent offences marked in black, other offences marked in grey; 285 actors; 505 links. Scale 1:8

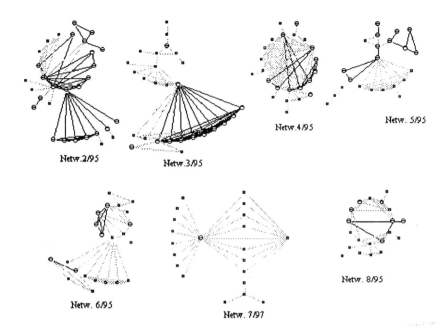

Netw.2/95

Netw.3/95

Netw.4/95

Netw. 5/95

Netw. 6/95

Netw. 7/97

Netw. 8/95

5.2 Youths suspected of offences in Stockholm in 1995 and their known co-offenders: the remaining seven large networks. Actors suspected of violent offences marked as circles, links consisting of violent offences marked in black. Other individuals marked as squares, other offences marked in grey; 172 actors in total; 332 links. Scale 1:4

consisting of violent offences, are marked for easy identification. It is clear that both violent and non-violent offences are to be found side by side in the same networks.

Network 7 is the least prone to violent offences. In this network the actors are in the main suspected of drug offences. One of the key actors responsible for pulling the network together is (alone) suspected of aggravated assault.

An examination of the material from 1995 shows that the proportion of actors suspected of violent offences increases with network size. Fifteen per cent of the individuals in networks comprising from 21 to 282 actors were suspected of at least one violent offence. This proportion falls gradually away with decreasing network size to just 2 per cent for pairs and isolates. These results coincide with the findings of Conwey and McCord (1997).

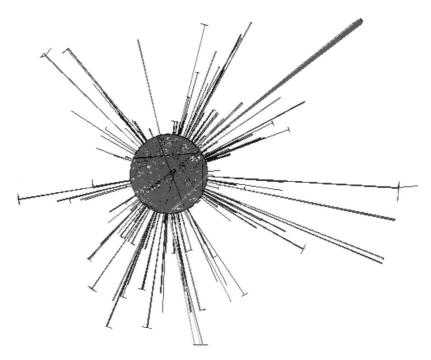

5.3 Youths suspected of offences in Stockholm between 1991 and 1995 and their known co-offenders: the Central Network. Links between members of the largest cluster marked in black, other links marked in grey. In total 4,130 individuals; 20,852 links. Scale 1:50

The graph in fact includes only 3,979 actors and 15,426 links. For technical reasons, a public order offence committed jointly by 151 actors has been excluded. The offence comprised 5,426 links and was linked into the Central Network via two of the participants (see the discussion in section 7.3 of this volume).

5.3 The Central Network 1991–1995

As has been mentioned, the size of the networks expands as we extend the period examined. If we conduct a network analysis of all 22,000 or so individuals who appear in the study at some stage during the period from 1991 to 1995, we find a large network comprising 4,130 individuals (figure 5.3), or just under 20 per cent of the entire study population, and 20,852 links, or 83 per cent of all the links that appear in the material. The remainder of the population is divided into a large number of isolates, and other networks comprising up to 71 actors. The networks that are not linked into the single large network are thus strikingly small. They are also short-lived. None of them spans more than two of the ten six-month study periods.

When we examine the network structure of the material as a whole, the large network assumes a central position. For this reason it will henceforth be referred to as 'the Central Network'. This Central Network would seem to be of considerable importance for the pattern of juvenile crime in Stockholm. It pulls together a disproportionately large percentage of the most delinquent youths; for example 95 per cent of the 274 individuals suspected of ten or more offences during the five-year study period are to be found here, and the actors linked into this network are together suspected of 39 per cent of all offence participations included in the study.

The Central Network contains forty-eight identifiable clusters with a significantly higher link density than the network as a whole. These clusters comprise just under half (46 per cent) of all the actors in the network. Forty-seven of the clusters contain between 4 and 117 actors (with 6 and 857 links respectively). The remaining cluster is extremely large, comprising 1,459 actors and 6,928 links (7 per cent of the individuals in the study but fully 27 per cent of the links). Of the individuals suspected of participation in ten or more offences, 73 per cent are to be found in this cluster, which can be seen as the nucleus of the Central Network.

Figure 5.3 shows that the Central Network is made up of a substantial core and a large number of smaller networks linked to members of this core. The links binding the core together primarily link the members in the largest cluster to one another, whilst the smaller clusters are usually to be found on the outside of the core. These lesser clusters are often tied to the core by means of one of their members having been suspected of offending together with a member of the core. In some cases several members of the largest cluster have been suspected of offending together with a group of individuals who lie outside the core. Figure 5.3 also contains individuals who are a part of the core, despite the fact that they are not members of the largest cluster, but rather are either members of other clusters or lie outside the clusters altogether.

The small scale $(1:50)^2$ used in figure 5.3 means that individuals who are linked to members of the core, but who are not themselves part of the core or of the central cluster, are not visible. The Central Network includes a large number of such individuals.

The longevity of links in the Central Network was considerably greater than in the material as a whole, although even here changes of co-offenders were very common. Of the links in the Central Network, 14 per cent survived longer than a single six-month period. The corresponding proportion in the material as a whole (as has already been mentioned) was 3 per cent.

There are a number of methods for examining the centrality of an actor's position in a network of delinquent relationships (Freeman 1979; Baron and Tindall 1993; Wasserman and Faust 1994). One such method is to count the number of known co-offenders to whom the actor in question is linked. Looking at the whole of the five-year study period we find that the individuals in the study population are linked to an average of 2.3 co-offenders each. Those actors who are linked into the Central Network have an average of 5.7 co-offenders, and those linked into the forty-eight clusters within the Central Network are more central than the rest almost to a man. These have an average of 8.8 co-offenders per actor.

These results are very similar to those from the Borlänge study (Sarnecki 1986). In Borlänge I also found a large network which was of central importance for juvenile crime in the town, and into which a large proportion of the town's most delinquent youths were linked. The Central Network in Stockholm is considerably larger than its counterpart in Borlänge (4,130 individuals as compared with 217 in Borlänge), but nonetheless comprises a smaller proportion of the whole population of suspects than was the case in Borlänge (20 per cent in Stockholm compared with 47 per cent in Borlänge).

Probably the most plausible explanation for this difference in the proportion of suspects linked into the central networks in Stockholm and Borlänge respectively is to be found in the lower clearance rates for juvenile offending in Stockholm in the 1990s compared with those in Borlänge, a much smaller town, in the 1970s and 1980s.

In this context, however, it is not the differences between Stockholm and Borlänge that are of most interest but rather the similarities. In both the smaller town and the relatively large city there seems to be a central network which draws together a large proportion of the area's most delinquent juveniles and which accounts for a disproportionately high percentage of the offence participations in the area.

5.4 Longevity of network composition

Even if it is rare for a co-offending relationship to last longer than a single six-month period (see page 43), it is possible that network composition might not change with the same degree of rapidity (since not all the members of a network are directly linked to one another).

In order to examine changes in the composition of the various networks over time, a 'macro-image' of the network data was produced. For the purposes of this analysis each network comprising six or more individuals from each of the ten six-month study periods is represented by a single symbol. The graph has been organised so that networks appearing during a certain six-month period (spring 1991, autumn 1991 etc.) are placed in the same column. Since the study covers ten six-month periods, there are ten such columns in the graph. Movements among the networks (i.e. when one or

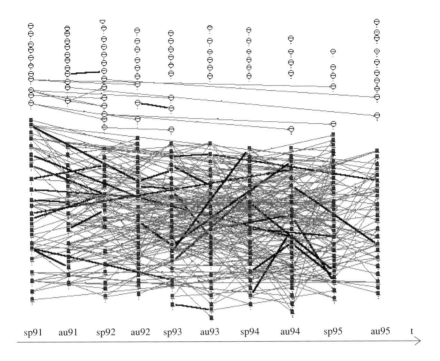

sp91 au91 sp92 au92 sp93 au93 sp94 au94 sp95 au95 t

5.4 Networks comprising six or more individuals suspected of offences in Stockholm between 1991 and 1995 (six-month periods) and movements between these networks. Movements comprising three or more individuals in black, the remainder in grey. Networks comprising a part of the Central Network represented by squares, other networks by circles.

more actors present in a certain network during one of the six-month periods turn up linked into a different network during a later period) are represented as links.

Despite having been simplified (networks comprising five individuals or less were excluded from the analysis), figure 5.4 is not easy to read. It comprises 327 networks (of six or more individuals) tied to one another with 728 links. The majority of these networks (around three-quarters) are linked together, which means that they are included in the Central Network. The remaining networks are among the smaller networks included in the graph, which for the most part appear only during the course of a single six-month period.

The point should once again be made that the links in this 'macro-analysis' represent individuals, and not offences as was the case in the earlier analyses. The graph indicates that it is rare for groups of offenders to move between networks. On average, each link represents 1.6 individuals. Links which represent the movement of three or more offenders are marked separately but, as can be seen, there are relatively few of these (eighty-nine, or 12 per cent of the total number of links).

These results coincide with findings from other studies (Reiss 1988; Reiss and Farrington 1991). Warr summarises the results of his own study of group delinquency in the following way: 'delinquent groups are short-lived groups, so short-lived that it may make little sense to even speak of delinquent *groups* at all, at least in any strict sense. The extreme instability of most delinquent groups means that offenders will normally have few opportunities to repeat their role in the same group and thereby develop a stable role structure' (Warr 1996: 33, original emphasis).

The results presented above also correspond with those of the Borlänge study (Sarnecki 1986). Mobility among different groups of co-offenders seems, however, to be somewhat higher in Stockholm than it was in Borlänge. In Stockholm we find hardly any long-lived, densely linked networks which turn up in several different periods containing the same individuals. Quite the reverse: in fact, the actively delinquent youths in Stockholm seem constantly to be switching to different co-offender groups.

However, there are a few exceptions to this. There is a group of nine boys aged from thirteen to fifteen who were jointly suspected of theft and mugging in both the autumn of 1992 and the spring of 1993. In autumn 1992 this group of boys was linked into a network comprising thirty-four individuals and in the following spring into another comprising twenty-three individuals. That is to say, that of the thirty-four actors present in the network from the autumn of 1992, nine turned up together in another network in the following spring. A further eight of these thirty-four individuals were suspected of offences in the spring of 1993, but in connection with different constellations of co-offenders and without being linked to one another.

The co-offending of the group of nine boys seems to have ceased after the spring of 1993. Two of them were suspected of a further joint offence (another mugging) in the spring of 1995, however.

In a few other cases, we find groups of between five and eight individuals suspected of co-offending in two separate periods, although these periods need not necessarily follow directly on from one another. Such groups are always linked into larger networks in both periods however, and it is rare for two, or at most three, individuals to appear together in more than two periods.

5.5 Summary and conclusions

The size of the networks is in large part dependent on the length of the period being studied. Dividing the data up into ten six-month periods produces 5,710 networks of varying size. The largest includes 151 individuals, whilst the smallest are made up of two individuals (dyads). Only 14 per cent of the individuals in the study were tied into a network of six or more individuals.

If the period being studied is extended to cover a whole year, the size of the networks increases. The largest network in 1995 included 285 individuals. This network linked together the individuals comprising the two largest networks of spring and autumn 1995, and also the members of a few other networks formed in these periods.

If we extend the period studied to cover the whole five years of the study, the largest network produces a total of 4,130 individuals, that is, almost 20 per cent of the study population. This large network was of central significance for juvenile crime in Stockholm (*inter alia* it included a large majority of the most delinquent youths) and was therefore named the Central Network. Although only one-fifth of all the individuals studied are members of this network, it includes 83 per cent of all the links to be found in the data. If the whole of the material is seen as a network, then the Central Network can be seen as its centre – a core.

But the Central Network has a core of its own too – a cluster that presents a significantly higher degree of link density than does the surrounding network. This cluster comprises 1,459 individuals. Just as individuals included in the Central Network have more known co-offenders than the average for the individuals studied, so individuals who are part of this network's central cluster have more known co-offenders than the average for the Central Network as a whole. The same applies to the level of delinquency. Members of the Central Network present a higher than average level of delinquency and members of the central cluster are on average more delinquent than other members of the Central Network.

The other networks produced when we study the whole of the five-year period are significantly smaller than the Central Network. And, in comparison with the Central Network, which is bound together by offences from all ten of the six-month study periods, they are not as durable.

As was shown in chapter 4, links among delinquent individuals are in most cases not particularly long-lived. The youths who continue with delinquent activities are constantly choosing new co-offenders. The networks too are in a constant state of flux: smaller networks are formed and then disappear again after a brief period, while within the larger networks the composition and constellations of the membership are constantly changing.

The general picture of delinquent networks in Stockholm is that, as in Borlänge, we see a large central network. This network, which is very probably much larger than the one produced here on the basis of register data, binds together a big proportion of the most actively delinquent juveniles in the area. Even though we find a number of different clusters within the Central Network, we may conclude that the most active delinquents in Stockholm are not divided up into a number of discrete groups in competition with one another.

Warr (1996), who like other researchers notes the low durability of groups of delinquent juveniles, questions whether it is correct in this context to talk of 'groups' in the social-psychological sense at all. For Warr, the low durability and the highly changeable membership composition makes it difficult to see how such groups could be expected to develop norms and identities of their own. Warr's results are confirmed by the findings produced in this study.

The conclusion may thus be that the youths in the networks we have studied are bound together by ties that are on the whole rather weak. This does not imply that the networks exert little influence on the occurrence and character of juvenile delinquency. As was mentioned in chapter 1, the concept of strong and weak ties was introduced by Granovetter (1974) in his study of how well-educated men from a suburb of Boston found themselves jobs. Finding employment took place to a large degree through informal personal contacts with people to whom the job-seeker had weak ties. Information concerning possible job opportunities seldom came from individuals, such as family members and close friends, to whom the person in question had strong ties. This was due to the fact that this latter group was both somewhat limited in terms of size, was also fairly closed, and characterised by dense contacts among its members. It was thus less likely that new impulses would come from this circle of individuals. Networks consisting of weak ties, on the other hand, were significantly larger and more open, thus increasing the likelihood that they would provide new information.

It is possible that the weak ties within the large Central Network of delinquent relations function in a similar way. The network comprises a large number of actors, many with an extensive and varied experience of delinquency, and a large number of new actors are recruited each year. In addition, the network is long-lived despite the fact that its composition is in a constant state of flux. This social structure may well have great significance for delinquent youths, providing them both with relevant new information and with contacts necessary for their continued delinquency.

CHAPTER SIX

The network connections of juveniles admitted to secure care facilities

This part of the study looks at the network attachments of a group of youths who were placed in secure care facilities in the county of Stockholm at some point during the period from 1991 to 1995. At this time there were five such institutions, admitting young people with serious social difficulties. The problems which result in placements in such facilities often involve violent or high frequency offending but also include a number of other more self-destructive behaviours such as alcohol and/or drug abuse and prostitution. In general, the level of problem behaviours manifested by youths admitted to these institutions is very high. Swedish legislation only allows the social services and the county administrative courts to submit an individual to compulsory institutional care when other measures have already been tried and failed, or when the conditions necessary for other (primarily voluntary) measures to have a fair chance of success are absent. Young people can only be placed in secure care facilities up to the age of 20, and they must be discharged before their twenty-first birthday (SFS 1990: 52).

According to the Swedish penal code (BrB), the age of criminal responsibility is 15 years (chapter 1, paragraph 6) and an individual cannot be convicted of an offence prior to having reached this age. Persons aged 18 or under can only be sentenced to prison if there are exceptional circumstances which merit such a sanction (BrB chapter 30, paragraph 5). In practice, persons below the age of 18 are very rarely sent to prison[1] (Sarnecki 1987). Use is made instead of the social services legislation which in its most intrusive form involves placement in a secure care facility of the kind mentioned above. We can thus assume that a large proportion of the youths aged from 15 to 17 who are known to the social services for serious and/or high frequency delinquency will be among those admitted to secure care facilities.

There are also legal restrictions on the use of the prison sanction for individuals who have turned 18 but not yet reached 20 years of age. These restrictions are somewhat less stringent, however (the law speaks here of 'special' rather than 'exceptional' circumstances). Prison sentences are used somewhat more frequently for this group, so we should assume that the majority of the most delinquent youths in this age group will not be found among those admitted to the secure care facilities, unless the placement took place prior to their eighteenth birthday. The youths who are admitted to secure care facilities are, however, likely to include those from this older age group who exhibit other kinds of delinquency related social problems, such as drug abuse, and thus these will be found in our material.

A comprehensive study was carried out of youths admitted to Stockholm's secure care facilities during the period from 1991 to 1995. The aim of the study was to examine the various problem profiles exhibited by the youths prior to placement, during their stay in secure care, and also over the course of a period of two years following their release from these facilities. The study also examined the measures taken by society as a result of the delinquency and other social problems exhibited by these youths (Sarnecki 1996).[2] The data came in part from the various authorities involved, and in part from interviews with the young people themselves. In total, 814 young people were included.

Of these 814 individuals, 540 (66 per cent) have been identified in the network data. The proportion of youths from the secure care facilities found in the network data is relatively low, owing to the fact that individuals placed in the facilities came from the whole county (and in some cases even from outside the county) while the network data covers only those individuals suspected of offences in the municipality of Stockholm. In addition, as was mentioned earlier, the behaviour of some of the young people placed in these institutions was of a self-destructive character, and thus not necessarily delinquent. A further reason is that the police data upon which the network study is based may differ in a number of respects from the information collected by the social services, which forms the basis for the decision to place an individual in secure care. The Swedish Official Secrets Act contains provisions denying the police access to information held by the social services.

6.1 Links among individuals admitted to secure care facilities

One question to which network analysis can provide an answer is to what degree admission to a secure care facility contributes to the formation of social ties among the most delinquent youths in Stockholm. It has occasionally been suggested that institutions which group together highly delinquent and antisocial individuals such as prisons, criminal psychiatric units and secure care facilities constitute schools of delinquent behaviour. Seen logically, there would seem to be a considerable risk that this type of institution would contribute to the formation of delinquent networks and to the transference of criminogenic information of all kinds.

This view of such institutions has been criticised by certain researchers, however. Murray and Cox (1979), for example, suggest that since they commit offences together, young delinquents already have an abundant source of access to the kinds of situation where delinquent behaviour can be learned. This considerably diminishes the 'attractiveness' of the institutions mentioned above as schools of crime. Murray and Cox's own research indicates that no learning of delinquency results from the arrest and detention of youths in connection with offences they have already committed.

In his review of the co-offending literature, Tremblay (1993: 23–4) makes the point that the conditions of institutional life may in fact be anything but favourable to the learning of delinquency. At the same time, however, he writes that the available data are insufficient to make a definitive judgement as to whether placement in such an institution can effect future delinquency by means of the establishment of new delinquent contacts. In this context, Tremblay cites the results of a study of adult co-offending networks carried out by Ianni (1975), which shows that a stay in prison affected the composition of co-offender networks to a larger extent among members of certain ethnic groups (blacks and Puerto Ricans) than among members of others (Italians). It is just this question of the extent to which placement in a secure care facility may affect the formation of co-offending networks, and thus also the delinquency of the individuals concerned, that will be discussed in this chapter.

6.1.1 The personal networks of young people admitted to secure care facilities

In order to study the co-offending patterns of individuals admitted to secure care facilities, personal networks were drawn up using the network data for each of the 540 secure care individuals present in the police data. The term 'personal network' is used here to refer to the network which is comprised of a specific actor and those individuals directly linked to this actor. Thus in this part of the study, the networks consist of those actors admitted to secure care facilities and their co-offenders. Individuals indirectly linked to these actors are not included.

The analysis of the personal networks of the 540 youths included a total of 1,880 individuals. Thus besides links to other youths admitted to secure care facilities, the young people placed in these facilities were directly linked to a further 1,340 individuals. The personal networks of the youths admitted to secure care facilities together comprise:

one large network made up of 1,181 individuals
79 smaller networks composed of between three and twenty individuals
68 pairs
126 isolates

The 540 individuals admitted to secure care facilities account for a total of 1,993 links. The number of links between two individuals, both of whom were placed in a secure care facility, is small, however – 203 or only 10 per cent of all the links between the actors studied and their co-offenders. The vast majority (90 per cent) of the secure care youths' known co-offenders were thus individuals who had not themselves been placed in such facilities during the period in question. Even at this stage we can state that co-offending with other individuals admitted to secure care facilities plays a relatively small part in the total known delinquency of the actors in question.

If a relation between two individuals (indicated here by joint participation in the same offence) is to be ascribed to their having spent time together in the same institution, three things are necessary. The individuals concerned must actually have been placed at the same institution, they must have been admitted at the same time,[3] and the offence or offences they committed together must have been committed after their stay in the secure care facility. An examination of data relating to secure care facility admittances shows that these conditions may have been met in at the most 28 cases (i.e. 28 of the 203 links between two individuals who had both been placed in secure care facilities may have resulted from the individuals having spent time together in the same institution). This leads to the conclusion that no more than 1.5 per cent of the links among individuals admitted to secure care facilities can have been established at the institutions in question. Thus the hypothesis that individuals placed in such facilities establish relations with other highly delinquent youths during their time in these institutions and that such relationships are continued after the individuals' discharge from the facilities is lent no support by the findings in this study.[4]

6.1.2 One large network

What we can say, on the other hand, is that highly delinquent youths who, as a result of this delinquency, are placed in secure care facilities are often linked through the joint commission of offences (both directly and indirectly) to other delinquent youths, many of whom have themselves been admitted to such institutions at one time or another. However, these links have been established independently of the institutional placement and ought rather to be ascribed to the fact mentioned earlier, that highly delinquent young people are often linked into the same network. This can be illustrated with the help of the largest of the networks produced in association with the drawing-up of the personal networks of the young people admitted to secure care facilities.

This network comprises 1,181 individuals of which 238 (20 per cent) had been admitted to secure care facilities. In total the network contains 3,950 links, of which 370 (9 per cent) bind together two individuals both of whom had been placed in a secure care facility. Of the remaining links, 1,759 bind individuals admitted to secure care facilities to other young people not themselves placed in such institutions. The other 1,821 links bind together pairs of individuals neither of whom had been placed in secure care, but both of whom were linked to one or other of those admitted to such institutions. The result is a dense and highly connected network with a visible core (cluster) comprising around half of the individuals and three-quarters of all the links. This network constitutes an important part of the study's Central Network comprising 4,130 individuals as shown in figure 5.3.

Thus of the individuals included in the network study, there were 540 (2 per cent of the total) who had been admitted to secure care facilities. Almost 63 per cent of these were members of the Central Network. Individuals admitted to secure care facilities are thus over-represented in the Central Network and in addition they take up significantly more of the central positions in this network than the average. The average number of co-offenders per individual in the Central Network is 5.7, while for the youths admitted to secure care facilities the corresponding figure is 8.9 co-offenders per actor.

6.2 Levels of delinquency before and after placement in secure care facilities

This section examines the possible effects of placement in a secure care facility from a network perspective. In order to study this question, the 111 individuals from the network data admitted to secure care facilities during autumn 1991 and spring 1992 were matched with a group of 'twins' from the principal population of the network study suspected of offences during autumn 1991 and spring 1992, but not admitted to secure care facilities. The

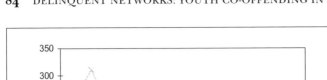

6.1 Number of suspected offence participations by 111 individuals admitted to secure care facilities in autumn 1991 and spring 1992, during the six-month period prior to their placement in a secure care facility; during the six-month period in which they were admitted; and during the seven six-month periods thereafter; and those by a matched control group comprising 111 individuals not admitted to a secure care facility, as well as the number of offence participations by the suspected co-offenders of both of these groups

matching was carried out on the basis of sex, age and level of recorded delinquency, both during the six months prior to admittance to secure care and during the six months in which the placement in a secure care facility took place. A comparison of these two groups, that is, the 111 youths admitted to secure care facilities and their 'twins', and of their respective co-offenders, is presented in figure 6.1.

As can be seen in this figure, the total number of offences for which members of the two matched groups and their co-offenders were suspected during the six months prior to the point when the first group were admitted to secure care facilities, during the six-month period during which these placements occurred, and during the seven six-month periods which followed, the number of offences committed by the youths who were to be placed in secure care facilities rose during the six-month period prior to their admission. It is probably this steep increase in delinquent behaviour that precipitated the decision to place them in secure care. The fact that the 111 youths who constitute the control group show the same pattern during the first two periods is a result of the matching procedure itself and the criteria used.

An examination of the continuing trend of registered offending by those admitted to secure care facilities shows a dramatic reduction in the level of delinquency during the following six-month period. It is unlikely that this reduction can be ascribed to the effects of placement in the secure care facility, however, since the level of delinquency of the control group members, who were not placed in such facilities (but were subject to a number of different forms of reaction) falls even more sharply. The longer-term trend of offending of those *not* admitted to secure care facilities seems to be somewhat more positive than that presented by the youths placed in these facilities. Those not admitted presented a level of offending that was on average 37 per cent lower during the following seven six-month periods than was that of the youths placed in the institutions. These results are hardly to be considered surprising. Similar studies show that individuals subjected to more intrusive social measures as a consequence of their offending tend to reoffend more often (see for example Börjesson 1968, Bondeson 1977). Interpretations of this type of result are controversial, as they can be understood to be the result either of the fact that institutional care is harmful, or of the fact that matching of this kind is very difficult to carry out correctly.

The network analytical perspective gives us another dimension when interpreting the data presented above. From this perspective, the youths placed in secure care facilities are part of a network in which they exert influence over and are in turn themselves influenced by others. If the authorities take measures against one of the individuals in such a network, this will affect not only the individual in question, but also the others in that individual's network.

A successful preventative intervention on the part of the authorities, which leads to an individual ceasing his or her delinquency completely, can in principle give rise to the following two scenarios:

If the individual is influential within the network, this may lead to the level of delinquency in the network as a whole being reduced or perhaps even ceasing altogether. Thus the effect will be greater than the reduction in delinquency brought about by the disappearance of the offences committed by the individual in question.

If the individual has rather less influence in the network, the intervention may perhaps lead to no reduction at all in the level of delinquency in the network. The offences which would have been committed with the participation of the individual in question are committed nonetheless in his or her absence. It is also possible, to consider an even more extreme scenario, that the individual had a restraining effect on the group's delinquency and that the delinquency of the group as a whole increases in the individual's absence (see Reiss 1980: 15–16).

It is possible to simulate a hypothetical outcome of the first scenario mentioned using a computer. Of the 111 individuals admitted to secure care facilities who were included in the follow-up study presented here, 66 were part of the Central Network which contained a total of 4,130 individuals and 20,852 links. Several of these individuals had central positions in this network and were linked to many other individuals in the network with whom they were suspected of committing several offences. If these 66 individuals had completely ceased their delinquency following their placement in a secure care facility (in autumn 1991 and spring 1992) and besides this had managed to influence their co-offenders in such a way as to get these to give up offending as well, this would have had a dramatic effect on the network. The network would have gone through a partial disintegration. The material would still contain a central network, but this new network would comprise only 2,836 individuals (thus being 31 per cent smaller) and 12,011 links (the number of links thus being reduced by 27 per cent). The number of offence participations would be reduced by 21 per cent, and the number of offences by 19 per cent.

It is thus likely that the complete rehabilitation or incapacitation of these individuals would have a considerable effect on juvenile delinquency in Stockholm. This hypothetical effect would be even greater if we also count the effects of the individuals' indirect influence, that is, the additional effect from co-offender to co-offender leading to a further possible reduction in delinquency. Reiss (1988: 118) indicates the need to take into consideration the dynamic processes that are played out in networks when estimating the effects of incapacitation on one or more individuals. Reiss and Farrington (1991) write: 'Just how many crimes are averted by incapacitation is a function of the replacement rate of incapacitated members, the rates of offending, and the deterrence effect of incapacitation on co-offenders who are not incapacitated' (367). This type of argument however, is extremely rare in the literature on the different dimensions of individual prevention such as incapacitation.[5]

In an attempt to illustrate this kind of effect, in addition to the delinquency of youths placed in secure care facilities and that of the matched control group, figure 6.1 above also presents the delinquency of the known co-offenders of these two groups. The figure shows that the co-offenders of the control group presented a significantly higher level of delinquency (measured as the number of offence participations) than the co-offenders of the youths admitted to secure care facilities. Over time, the trend in delinquency levels presented by the co-offenders of the control group follows that of the control group (and the study group) itself, even if it lies at a higher level to begin with. After period four, the delinquency level presented by this group as it were 'touches down' at the level presented by the other groups.

The picture is quite different for the co-offenders of those admitted to secure care facilities. The delinquency level presented by this group was more or less identical to that of the study group during the period prior to the placements in secure care facilities. While the level of delinquency of the other groups shown in figure 6.1 rose during period two (the period when members of the study group were admitted to secure care facilities) the delinquency level presented by the co-offenders of the study group dropped somewhat during this period, and then fell further during the following period.

Since figure 6.1 shows the total number of offence participations in the two groups of co-offenders, the differences may be the result of differences in the size of the two groups. This was true of the period prior to the placement of the study group in secure care facilities, since at this point the number of co-offenders linked to the control group was larger than the number linked to the study group. During the period when the study group was admitted to the secure care facilities, however, and during the following periods, the number of co-offenders linked to the two groups was more or less the same. The differences in the delinquency levels of the two groups of co-offenders during these periods were thus the result of the fact that the average number of offence participations, per individual, was larger for the co-offenders of the control group. The number of suspected offence participations for the co-offenders of the two groups are presented in figure 6.2.

Figure 6.2 shows that according to the police data, the co-offenders of both groups presented the same average levels of delinquency before the members of the study group were placed in secure care. During the period when the study group were admitted to secure care facilities, the delinquency level of this group's co-offenders fell considerably, whilst the delinquency level of the control group's co-offenders increased. During the period following the study group's admittance to secure care facilities, the delinquency levels of both groups of co-offenders increased. The delinquency level of the study group's co-offenders was now as high as (or even a little higher than) that presented by this group's co-offenders prior to the placements in secure care facilities. Nonetheless, the delinquency level of the control group's co-offenders was still significantly higher. During

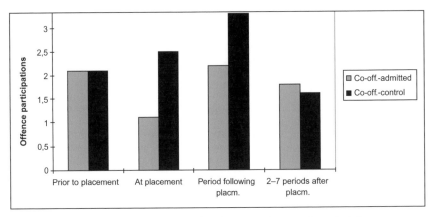

6.2 Average number of offence participations per six-month period for co-offenders of individuals admitted to secure care facilities in autumn 1991 and spring 1992 and for co-offenders of a matched control group. The figure covers the six-month period prior to placement, the period during which placement took place, the period following placement, and the remaining six-month periods after placement, taken together

periods two to seven after admission, the average delinquency levels of both groups of co-offenders fell. There was thus an equalisation of the delinquency of the two groups of co-offenders which once again presented very similar average delinquency levels.

One way of interpreting this trend is to see the members of the networks of those admitted to secure care facilities as having been affected by the way their friends have been dealt with by the authorities. The eventual equalisation between the two groups of co-offenders can also be understood from this perspective. We know that the composition of co-offender groups changes very quickly, so that only a few of the co-offenders of the individuals in the study group continue to commit offences with these individuals in the longer term. If the placement of the study group in secure care had an effect on this group's co-offenders, then logically it is those individuals who were members of the study group's networks either at the time of placement in a secure care facility or shortly thereafter who must have been affected.

There are, of course, objections to this interpretation of the results. An alternative interpretation would be that the youths admitted to secure care facilities chose less highly delinquent co-offenders after the time they spent in these institutions.

The question remains, however, why it is not the delinquency of those placed in secure care facilities that is affected by this placement, but rather that of their co-offenders (or alternatively the choice of co-offenders made by the study group)? The conclusion that the youths admitted to these facilities were not affected by the placement may be somewhat hasty. We do not of course know how the level of delinquency presented by these individuals would have looked if they had not been admitted to the institutions in question. While their delinquency increased during the period in which they were admitted to these facilities, this increase may be the result of offences committed immediately prior to placement (the data available were not sufficiently detailed as to allow for this question to be examined). And it cannot be ruled out that the level of delinquency presented by these youths would have been even higher had they not been placed in secure care facilities. Interpreting these results is a tricky business. More research, using more detailed data, is needed into the network effects of official measures against active delinquents.

6.3 Profile groups

Here we examine the relationship between the type of asocial behaviour exhibited by specific delinquents, and behaviour exhibited by the individuals and networks to which these delinquents are linked. The question examined is thus that of specialisation, either between different networks, or in different dyads of the same network. It is possible that even if specific individuals exhibit a fairly varied pattern of offending, co-offending groups may present a much higher degree of specialisation (see Warr 1996: 33). The opinions of academics who have studied groups of delinquent youths vary as to the degree to which these groups specialise in offences of various types. As we saw earlier (p. 16), Klein (1995) refers to the offending pattern of street gangs as 'cafeteria style delinquency' (a little of this, a little of that, a little of the other) while Sanchez-Jankowski (1991), for example, writes of more specialised gangs.

The study of young people admitted to secure care facilities included an analysis of the various problem profiles exhibited by the youths in question (Sarnecki 1996). The data on which this analysis was based came in part from the applications made by the social services to have the youths admitted to secure care, in part from investigations into the youths' problems undertaken in connection with their admission to the facilities, and in part from interviews with the young people themselves. The data on crime, other deviant behaviours and difficulties[6] collected from these various sources was then subjected to a factor analysis.

The factor analysis produced five factors, and on the basis of these the youths in the study were classified into five problem profiles:

Crime profile
Substance-abuse profile
Psychological disturbance profile
Sexual disturbance profile
0-profile (containing youths with no easily identifiable problem profile)

The crime profile comprised individuals whose major problem was that they were active criminals often committing serious offences. The group contained both individuals who committed a large number of offences and individuals whose level of criminal activity was slightly lower, but whose offences were very serious. A high proportion of these individuals had committed different types of violent offences. Any attempt to further divide this group into a number of subgroups on the basis of different offence types was rendered meaningless by the fact that the group did not contain any individuals who committed only a single, or a very few, types of offence.

Within the substance-abuse profile, too, attempts at a further division into alcohol abusers and drug abusers proved pointless, since it was common for the youths in this profile group to abuse a variety of substances.

The youths classified in the psychological disturbance profile exhibited a number of different psychological disorders (personality disorders, brain injuries, borderline syndrome etc). Substance abuse and criminality also came into the picture but were felt to be of secondary importance.

The sexual disturbance profile comprised individuals who had been taken into care as a result of prostitution and/or because they had been exposed to other forms of sexual abuse and exploitation.

Youths presenting a more splintered and diffuse problem profile, who could therefore not be classified in one of the profile groups described above were classified instead as profile group 0.

This section takes a closer look at the data contained in the network material concerning the individuals with these problem profiles and their known co-offenders.

The proportion of the individuals classified into the different profile groups who were suspected of offences in Stockholm between 1991 and 1995 and who are thus identifiable in the network data varied between 69 per cent in the crime profile group and 47 per cent in the sexual disturbance profile group. The remainder of the classified individuals were not suspected of offences in Stockholm during this period.

Table 6.1 shows that the average age of the members of the various profile groups did not differ markedly from that of the principal population as a whole. Individuals classified in the substance-abuse profile and the

Table 6.1: *Number, average age at first registered offence, proportion of females, and average number of co-offenders and offence participations for youths in secure care facilities classified into one of the problem profile groups and suspected of offences in Stockholm between 1991 and 1995, and for their co-offenders, as well as the corresponding data for all youths suspected of offences in Stockholm during the same period*

	Crime prof.	Subst. ab. prof.	Psych. prof.	Sex. prof.	0 prof.	Total	All suspects
Actors							
Number of actors	184	118	64	33	141	540	19,617
Average age	16.7	17.3	17.0	16.6	15.8	16.6	16.7
% females	12.1	35.8	34.7	75.7	25.4	27.3	27.0
Average no. offence participations/ individual	5.6	5.1	5.1	2.7	5.2	5.2	1.7
Average no. co-offenders/individual	4.6	3.1	3.2	1.7	4.6	3.9	2.3
Co-offenders							
No. of co-offenders	672	337	219	64	618	1,910	13,262
Average age	19.3	21.3	21.2	20.7	19.8	20.1	18.0
% females	9.1	10.2	10.0	28.6	10.6	10.5	23.0
Average no. offence participations/ individual	2.9	2.5	4.1	2.7	2.8	3.0	2.0
Average no.co-offenders/individual	3.6	3.2	3.3	2.4	3.4	3.4	3.9

psychological disturbance profile were a little older than the others, whilst those classified in the 0 profile were a little younger.

With regard to the proportion of females, the crime profile is noteworthy for the low proportion of females classified into this profile group, whilst the proportion of females in the sexual disturbance profile is very high.

On average, the youths classified into the various profile groups presented a higher level of delinquency than the average for the principal population between 1991 and 1995, and this was true even for those individuals whose problems were not judged to be primarily crime related, such as those classified in the sexual and psychological disturbance profiles. The individuals classified in the sexual disturbance profile nonetheless presented a level of delinquency that was on average significantly lower than that of the other groups. (Another factor indicating that this group is less delinquent than the others was that a smaller proportion of this group was found in the police data covering persons suspected of offences).

The youths classified in the various problem profiles had more known co-offenders and thus more central positions in their respective networks than the average for the principal population. The young people in the sexual-disturbance profile represent an exception here, having fewer known co-offenders than the average, which is probably due to the fact that most of the members of this group were girls, who on the whole had less central positions in the networks studied. Not surprisingly, the individuals classified into the crime profile and the 0 profile (i.e. the two groups presenting the highest levels of delinquency) had the most known co-offenders (4.6 per individual).

On average, the co-offenders chosen by members of the different profile groups were older than the actors themselves. As has been mentioned, this age difference is natural, since, unlike membership of the principal population, membership of the co-offender group is not defined on the basis of age. The average age difference between the profile group individuals and their known co-offenders lies at around four years. The exception is the crime profile group where the co-offenders are on average 2.6 years older. The age difference among the youths classified into the different profile groups and their co-offenders is considerably larger than the average age difference among members of the principal population as a whole and their co-offenders, however. The general trend in the data is that more highly delinquent youths have older co-offenders more often than their less delinquent counterparts.

The proportion of females among the co-offenders for all the profile groups is lower than the proportion of females classified into the different profile groups. This is an interesting finding. One might expect the opposite to be true, at least for the crime profile group, since the girls in the study as a whole seem more often to commit offences together with more highly delinquent boys or with other girls. The most highly delinquent girls, however (those classified into the crime profile group), seem on the whole to have male co-offenders who according to our data present a lower level of delinquency than the girls themselves.

The level of registered delinquency for the co-offenders was lower than that for the youths placed in secure care facilities. It is interesting to note the fairly low level of delinquency presented by co-offenders of the youths in the substance-abuse profile group. Many of the delinquent connections formed by the youths classified as substance-abusers seem to be with individuals suspected of relatively few offences. Some of these offences relate to the sale of drugs. The high level of delinquency presented by the co-offenders of individuals classified in the psychological disturbance profile is also interesting. The youths in this profile group apparently tend more often than the other groups to choose co-offenders from among more highly delinquent persons.

6.3.1 Offence types committed by profile group members and their co-offenders

Table A8 in the appendix presents the offence participations of the members of the different profile groups and their co-offenders on the basis of the different offence types committed. The table also shows the distribution of the various offence types for all those included in the study. The most striking impression when one compares across the different profile groups is that the differences between the profile groups are relatively small. Even if the youths are seen by the responsible authorities to have different fundamental problems, their delinquency, as registered by the police, looks on the whole to be of a fairly similar type. Thus the offence type distribution for all of the profile groups is dominated by various types of theft offences, whilst drug offences, for example, are relatively uncommon, this being true even for the substance-abuse profile.

What is interesting from the point of view of this study is the similarity or dissimilarity of the character of the offences committed by the members of the different profile groups and their co-offenders respectively. Some of the similarity in the offending patterns shown by members of the profile groups and their co-offenders can be ascribed to the fact they participated jointly in a number of these offences. Such joint offences only account for a fairly small proportion of the total number of offence participations, however (just under 15 per cent).

Table 6.2 shows the average delinquency levels in terms of suspected offence participations for offences against the person,[7] property offences,[8] and drug offences[9] for individuals from the five profile groups and their co-offenders. In general the picture is fairly unequivocal. The members of the different profile groups presented levels of delinquency that were consistently higher than those of their co-offenders for all three offence categories. There were two exceptions. Co-offenders of the individuals with the sexual disturbance profile presented a higher level of offences against the person than did the profiled individuals. The level of offences against the person was rather low among those with a sexual disturbance profile in comparison with the other profile groups, however. The second exception

Table 6.2: *Average level of delinquency in the form of offences against the person, offences against property and drug offences (number of suspected offence participations) per individual 1991–1995 for individuals with different problem profiles and for their suspected co-offenders*

	Crime profile	Substance abuse profile	Psych-problem profile	Sexual disturbance profile	Profile 0
Offences against the person					
Actors	2.3	1.7	1.7	0.9	1.9
Co-offenders	1.1	1.1	1.3	1.2	1.0
Offences against property					
Actors	2.6	2.1	2.6	1.2	2.5
Co-offenders	1.4	0.8	2.1	1.1	1.4
Drug offences					
Actors	0.3	0.5	0.3	0.2	0.4
Co-offenders	0.2	0.2	0.4	0.1	0.2

relates to the co-offenders of individuals with a psychological disturbance profile, who presented a somewhat higher level of drug-related delinquency than did the members of the profile group in question.

In addition, table 6.2 shows that although the members of the crime profile are more delinquent when it comes to crimes against the person than the other profile groups, their co-offenders are no more delinquent as regards this form of offending than are the co-offenders of members of the other profile groups. On the contrary, co-offenders of the members of the crime profile seem to commit fewer crimes against the person than do the co-offenders of members of both the psychological and sexual disturbance profiles.

Members of the psychological disturbance profile group seem to be somewhat more active when it comes to property offences than the members of the crime profile group. And their co-offenders commit considerably more property offences than do the co-offenders of members of the crime profile group.

The co-offenders of members of the substance-abuse profile do not seem to commit an exceptionally high number of drug offences. Once again the co-offenders of members of the psychological disturbance profile appear on average to be suspected of drug offences more often than the members of the psychological profile group themselves.

The results presented above suggest that those youths in the profile groups who themselves present relatively high levels of delinquency tend to commit offences with other fairly highly delinquent individuals, even if these co-offenders seem to be somewhat less delinquent than the profile group members themselves.[10] The delinquency levels of members of the different profile groups do not vary greatly between the various profiles although certain offence types which are specifically related to the different profiles are somewhat more common among members of the profile group in question than among the other profile groups. These profile-typical offences do not seem to be any more common among the co-offenders of the specific profile groups in question than they are among the co-offenders from the other profile groups, however. Thus the delinquency patterns of the co-offenders do not seem to be more similar to the patterns presented by the specific profile groups with whose members they co-offend than we would expect of any other highly delinquent individuals.

The analysis of the delinquency of the profile group members and that of their co-offenders carried out on the basis of the network data leads to the conclusion that our material does not contain definite groups of youths who specialise in certain types of offence. It is worth looking a little more closely at this conclusion, however.

6.3.2 Offending patterns in the networks of youths in the crime and substance-abuse profiles

This section examines the delinquency of youths from the crime and substance-abuse profiles as well as that of the individuals with whom they are linked. These two profile groups were chosen for closer examination partly because they constitute the largest of the profile groups and partly because their principal problems are related to delinquency.

Within the framework of the project, these two groups were studied by Shannon (1998). He discusses, amongst other things, whether it is really a question of two distinct profile groups, or whether the profiling mechanism might rather have identified two different stages in a career that many of the individuals have in common. Despite the fact that there are certain similarities among the offending patterns presented by members of the two groups at younger ages, Shannon finds that when comparing the structure of their respective delinquency patterns at age 19 and above the differences between the two groups are sufficient to support the conclusion that we are in fact looking at two different career trajectories. Violent offences are much more common among individuals from the crime profile, for example, whilst at the same time these youths are seldom suspected of drug offences. The offending pattern of the individuals from the substance-abuse profile, on the other hand, is more focused on drug and theft offences.

Unlike the presentation in the preceding section, the data studied here are not the offence participations of the actors in question, but rather the links which tie these individuals to their known co-offenders. The examination of links is not restricted to those in the individuals' personal networks (i.e. those linking them to their immediate co-offenders) but also covers indirect links, in steps of one link at a time, up to a distance of eight such steps from the individual in question.

As was mentioned above, the individuals in the crime profile were suspected of violent offences to a greater extent than other individuals in the study. Two offences of which these individuals were commonly suspected were those coded by the police as common assault (i.e. less serious) on an adult male, outdoors, and muggings, without firearms. The following analysis examines links between individuals from the crime profile and their co-offenders which are comprised of incidents coded by the police into these two offence categories.

Of all the links included in this part of the study, 4.9 per cent contained the type of assault examined here, and 3.6 per cent muggings.[11] In total we are looking at 8.2[12] per cent of all the links covered in this section of the study. Figure 6.3 shows how large a proportion of all the links contain these two offences, at each step taken away from the 184 crime profile individuals in their respective networks. Step one refers to the links between the individuals from the crime profile and their immediate co-offenders, whilst step two refers to links between these co-offenders and *their* co-offenders, and so on all the way to step eight.[13]

Figure 6.4 shows that the proportion of links containing muggings and assaults of the type studied varies little in the first three steps taken away from the crime-profile individuals. The proportion of links containing these offences is considerably higher than the average for the material as a whole in these first three steps. The proportion then drops markedly as we move further away from the members of the crime-profile group. After step five, the proportion of links containing these offences is lower than the average for the material as a whole.

A corresponding analysis for the 118 individuals from the substance-abuse profile produced results that were in part very similar. The offences that were studied in this instance were partly possession and consumption of illicit drugs and partly all other forms of contact with such substances, with the exception of manufacture. This last category primarily covers offences that would be referred to as 'drug dealing' in everyday parlance.

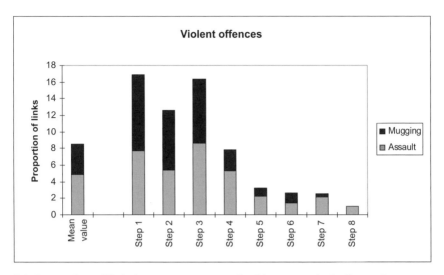

6.3 Proportion of links between persons under 21 suspected of offences in Stockholm between 1991 and 1995, containing 'common assault on an adult male, outdoors' and 'mugging'. Links divided into network distance 'steps' from members of the crime profile group.

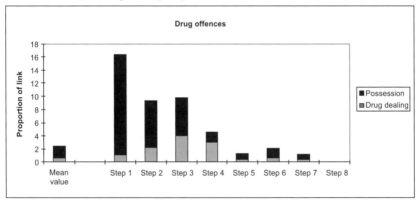

6.4 Proportion of links between persons under 21 years suspected of offences in Stockholm between 1991 and 1995 including the offences of 'possession and use of drugs' and 'other contact with drugs besides possession, use and manufacture'. Links divided into network distance 'steps' from members of the substance-abuse profile group.

These two offence categories were relatively rare in the data as a whole, with possession/use offences in total comprising 1.8 per cent of all links, and dealing comprising 0.6 per cent of links. Between them, these two offence categories comprised 2.1 per cent of all links covered in the study.

The proportion of links between youths in the substance-abuse profile and their co-offenders which contain dealing offences are only very slightly higher than the average for the study material as a whole. This is perhaps not so surprising, since these youths' problems have primarily to do with substance abuse rather than with drug-dealing. The proportion of links containing dealing offences rises as we move a little further from the individuals in the substance-abuse profile, and is highest at step three, that is, at a network distance of two steps from the individuals in this profile group.

The picture is different for possession offences and thus (since these constitute the majority of drug offences) also for drug offences as a whole. The proportion of links containing drug offences was much higher among individuals in the substance-abuse profile and their immediate co-offenders than in the links of the subsequent steps. Up until step four, the proportion of drug offences was higher in the networks surrounding the 118 members of the substance-abuse profile than was the average for the study material as a whole, whilst at distances further than this from the profile individuals, the proportion of links containing drug offences was lower in these networks than the average.

Thus the levels of suspected drug offences in the networks around the substance-abuse profile seem to be similar to the levels of suspected violent offences in the networks around the youths from the crime profile. Just as there appears to be a circle of individuals linked to one another by, in addition to other offence types, an extensive amount of violent offending, we find a group of individuals linked to one another with a high proportion of drug offences. The offences which link together individuals outside these groups contain considerably lower proportions of violent and drug offences respectively than those linking together the individuals within these groups.

Perhaps the most important result of this particular analysis, however, is that these two groups of individuals – those linked by relatively high proportions of violent offences and drug offences, to a large extent constitute *one and the same group* of linked individuals. Several of these actors were members of the Central Network. In fact, of the Central Network's 4,130 members, 2,647 (64 per cent) were to be found at a distance of three steps or less from the individuals in the crime and/or substance-abuse profile groups.

If we use network analysis to identify those individuals lying within three network steps of members of one of the two profile groups, we find that 67 per cent of the members of these two groups in fact comprise the same individuals.

Shannon (1998), who also studied the known offending patterns of youths from the same networks as members of these two profile groups, found no support for the hypothesis that the youths in the networks of these two groups were members of different kinds of network or moved in different offending environments. He suggests that if it is in fact possible to differentiate two distinct problem profiles in the individuals studied, whilst at the same time noting that these profiles have evolved in similar (or as I have shown in more-or-less the same) social environments (networks), then explanations of the differences in the deviant behaviours presented by the young people in question ought to be sought primarily at the level of the individual. This conclusion may be correct, provided that the networks of these two groups do not differ significantly along other dimensions which it has not been possible to study given the method used here. It is possible, for example, that there might be differences in family circumstances among individuals from the different profile groups.

A close examination of the problems presented by the parents of those included in the profile groups, as well as of the youths' relations with their parents, the youths' values, their behaviour in the secure care facilities and so forth (Sarnecki 1996) suggests that there were only a few significant differences between the youths from the crime and substance-abuse profile groups. The following differences may be of interest in this context:

The substance-abuse group contained a higher proportion of girls than the crime profile group (36 per cent as compared with 12 per cent).[14]

The proportion of youths with parents presenting drink problems was higher in the substance-abuse profile than in the crime profile (36 per cent as compared with 26 per cent for fathers; 20 per cent as compared with 14 per cent for mothers).

The proportion of drug abusers is also slightly higher among parents of the substance-abuse profile group as compared with the crime profile group.

Besides these, differences were small to the extent that they presented themselves at all. Youths from both the crime profile and the substance-abuse profile often came from backgrounds that were very difficult, as was indeed the case with the young people classified into the other problem profiles as well.

A comparison between the youths from the two profile groups cannot refute the hypothesis that in the context of similar influences from the delinquent environment, it is individual characteristics that lead to different types of delinquent career. It is possible, for example, that girls and persons with parents who are substance-abusers more often become substance-abusers themselves, whilst boys from difficult home environments where substance abuse is not as common more often evolve into delinquents with a tendency towards the use of violence. And this despite the fact that both groups are members of delinquent networks where models and opportunities for both types of behaviour are readily available. This does not exclude the possibility that belonging to a delinquent network of this type increases the likelihood of the onset of deviant behaviour and also of its becoming more frequent and permanent.

6.4 Summary and conclusions

Of the individuals included in the network study, 540 were admitted to secure care facilities as a result of serious delinquency and/or other forms of antisocial behaviour. This chapter has taken a closer look at the networks of these individuals.

We can assume that the youths admitted to secure care facilities in most cases number those among the most socially disadvantaged individuals covered by the network study as a whole. It is therefore hardly surprising that these youths often assumed central positions in the networks studied. A large proportion of these youths were also members of the Central Network.

Even if many of the young people admitted to secure care facilities were members of the same network (which itself constituted part of the Central Network) it was nonetheless relatively unusual for these youths to be linked directly to one another by means of joint participation in offences. Of all the links tying these youths to their co-offenders, only 10 per cent involved links between individuals both of whom had been admitted to secure care facilities.

Ties between individuals who were at the same secure care facility at the same time were even fewer, comprising only 1.5 per cent of all links among youths admitted to these institutions and their co-offenders. This suggests that a stay in such an institution has little significance for the formation of new delinquent relations and thus plays no great role in the continued delinquency of youths placed in these facilities.

The reoffending of youths admitted to secure care facilities was compared with that of a matched control group. The results show that youths admitted to secure care facilities reoffended somewhat more often than those in the control group, who were similarly delinquent to begin with but who had not been the target of such radical interventions on the part of the authorities.

A comparison of the levels of delinquency between registered co-offenders of those admitted to secure care facilities and co-offenders of the control group showed, however, that the co-offenders of the youths admitted to secure care facilities committed fewer offences during the period following the placement of their co-offenders in these facilities than did the co-offenders of the control group. One possible interpretation of this result is that societal interventions focused on young delinquents produce a network effect such that the delinquency levels of their co-offenders are reduced. Even if this interpretation is open to question, it seems clear that more research is needed into the network effects of different forms of societal intervention aimed primarily at individuals.

Individuals admitted to secure care facilities were divided into five groups on the basis of the specific types of problem which dominated their patterns of antisocial behaviour. A study of the registered delinquency of these groups showed certain offending patterns to be typical of the different problem profiles. It is difficult, however, to identify any major differences in the character of the offences committed by the co-offenders of the youths in the various profile groups.

The networks of members of two of the problem profile groups, that is, the crime profile and the substance-abuse profile, were the focus of a more detailed analysis. This showed that links at a distance of fewer than four network steps from members of the crime profile contained a considerably higher proportion of violent offences than the remainder of the links. A corresponding pattern, this time in relation to drug offences, was found in the networks surrounding the substance-abuse profile group. Links closer than three or four network steps from the members of this profile group contained a much higher proportion of drug offences than the average level for all links. Thus the networks studied contain areas where violent offences and drug offences are more common than they are in other areas.

A closer examination shows, however, that the areas of the networks where these two offences were more common to a large extent were comprised of the same individuals. Thus youths classified into the crime profile and/or the substance-abuse profile were positioned in those parts of networks where both violent and drug offences were considerably more common than they were on average.

Youths with somewhat different problems were thus to a large extent found to belong to the same delinquent networks. One possible conclusion is that whilst these youths' problems on a more general level were related to their membership of delinquent networks, the specific character of their problems owed more to conditions at the level of the individual. Girls and individuals whose parents were substance-abusers tended more often to develop a substance-abuse profile, whilst boys whose parents were not substance-abusers tended more often to become violent, despite the fact that both groups of youths belonged to the same networks where models for both types of behaviour were available.

The conclusion drawn from the analyses described here is that the material does not contain groups formed around the more actively delinquent individuals who have visibly specialised in violent[15] or drug offences. What we do find, on the other hand, is a group of highly active delinquent youths who to a larger extent than others spend their time in the commission of more serious offences. This group assumes a central position in the networks of delinquent youths found in Stockholm and contains youths with different problem profiles. It is thus the individuals rather than the networks that, to a certain extent at least, present some degree of delinquent specialisation.

CHAPTER SEVEN

Football hooligans in the networks

In this and the following chapter, the focus is on groups of suspected offenders whose choice of co-offenders and network membership might be expected to follow a different pattern from usual. This chapter looks at football hooligans, whilst the following chapter focuses on members of extremist political groups.

Over recent years, football hooliganism has become a focus of attention both in the criminological literature and elsewhere (Kerr 1994; Armstrong 1998; Pettersson 1998a; du Rées Nordenstad 1998). It is an interesting phenomenon because it differs from other types of delinquency in many respects, not least by way of the expressive nature of the offences concerned. Such offences are committed in large groups, are often organised to some degree, and are characterised by levels of violence and a hatred which are incomprehensible to many. The literature features discussions of whether football hooligans are ordinarily delinquent males exploiting the instability characteristic of emotionally charged masses, or whether their hooliganism is a question of normally law-abiding individuals allowing their strong emotional commitment to their team to explode into violence (Ahlberg 1985).

In Sweden, serious attention was focused on football hooliganism for the first time during the 1980s (Ahlberg 1985; Brottsförebyggande rådet 1986). The size of the problem varies from year to year but at the moment is felt to be on a downward trend (du Rées Nordenstad 1998). Conflicts among supporters of the more successful teams are not uncommon before, during and after matches if groups of agitated supporters (often under the influence of alcohol) come into contact with one another. In order to increase the safety of both the general public and these groups themselves, a number of measures are taken in connection with the more important matches to keep

groups of rival fans apart. It happens, however, that certain groups of supporters go looking for each other with the express intention of fighting. It
is primarily individuals from these groups that are referred to as football
hooligans, individuals with an intense, almost fanatical commitment to their
team and a high propensity for violence at matches (du Rées Nordenstad
1998).

In Stockholm, the police view is that football hooligans are to be found
among the supporters of three of the city's more prominent football clubs:

Allmänna Idrottsklubben (AIK)
Djurgårdens Idrottsförening (DIF)
Hammarbys Idrottsförening (HIF)

The strong ties to a specific team and the presence of some degree of organisation make the different groups of hooligans interesting as networks. In
this chapter, a network analytical examination will be carried out of groups
of individuals adjudged by the police to be football hooligans.

7.1 103 football hooligans

In 1997 a study of football hooliganism and the societal response to this type
of problem was carried out at the Criminology Department of Stockholm's
University (Pettersson 1998a; du Rées Nordenstad 1998). The study was
undertaken in co-operation with a special unit within the Stockholm Police
force that was assigned the task of preventing violence at and around sporting events. One of the methods employed by this police unit was to identify
and keep a close eye on the most violent supporters from the three most successful football clubs in Stockholm. In 1997, when the study was carried out,
the police had under observation a group of 103 individuals judged to be
football supporters particularly prone to violence. It is these individuals that
are here referred to as football hooligans.

Pettersson (1998a: 112, 113) interviewed a number of informants with an
extensive knowledge of the problems associated with football hooliganism.
The information provided by these people confirmed the validity of the
police document listing the most violence-prone football supporters.
According to the informants, the core of the group of football hooligans in
Stockholm had not changed very much since the first half of the 1990s.

Of the 103 football hooligans, eighty-seven (85 per cent) were born
between 1970 and 1978 and would thus be found among the principal population of the network study provided they were suspected of offences
during the period from 1991 to 1995. Of these, sixty-nine (67 per cent) have

actually been identified in the network study data. These individuals were distributed among the supporters of the three football clubs in question in the following way:

47 per cent were supporters of AIK
32 per cent were supporters of DIF
21 per cent supported HIF

7.1.1 The personal networks of AIK supporters

The thirty-three AIK supporters on the police list of football hooligans who were both aged under 21 at some stage during the period from 1991 to 1995 and also suspected of offences in Stockholm during this period, together had twenty co-offenders registered in RAR who were not on the list of AIK hooligans provided by the police. Two of these co-offenders were on the police list of DIF supporters, however, and one was on the police list of HIF supporters.

Figure 7.1 shows the personal networks of the AIK supporters studied, that is, the networks comprising the hooligans themselves and their known co-offenders. During the period from 1991 to 1995 seven such networks can be identified, of which two are somewhat larger than the others, whilst two comprise only pairs of actors. A further seven AIK supporters turned up in the network data as isolates and are therefore not presented in the graph.

The largest network in figure 7.1 consists in part of twelve AIK supporters who were together suspected of participating in a disturbance near one of Stockholm's bridges in autumn 1994. Twenty-one of the total of fifty-seven links binding the members of this network to one another are related to this single event. The disturbance occurred in connection with a football match. For several of the AIK supporters, this was the only offence for which they were registered in RAR during the period from 1991 to 1995.

Several other individuals who are members of this network are linked into it by means of the robbery of a taxi-driver, which they were suspected of having committed together with two of the AIK supporters in autumn 1993. One of the participants in this robbery was a person listed by the police as one of the DIF hooligans. The network also contains an individual listed as an HIF hooligan. This individual is tied into the network by means of suspected participation in two other public-order disturbances in spring 1992 and spring 1993, together with one of the AIK supporters and a further individual. The HIF supporter, who was born in 1974, had a total of forty known co-offenders and was registered for offences in seven of the ten six-month periods covered by the network study. His delinquency consisted partly of

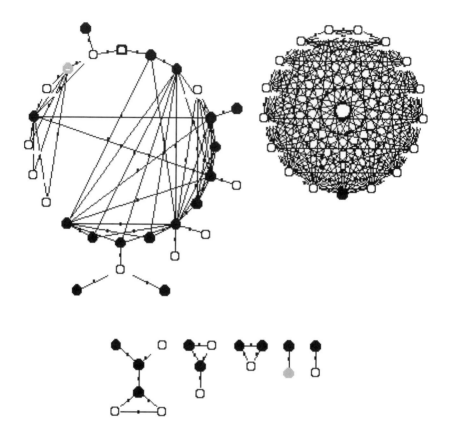

7.1 Personal networks in Stockholm between 1991 and 1995 of AIK supporters from the list of football hooligans provided by the police. AIK supporters marked with black circles, DIF supporters marked with grey circles, HIF supporters marked with squares, others marked with white circles. Scale 1:3

football-related public-order offences, but he was also suspected of a considerable number of other violent offences, such as common assault, assaults on public servants, and vandalism.

The other large network comprises a single vandalism offence in the centre of Stockholm involving the destruction of a number of cars. Only one of the individuals on the police list of football hooligans participated in this offence, and the remaining sixteen participants were youths aged from 16 to 19 years. A number of these were suspected of other offences either prior to or after the vandalism of the cars. The event bears many of the characteristics of a public-order offence, but is not related to football.

The graph contains two further events of the type described above: a smaller disturbance at one of Stockholm's sporting arenas involving three AIK supporters and three others, and a trespass offence at a public baths where two AIK supporters and two other individuals were suspected.

The remainder of the offences included in figure 7.1 were primarily car thefts and assaults for which AIK supporters were suspected, together with one another and with co-offenders not present on the police list. These offences are probably not football-related. This is also true of a vandalism offence at a restaurant in the centre of Stockholm for which an AIK supporter and a DIF supporter were suspected.

7.1.2 The personal networks of DIF supporters

The 22 DIF hooligans had a total of 158 known co-offenders. The large majority of these are to be found in a single large network which comprises a few football-related incidents which took place during spring 1992 and spring 1993. A total of 145 individuals were registered by the police in association with these two disturbances, of which 24 are on the list of football hooligans (14 were DIF supporters, 8 were HIF supporters and 2 were AIK supporters). The remaining 107 individuals suspected in connection with these offences were not on the police list of football hooligans.

It is important to note that for most of the individuals (68 per cent) suspected in connection with these two events (and who were under 21 at the time) participation in one of these disturbances is the only offence for which they are suspected, according to our data. Some of those involved present a high level of delinquency, however (7 per cent are suspected of having committed five or more offences). The supporters (DIF and HIF) who are present on the police list of hooligans and who are also present in this network were on average more delinquent than the others. The types of offence for which they were suspected varied, and besides participation in public-order offences, vandalism and assaults on public servants, they were also suspected of other forms of violent offence and a considerable amount of property crime.

Besides being members of the large network described above, one or two of the DIF supporters are linked into two smaller networks (comprising nine and eleven individuals respectively) and two dyads. One of the smaller networks is also constituted in part of a football-related disturbance (spring 1993). The remaining links connecting known DIF hooligans to their co-offenders concern offences which do not appear to be football-related.

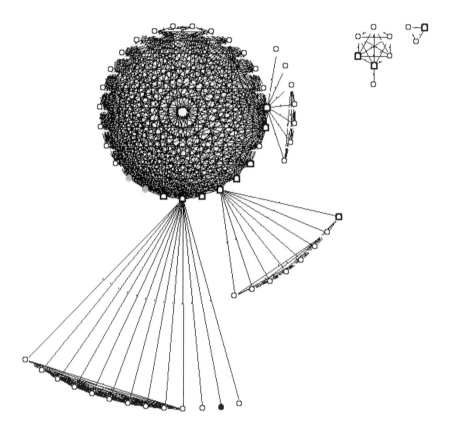

7.2 Personal networks in Stockholm between 1991 and 1995 of HIF supporters from the list of football hooligans provided by the police. AIK supporters marked with black circles, DIF supporters marked with grey circles, HIF supporters marked with squares, others marked with white circles. Scale 1:4

7.1.3 The personal networks of HIF supporters

The HIF supporters are linked together in one large network comprising fifty-five individuals and two smaller networks comprising seven and three individuals respectively. The largest network containing HIF supporters formed around the same incident at the South Stadium in spring 1993 that was partially constitutive of the largest network of DIF supporters discussed above. Seen from the perspective of the HIF supporters, the network contains eight HIF supporters, two DIF supporters and seventeen individuals not present on the police list of hooligans (see figure 7.2). Three of the HIF supporters were then suspected of one offence each (during spring 1991 and spring 1992) which also had the character of public-order disturbances. One of these offences was the trespass at the outdoor public baths already referred to in connection with the examination of the AIK supporters' offences.

The network comprising seven individuals arose as a result of two HIF supporters and five other individuals participating in another football-related disturbance in spring 1991. Links between HIF supporters and other individuals which are not related to football hooliganism or other types of public-order offences are rare.

7.2 Football hooligans in the Central Network

Forty-five per cent of the AIK supporters, 77 per cent of the DIF supporters and 79 per cent of the HIF supporters found in our data were linked into the Central Network. In total, 69 per cent of all the football hooligans under age 21 who were both mentioned on the police list and suspected of offences in Stockholm between 1991 and 1995 were members of the Central Network. This might be seen to indicate that a significant proportion of the individuals who were judged by the police to be football hooligans in 1997, assumed fairly central positions among suspected juvenile delinquents between seven and two years earlier. The proportion is high given the fact that only 20 per cent of all young people suspected of offences during this period were tied into the Central Network.

Such an interpretation may represent an overestimation of the significance of football hooligans for juvenile offending in Stockholm. The public-order offences for which football hooligans[1] were suspected were of a very special nature, not least from a network perspective. Many of these offences involved a large number of individuals and thus generated a lot of links. It then takes only one of the individuals suspected of participating in the public order disturbance to be suspected of an offence with another individual who is in turn linked into a larger network for all participants in the original disturbance to be counted as members of this same network. It was through associations of this kind that a considerable proportion of the football hooligans listed by the police were linked into the Central Network. Of the 4,130 members of the Central Network, 764 (18 per cent) were suspected of participating in public-order disturbances of one kind or another, some of which were related to football hooliganism whilst others were of a different nature, occasionally political. Of 20,852 links in the Central Network, 8,037 (or 39 per cent) contain this type of offence. The majority of the individuals who participated in such disturbances had peripheral positions in the Central Network. However, this group also contains individuals with central positions who, in addition to their participation in public-order offences, were also suspected of several more traditional offences.

The large number of individuals, and particularly links, in the Central Network that are related to different types of public order offences raises the question of whether it is just such individuals and links, representing 'atypical' offences, that hold the Central Network together. The types of interaction among individuals involved in these offences are of a rather special kind (see pp. 71–4), and if such offences are of essential to the connectivity of the Central Network, then the whole thesis on the major significance of the Central Network might be called into question. The fact is, however, that individuals linked into the Central Network only through public order offences of this kind are not of any major significance for the network. In figure 5.3 (chapter 5), a considerable proportion of these individuals (151 individuals, or 20 per cent) and the majority of the links connecting them (5,426 links, or 68 per cent) were excluded for technical reasons (relating to the capacity of the computer program) without having an effect on the remainder of the network. If the remaining actors who are linked into the Central Network exclusively by means of participation in public disturbances are excluded, the Central Network would still comprise 3,768 individuals. These individuals would be connected by a total of 12,857 links. The number of offence participations, and particularly the number of offences for which the network is responsible, are only marginally affected.

An interesting discovery is that one of the more peripheral parts of a network generated in connection with a certain politically inspired disturbance is bound to the Central Network by means of the fact that a number of the participants at this political disturbance were also involved in the disturbance at the South Stadium mentioned earlier. There are thus apparently a number of young people who join in with public-order disturbances somewhat irrespective of the character of the disturbance in question. These youths are then linked with other more traditionally delinquent areas of the Central Network by means of other types of offending.

According to our data, a majority of the individuals suspected of participating in politically inspired disturbances, and perhaps more surprisingly a majority (albeit a smaller one) of those suspected of participation in football-related disturbances, have not been registered in connection with any other delinquency than just these public order offences.

The relatively low (known) level of other types of offence than solely 'football hooliganism' and the like is somewhat surprising. Pettersson (1998a) studied the same group in 1997 and found them to be more involved in other types of offending than they were in football-related offences. We have no option but to state that in our data we have found networks that specialise in this type of offence and that although they are linked to networks with different offending profiles, they are nonetheless relatively self-contained. Hooliganism seems also to be relatively persistent over time, since, as was mentioned above, we find individuals from the hooligan list generated in 1997 turning up in connection with football-related disturbances as early as 1991.

Thus football hooliganism in some ways constitutes an exception to the principles that have been described earlier in this study.

7.3 Summary and conclusions

This part of the study was based on a list, provided by the police, that contained the names of 103 of the most violence-prone supporters of Stockholm's three most successful football teams. Sixty-nine of the individuals on this list could be identified in the network study data.

Three separate analyses were carried out on the personal networks of these sixty-nine individuals during the period from 1991 to 1995. The analyses confirm that many of these individuals were in fact involved in public order disturbances and other offences related to football matches. The results also suggest that the young people identified as football hooligans had on several occasions also been involved in other types of disturbance not directly linked to their sporting interests. A number of these individuals were also suspected of other more traditional offence types, and some presented high levels of delinquency.

A large number of individuals were suspected of having participated in football-related disturbances together with the hooligans identified by the police. For most of these, their participation in the disturbances in question represented the only offences for which they were suspected. However, in this group too there was a small number of more highly delinquent individuals. By means of the fact that the football hooligans were linked to these highly delinquent individuals, the hooligans' personal networks were tied into the Central Network. Around 18 per cent of the members of the Central Network comprised individuals who had participated in some or other (often football-related) public-order disturbance. Many of these people are not known as delinquents outside of their participation in such disturbances and are thus not typical of members of the Central Network. In most cases, though, these individuals assume marginal positions in the Central Network. If they were to be excluded it would certainly mean a considerable reduction in the number of links comprising the network, but any other effects would be insignificant.

Some of the football hooligans and their co-offenders appear to differ from the other youths studied in that they seem to be members of special-ised networks. At the same time, when Pettersson (1998a) studied the same group of hooligans and their co-offenders a few years later, she found that several members of the group were also suspected in connection with other offences. This might indicate that the levels of offending of those studied, and their contact with other actively delinquent individuals, increase as they become older. It is even possible that the increase in the extent and diver-sity of the offending patterns of these individuals might be related to their connection to the Central Network.

Football-related disturbances are untypical of the offences in our study in another way too. Persons who participate in one and the same disturbance and are thus linked together in the same network are often members of dif-ferent groups that are hostile to one another. As has been described above, for example, the 'mortal enemies' among the supporters of HIF and DIF are registered as having committed public order offences together. Some of the co-offenders in such offences can be said to occupy the same role as that of the victim in other more traditional types of delinquent networks. This antagonistic relation between co-offenders participating in one and the same offence is of course a complicating factor when it comes to interpret-ing the networks. It is no longer a question of transferring the same kind of techniques, attitudes and values as when individuals in another context together commit a burglary or an assault, for example.

At the same time we can assume that even here there exists a mechanism whereby different groups of football hooligans exert influence over one another. Their behaviours are essentially the same and this is also true of their attitudes and values. The learning of delinquent behaviour can in fact take place in situations characterised more by harsh and implacable confron-tation than by the intimate co-operation between the participants that we are perhaps more used to imagining. In spite of the antagonism among the indi-viduals concerned, our discovery that 'enemies' often belong to the same network in fact represents another example of the way the assumptions on which the study is based manifest themselves in practice. Even here there is a transference of norms, values and delinquent techniques taking place. Through participation in the same offence the young people learn from one another how such offences are committed, even though this process takes place whilst the actors concerned are involved in a violent confrontation.

It should be added that even if associations with a certain group of sup-porters appear to be both committed and long-term, this does not prevent 'enemies' from committing other more traditional types of offence together (at least on occasion) in other contexts.

CHAPTER EIGHT

Politically and ideologically motivated offences

This chapter is also devoted to a specific and in some ways atypical group among the delinquent youths studied, namely individuals who during the last six months of 1995 were suspected of crimes described by the Swedish state security police as 'national security related' (Säkerhetspolisen, State security police 1996, 1997, 1998). Members of the research project made an application for and were granted permission to examine the extent of these individuals' involvement in networks of young delinquents in Stockholm between 1991 and 1995.

The analysis is based on a list provided by the security police containing information pertaining to ninety-seven individuals. The list included:

eighty-two persons suspected of extreme right-wing offences[1]
fourteen persons suspected of extreme left-wing offences[2]

In criminological terms, the offences for which these individuals were suspected would fall under the rubric of 'hate crimes' (Hamm 1994) and/or political crimes with more-or-less clearly defined ideological motives. Information concerning these individuals' crimes came from offence reports recorded in the police's RAR register, that is, the same register as that from which the network study data was drawn. Each county police authority (including Stockholm) employs someone to carry out a continual examination of RAR reports in order to pick out 'national security-related' offences with the aid of specific criteria. These sweeps cover eighty-one different offence codes. One of the units within the security police then has the responsibility of maintaining a register of all the relevant offence reports (State security police 1998: 5). The information provided is further examined by this unit and constitutes the basis for yearly reports (State security police 1996, 1997, 1998).

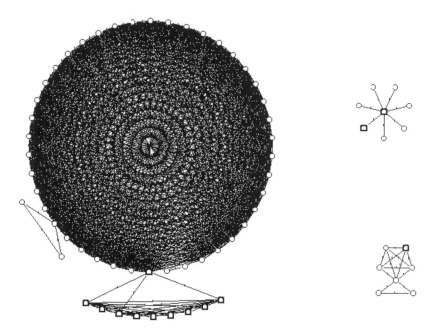

8.1 Persons suspected by the state security police of extreme left-wing offences during autumn 1995 and their known co-offenders between 1991 and 1995 at one and two network steps from the individuals concerned. Persons suspected of extreme left-wing offences marked with squares, others marked with circles. Scale 1:5

The suspected extreme right- and left-wing offenders included on the list were born between 1920 and 1980. Only fifty-three of them were born in 1971 or later and could thus at some point have found their way into the network study's principal population.

A total of forty-two individuals from the list were identified in the network data, twenty-eight were suspected of right-wing offences and fourteen were suspected of left-wing offences. Most of these were members of the principal population, but a few of the older individuals from the police list were also present by virtue of having been suspected of offences together with members of the principal population.

8.1 Left-wing extremists

According to the state security police, most of the left-wingers on the list belong to one or other of 'a number of loose knit single issue groups with a shared core ideological viewpoint' (State security police 1998: 4).

The networks drawn up around actors suspected of extreme left-wing offences comprise the suspected left-wing extremists, their immediate co-offenders, and also the co-offenders of this first group of co-offenders (i.e. individuals who lie two network steps from the suspected extremists).[3] In all, we are looking at networks comprising sixty-eight individuals, fourteen of whom were on the security police list.

The average age of the members of these networks (at the time of the first offence during the period from 1991 to 1995) was rather high, at 19.8 years, the individuals being between 14 and 39 years of age (SD = 4.8). Females made up 26 per cent of the group. Data relating to where these individuals lived was extremely patchy.

Three networks containing one or more persons suspected of extreme left-wing offences were identified, of which the largest comprised a total of fifty-three individuals. These were linked together by means of only two incidents; however, one was a large disturbance in autumn 1991 in central Stockholm for which forty individuals were suspected. Only one of these suspects was to be found on the security police list of suspected left-wing extremists, a young woman born in the mid-1970s and living in Stockholm who was also suspected of a further (unspecified) public order offence just over four years later, in autumn 1995, this time together with nine other individuals. According to the RAR register, this offence was committed at the university underground station. All ten of the persons suspected of this offence (comprising an additional woman and eight men, all in their twenties) were to be found on the security police list of persons suspected of extreme left-wing offences in autumn 1995, and it was obviously just this offence that led to their names being on the list.

Of the remaining two networks, one was comprised of an unspecified petty offence for which two individuals from the police list and a further six people were suspected, and the other of a trespass offence in autumn 1993 for which one individual from the police list was suspected together with four others. One of these four people was suspected in connection with a further trespass offence during the same period. The first of these two offences was obviously political in character, the youths in question protesting against the building of a new road. As regards the second, it is not altogether clear but nonetheless quite possible that it was also of a political nature.

All in all, every crime committed by the extremist left-wing youths seems to have been politically motivated. The data show no sign of any network ties to other groups of 'ordinary' criminals. The average number of offences per individual was very low at 1.1, the vast majority thus being suspected of participating in a single offence only.

8.2 Right-wing extremists

The networks of individuals suspected of extreme right wing offences (figure 8.2) are different in some ways from those of the suspected left-wing extremists. Here we find a greater number of networks and their structure is less clear.

The twenty-eight individuals suspected of extreme right-wing offences were linked to a total of eighty-six co-offenders within two places of themselves in the networks. The average age was somewhat lower than that of those suspected of extreme left-wing offences (18.7 years) and the variation in age was also somewhat smaller (SD = 3.3). The proportion of females was considerably lower (7 per cent).

The largest network comprised thirty-one individuals aged from 15 to 27 years (average age 19), who were linked together via a large number of offences committed during 1994 and 1995. Five of the members of this group were to be found on the police list of extreme right-wing offenders. The types of offence for which the members of this network were suspected varied somewhat, but they consisted primarily of crimes against the person such as threats, unlawful entry, several cases of common and aggravated assault against males unknown to the perpetrator, threats against public servants, unlawful possession of weapons (other than firearms) and vandalism of public property. The group does not seem to be based in any particular area, its members coming from a number of different parts of Stockholm.[4]

The offending of this group was concentrated primarily in central Stockholm, the offences often being committed in the Old Town. A number of offences occurred at a place known to be a rendezvous for skinheads, and the character and offending pattern of the group indicates that it is in fact a gang of skinheads.

This group constitutes part of the Central Network, and as such is linked into an extensive network of young offenders in Stockholm.

The second largest network in figure 8.2 was of a different character. It comprised thirteen members of whom three were registered as suspected of extreme right-wing offences. All of the members seem to live in the same part of central Stockholm, and they seem to have offended together over an extended period of time (first joint offence in spring 1992, last in autumn 1995). The group appeared in the network data for the first time when the boys were from 13 to 14 years of age. The types of offence vary, but include both assaults on juveniles and adults with whom they were acquainted, unlawful possession of weapons (other than firearms), car thefts and break-ins at schools. All the offences seem to have been committed in and around the part of town where the boys lived. The group thus

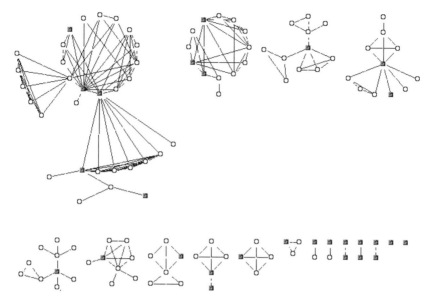

8.2 Persons suspected by the state security police of extreme right-wing offences during autumn 1995 and their known co-offenders between 1991 and 1995 at one- and two network steps from the individuals concerned. Persons suspected of extreme right-wing offences marked with squares, others marked with circles. Scale 1:5

seems to have the character of a locally based network engaged in all-round delinquency.

The following four networks were each formed around one individual (or in one case two individuals) from the police list of suspected right-wing extremists. The principal individuals in each of the networks were highly delinquent in a variety of offence types ranging from trespass, threat and assault to all manner of theft offences and in one case also drug offences. One of the networks contains five individuals who were included on the police list of football hooligans, four DIF supporters and one AIK supporter. One of the DIF supporters and the AIK supporter are also included on the security police list of individuals suspected of extreme right-wing offences. These two individuals were suspected of together having committed a number of anti-Semitic offences. Their differences regarding which of the two football teams was best did not get in the way of them together express-ing their hatred of all things Jewish.

It would be pointless to go through the remaining networks, since the pattern is already clear. Unlike the individuals suspected of extreme left-wing offences, youths suspected of right-wing offences, and those co-offenders lying within a distance of two network steps of these individuals, present

Table 8.1: *Suspected offence participations in Stockholm 1991–1995 for individuals suspected of extreme right-wing offences in autumn 1995 and the members of their networks broken down into different offence categories. Per cent*

Offence type	%	N
Assault, attempted murder, murder	33.3	73
Sex offences	—	—
Mugging	4.1	9
Other crimes against the person	16.1	35
Shoplifting	1.0	2
Other theft offences	20.5	45
Vandalism	5.0	11
Other property offences	3.2	7
Drug offences	2.7	6
Public-order offences, assaults on public servants etc.	8.2	18
Other offences	5.9	13
Total	100.0	219

high levels of delinquency unrelated to their political views and activities. Table 8.1 presents the distribution of the offence participations for which the individuals presented in figure 8.2 were suspected during the years from 1991 to 1995, broken down into offence categories.

Crimes of violence and other offences against the person, particularly different forms of assault, comprise a very high proportion of this group's delinquency. But the level of property offences, including various kinds of theft, was also fairly high. The participation in public-order disturbances so common among the youths suspected of extreme left-wing offences was relatively rare among the right-wing extremist group. Generally speaking, the right-wing extremists seem to participate in all kinds of offence of which a small proportion may be motivated by politics or perhaps rather by hate.

The largest network containing individuals from the police list of right-wing extremists, which at least in part was clearly comprised of skinheads, was linked into the Central Network.

8.3 Summary and conclusions

Considerable differences were observed between the networks of those youths suspected by the security police of having committed extreme left-wing offences during autumn 1995 and those suspected of extreme right-wing offences during the same period. According to the available data, the members of the first group devoted themselves exclusively to political offences, and their offending levels as recorded in the RAR register were low.

Those youths suspected of extreme right-wing offences during the same period, on the other hand, were principally involved in various kinds of traditional offences featuring a considerable amount of violence. Only a small proportion of this group's offences were obviously politically motivated.

Several of the young people suspected of extreme right-wing offences were members of the Central Network earlier identified in the network data, which was not true of the youths suspected of extreme left-wing offences.

A study of males who were active delinquents during the 1970s and at the beginning of the 1980s (Sarnecki 1990b) showed that many of these delinquent men had obvious left-wing sympathies. On average, their political views were somewhat to the left of those of the average male of the same age. Many of these men had also participated in illegal activities organised by the extreme left. The current network study examines a generation of youths that will be of the same age as the children of the men described. Among the delinquent youths in this younger generation we found groups who were obviously acting out extreme right-wing sympathies. There were no such groups to be found during the earlier period.

This observation is interesting in the light of the general social changes seen in Swedish society during this time. The powerful and occasionally quite radical left-wing movement, which for a while successfully influenced social discourse in Sweden, has become successively weaker and has made room for various right-wing groups, some of which are of an extremely radical nature, and which now seem themselves to exert influence within the ongoing social discourse. It is possible that the perspective on society held by antisocial males (and it is almost exclusively a question of males) is more affected by the 'spirit of the age' in which they grow up than we imagine. During the 1970s there were individuals on the outskirts of the left-wing movement who over-internalised the ideology of the left, to such an extent that it became a destructive influence in their lives. Sarnecki (1990b) contends that a considerable proportion of Stockholm's heavy drug-users came from just this group of individuals. The situation today may well be similar, except that individuals with obvious adjustment problems now more often find their way into groups professing extreme right-wing views. Life in a group of skinheads, for example, leads then to further destructive and delinquent behaviour. The difference between the 1970s and the 1990s is that the nature of right-wing ideology means that not all individuals with adjustment difficulties will be able to find a home in these groups. This path is usually not open to immigrant youths, for example, particularly those from countries outside Europe.

The obvious politicising of a certain proportion of highly delinquent youths is an interesting phenomenon in itself. One might ask why a number of delinquent young people should 'spice up' their already highly deviant existence with a deviant ideology. The most credible explanation is probably to be found in a need to neutralise or rationalise certain types of delinquent acts which is characteristic of young people (compare Matza 1964). By referring to some form of extreme political ideology, it becomes easier to justify various types of offence to oneself and one's social network. The spread of such 'neutralising ideologies' may very well be one of the more important functions of the right-wing networks examined here.

It should be added that the relatively isolated groups of youths who carry out extreme right-wing offences are often linked into the same network (the Central Network) which includes a considerable proportion of youths with a non-European background (see chapter 9). Within the Central Network, just a few steps away from the individuals committing racist offences, we find young people who are potentially victims of such offences.

CHAPTER NINE

Ethnicity

The employment of a racial/ethnic perspective on crime is something that is taken for granted in much of the American-inspired social science literature. American criminologists appear to agree that there is an ethnic dimension to the crime problem in the USA, as is evidenced *inter alia* in the criminological literature on American gangs where there is apparent consensus that the majority of gangs are ethnically homogeneous (e.g. Knox 1991: 2, 18; Klein 1995: 105, 106).[1] Gang formation is viewed as a coping mechanism employed by young people from ethnic minorities in the context of oppressive majority rule (Spergel 1995). But ethnic homogeneity in the choice of co-offenders in America is not limited to gangs. In other contexts too it is relatively unusual for individuals from different racial backgrounds to commit offences together. According to the statistics produced by the US Bureau of Justice (1984 table 49), individuals from different ethnic backgrounds were involved in only 6 per cent of reported violent offences. Reiss (1988: 135) compares these statistics with data on the gender composition of groups of perpetrators linked with these same offences and finds that it is less common for perpetrators of violent offences to come from different racial backgrounds than it is for them to come from the different gender groups, which is in itself also very unusual. Reiss and Farrington's study of youths in London (1991: 391) indicates[2] that here too choices of co-offenders from different ethnic backgrounds are very rare.

American criminology exerts a very strong influence over European and perhaps particularly Swedish criminological research, and the bibliography at the end of this volume speaks for itself, the vast majority of the theoretical perspectives and empirical studies on which my own presentation is based coming from the USA. In most contexts this would not constitute too much of a problem, since many of the mechanisms underlying crime are reasonably universal at least in the context of the western world. There are, however, exceptions to this rule, and the ethnic dimension of delinquency would appear to constitute one of these exceptions.

There are clear differences between the American discourse on ethnicity and its Swedish counterpart. Even the conceptual apparatus employed is different in a number of respects. Since the collapse of Nazism in the 1940s, for example, the concept of race has been used only very rarely in the context of social scientific research in many European countries. In the USA, on the other hand, the use of the concept is regarded as quite natural. The reasons for such conceptual differences are not purely ideological but also have to do with the fact that the racial backgrounds of many of the minority groups in European countries are not as easily defined as are the large African- and Latin-American minorities in the USA.

Another difference between the USA and Europe lies in the fact that discussions of the ethnic dimension of criminality have a significantly longer tradition in North America. During the last few decades, however, as more West European countries have come to play host to increasingly multiracial populations, and in particular as more and more people have come to these countries from distant parts of the world, attention has become increasingly focused on the question of ethnicity and crime in Europe too (Killias 1989, Junger 1990, Marshall 1997, Tonry 1997).

Compared with many other countries, Sweden's population was for a long time relatively homogeneous in ethnic terms. In modern times, immigration to Sweden began to increase sharply only after the Second World War (von Hofer *et al.*1997). Today, though, a considerable proportion of the population (about 18 per cent) comes from an immigrant background (Westin and Dingu-Kyrklund 1998). The vast majority of the population is still comprised of ethnic Swedes, however, and as a result discussions often revolve around Swedes and immigrants (or people with an immigrant background) without any attempt being made to differentiate the latter group into its many, often small, constituent ethnic minorities. This terminology, however problematical it may be, will also be employed here.

The immigrants living in Sweden are over-represented among persons convicted of criminal offences (they are about twice as common) in relation to their proportion in the population. Today this over-representation of immigrants in the crime statistics is often taken up and exploited by the Swedish media, but this has not always been the case. Just over thirty years ago, the Swedish Immigration Authority ran an advertising campaign which claimed that immigrants did not commit more criminal offences than

Swedes (Hedenbro 1977), a contention that was false according to all the statistics available (Sveri 1980; von Hofer et al 1997; Martens 1998; Ahlberg 1996). The incident serves to show very clearly how sensitive a question the issue of immigrant criminality has been, and indeed remains, in Sweden.

Over the last few years, the media have reported that the major Swedish cities are characterised by ethnic segregation on a grand scale. One of the ways in which this segregation is often thought to manifest itself is in the formation of ethnically homogeneous groups of youths from different ethnic backgrounds, which then find themselves in conflict both with other such groups and with Swedish youths. In its attempts to put a name to this phenomenon, the press has coined a new phrase: 'low intensity race war' (Ohlsson 1997). The fear was that Sweden was headed for the same fate as America, with ethnically homogeneous gangs in a constant state of conflict with one another. Against this backdrop, it may be of interest to study the ethnic composition of the delinquent juvenile networks in Stockholm.

9.1 The ethnicity study in the network project

Within the framework of the network project, Pettersson (1998b) carried out a study of all individuals from the principal population who were suspected of violent offences[3] at some point during 1995. The results are unequivocal on one point: delinquent networks in Stockholm are comprised of individuals from a mixture of ethnic backgrounds. There is no room for any doubt as to the absence in Stockholm of networks made up of individuals from a single ethnic minority. In this respect Stockholm is very different from the metropolitan areas of North America.

In the course of her study, Pettersson identified the ethnic background[4] of the members of eighty-six co-offending networks (connected components) comprised of three or more members. Of these networks, twenty-two consisted of individuals with a Swedish or other Nordic background, of which half were comprised solely of Swedes. Twenty-three networks consisted of youths from a variety of immigrant backgrounds, and contained no Swedes at all. Eight of these networks were comprised of individuals all of whom were born outside Sweden – that is, of first-generation immigrants. Almost half of the networks, forty-one to be precise, comprised individuals from both Swedish and immigrant backgrounds (Pettersson 1998b: 61).

Pettersson contends that in reality the networks studied were in actual fact fewer and larger than those that turned up in the data, since the individuals examined were also linked to one another with offences of other types than the violent offences which formed her sampling base. This being the case, the ethnic composition of the networks would be even more heterogeneous.[5]

Through a closer examination of the networks, Pettersson has found that networks comprised of individuals from a single ethnic minority (both first and second generation) are extremely rare in her material. Of the eighty-six networks studied, only five were of this kind, the largest of which comprised only four persons. The members of each of these networks were suspected of joint participation in a single offence. The larger networks and networks containing individuals presenting a higher level of delinquency (as has been shown, the more highly delinquent individuals often belong to the larger networks) were ethnically heterogeneous and were comprised of both Swedes and immigrants.

9.2 The choice of co-offenders and victims viewed from an ethnic perspective

The calculations below are based on all persons aged 20 years or under suspected of violent offences during 1995, as well as their victims and suspected co-offenders. The data on the individuals' ethnic backgrounds are taken from Pettersson's study. I have, however, modified her data somewhat by excluding persons suspected of threats and assaults directed at public servants.

This part of the study will examine not only the choice[6] of co-offenders but also that of victims. Counting is based on the understanding that when two individuals aged under 21 choose each other as co-offenders, this constitutes a reciprocal 'choosing', and thus represents two choices. As was described in chapter 4, such mutual choices produce two pairs. When an individual chooses a victim, this represents a choice from the perpetrator's side alone. This type of choice produces one pair.[7] The material contains 1,225 suspect–suspect pairs and 1,998 suspect–victim pairs, where data is available on the ethnic background of both individuals contained in the pair.[8]

As was mentioned above, it is not always easy to classify an individual's ethnic background, particularly when such individuals must be placed into dichotomous categories, as is the case here. There are several problems with a classification of this type. The fact that two individuals come from the same country does not inevitably mean that they have the same ethnic background with regard to language, religion or any of a number of other cultural elements. Immigrants in Sweden who moved here from Turkey, for example, may be ethnic Turks or Kurds, whilst immigrants from Poland might have a Polish-Catholic, Gypsy, or Jewish background (or a combination of two of these). At the same time, it is possible that individuals from different countries, and sometimes even from different continents, can have very similar ethnic backgrounds, as is also the case with many immigrants from Kurdish and Jewish communities. Since many of the ethnic classifications made here are of practical necessity based on the countries of origin of the individuals concerned and their parents, errors of this kind are unavoidable.

Another problem is that it is commonly the case that an individual's ethnic background will span a number of different ethnic groups. A considerable proportion of the youths studied here had parents from two completely different countries. In many cases, one of the parents was Swedish, and the other from one of Sweden's ethnic minorities. There are thus many young people in the data who were born in Sweden of a Turkish father, for example, and a Swedish mother. A mechanical classification of these youths into one of the two ethnic groups to which their parents belong would probably be rather meaningless, and asking such young people about their background produces a wide variety of answers depending on the circumstances.

Two different classifications of this group are employed here. In the first instance, two youths are classified as having the same ethnic background if at least one of the parents[9] of each individual come from the same country. This would mean that if the mothers of two youths are both born in Sweden, for example, the pair is counted as comprising individuals from the same ethnic group. Using this first classification, we find that the majority of both suspect–suspect (70 per cent) and suspect–victim pairs (71 per cent) comprise members of the same ethnic group.

The second method of classification only defines pairs as ethnically homogeneous if all four parents are born in the same country. In the extreme case this would mean that if two Swedish youths were suspected of a joint offence and one of them had a Norwegian father, then the pair would be classified as containing individuals with different ethnic backgrounds.[10] Using this method of classification, the majority of all suspect-suspect and suspect-victim pairs (55 and 59 per cent respectively), contained individuals from different ethnic groups.

Of the results described above, the most relevant for this study is the fact that irrespective of the classification method used, the proportion of ethnically homogeneous or heterogeneous pairs is virtually identical for suspect–suspect pairs and for suspect–victim pairs.

9.3 Swedes/immigrants

In Table 9.1, suspect–suspect pairs are compared with suspect–victim pairs with respect to the proportions comprised of two Swedes, one Swede and one immigrant, and two immigrants. In Classification 1, all individuals with at least one Swedish-born parent are counted as Swedes. Classification 2 reckons as Swedes only those with both parents born in Sweden.

Table 9.1 shows that the network ties presented by delinquent immigrant youths in Stockholm are open to widely different interpretations depending on how the concepts Swedish and immigrant are defined. According to the first method of classification, the majority of suspect–suspect pairs were comprised of Swedish youths. The proportion of pairs comprising two immigrants was very low, 21 per cent of co-offending pairs, and 9 per cent of suspect–victim pairs. From this perspective, it could be contended that violent offences committed by youths in Stockholm are to a large extent a Swedish rather than an immigrant problem irrespective of whether one looks at the perpetrators or the victims. Around half of the suspect–suspect and more than half of the suspect–victim pairs were comprised of two Swedes.

The picture is rather different when 'Swedishness' is defined using the second definition. If one only counts as Swedes those individuals with a 'completely Swedish' background, the proportion of Swedish suspect–suspect pairs drops to around 23 per cent and the proportion of suspect–victim pairs where both individuals are Swedes falls to 27 per cent. This means that 77 per cent of all suspect–suspect pairs contain at least one immigrant. The corresponding proportion for suspect–victim pairs is 73 per cent. From this perspective, violent juvenile offending in Stockholm begins to look very much like an immigrant problem.

Table 9.1 shows that the proportion of suspect–suspect pairs comprising one Swede and one immigrant was 32 per cent irrespective of the classification method used. The proportion of suspect–victim pairs comprising one Swede and one immigrant varied with the different classification methods, however. Irrespective of the classification method employed, the proportion of pairs where Swedes were the victims of violent offences perpetrated by immigrants was greater than the proportion of immigrants victimised in this way by Swedes. The proportion of pairs where Swedes were victimised by immigrants was greater when using classification 2, that is, when the concept 'immigrant' was given a wider application.

The results presented above indicate that manifestations of a supposed ethnic conflict between the majority and immigrant populations could not account for very many of the violent offences studied. The fact that the pro-

Table 9.1: *Choices of co-offenders and victims. Youths under 21 years of age suspected of violent offences in Stockholm in 1995, their co-offenders and victims, presented on the basis of ethnic background (Swedish or immigrant). Classification 1: persons with at least one parent born in Sweden counted as Swedes; Classification 2: only persons with both parents born in Sweden counted as Swedes. Per cent*

Classification	Classification 1		Classification 2	
Type of pair	Suspect–Suspect	Suspect–Victim	Suspect–Suspect	Suspect–Victim
Immigrant–Immigrant	21	9	45	27
Immigrant–Swedish	{32	25	{32	34
Swedish–Immigrant		11		12
Swedish–Swedish	47	55	23	27
Total	100	100	100	100
N	1,225	1,998	1,225	1,998

portion of Swedes victimised by immigrants is larger than the proportion of immigrants victimised by Swedes is almost certainly due to the way in which immigrants were in general more over-represented among the perpetrators of violent offences than they were among the victims of such offences (compare von Hofer *et al.* 1997)

9.4 The choice of co-offenders and victims in eight ethnic groups

In her study of violent offences in the network data from 1995, Pettersson (1998b) classified the individuals studied into eight large ethnic groups (Swedes and seven sub-groups of immigrants): 'Swede' is defined in a more narrow sense. Pettersson counts those persons with at least one parent born outside Sweden as having a foreign background (1998b: 59).

For each of the ethnic groups, a calculation was made of the proportion of pairs in which the individuals studied chose another individual from the same ethnic background (as a co-offender or as a victim respectively) and the proportion in which the co-offender/victim was chosen from each of the other ethnic groups. These choices were then expressed in relation to the proportion of co-offenders/victims from each of the ethnic groups that one would expect to find if such choices were made on a purely random basis. One can make such a calculation in one of two ways, depending on how one approaches the notion of choice of co-offenders and victims:

Individuals can be seen to choose co-offenders and victims from among those actually suspected of offences (or registered as victims of the offences in question).

Individuals can be seen to choose co-offenders and victims from among the population of Stockholm in its entirety.

If we then divide the proportion of actual choices made of individuals from the same ethnic group, and from the other ethnic groups, with the proportion of choices that we would expect to be made of individuals from each of these groups if such choices were completely random, we arrive at a measure of the extent to which a certain ethnic group is over- or under-represented in the actual choices made. The measures describing choices of co-offenders and victims from the same ethnic group as the perpetrator, expressed in terms of the ethnic distribution in the populations of suspects and victims respectively, and then in terms of the total population of Stockholm, are presented in tables 9.2 and 9.3.

9.4.1 Choices of co-offender

On the basis of Pettersson's classification of eight ethnic groups, we find that 41 per cent of the co-offender choices studied concerned two individuals from the same ethnic background. Of these ethnically homogeneous choices, 57 per cent were made by Swedish youths choosing other Swedish youths as co-offenders. The majority (59 per cent) of all co-offender choices included in the data could be termed ethnically heterogeneous. If we restrict ourselves to looking at choices of co-offender made by youths with an immigrant background, the proportion is even larger. Of all the choices of co-offender made by youths from the various ethnic minorities, only 29 per cent concerned two youths from the same ethnic group. It must be remembered, in this context, that the eight ethnic groups are themselves fairly heterogeneous in terms of ethnicity and each include individuals from various, often very different, minority groups. This means that the ethnic heterogeneity in choices of co-offender was in fact even greater than is indicated by the results presented here. Tables 9.2 and 9.3 should be seen against this backdrop.

The measures presented in table 9.2 should be interpreted in the following way: a value of one indicates that the choice of co-offenders gave the same result as would have been expected if it took place on a completely random basis. A value of less than one indicates that individuals from the ethnic group in question are under-represented among the co-offenders chosen by individuals from that same ethnic group, whilst a value greater

Table 9.2: *Individuals under 21 years of age suspected of violent offences in Stockholm 1995. Proportion of choices of co-offender from the perpetrator's own ethnic group, divided by the proportion of such choices that would have been made if the choice of co-offender were made completely at random from the group containing all the co-offenders studied, or from the whole of the population of Stockholm respectively*

Individuals with a background in:	In relation to all co-offenders	In relation to the population of Stockholm	Total number of actual choices made
Sweden	1.3	0.8	527
Scandinavia excluding Sweden	1.7	2.3	176
Europe excluding Scandinavia and Turkey	1.7	2.6	150
The Middle East, Turkey and North Africa	2.3	2.2	248
Africa excluding North Africa	4.7	19.0	119
Asia excluding the Middle East	1.7	0.5	65
South- and Central America	4.5	17.5	77

Notes:
(Calculations based on Pettersson 1998:34, and on table A9 in the appendix)

than one indicates that individuals from the ethnic group in question are over-represented. The higher the value, the greater the level of over-representation. A value of two, for example, indicates that individuals from a certain ethnic group are chosen as co-offenders twice as often as would be expected on the basis of chance.

The question as to which of the two bases for comparison is more suitable for calculating the proportion produced by totally random choices (the entire group of co-offenders or the whole of the population of Stockholm) is not an easy one to answer. If we use the entire group of co-offenders as the basis for comparisons, the implicit assumption is that the individuals who committed offences would have done so anyway, even if their co-offenders were different individuals. This assumption does not fit too well with the principal theme of this study. Using the ethnic composition of the population of Stockholm as a whole as the basis for comparisons, on the other hand, implies assuming the opposite, namely that everyone living in Stockholm is capable of committing offences to the extent that they are chosen as co-offenders by the actors studied. This too is a fairly unreasonable assumption. The truth regarding the processes that led to certain individuals participating in delinquent activities lies somewhere between these two extreme assumptions. As can be seen from table 9.2, however, the results indicate similar tendencies irrespective of which of these two bases is used for the comparison.

In addition, the results show that suspects from more or less all the ethnic minority groups chose individuals with the same ethnic background as themselves as co-offenders for violent offences more often than would be expected on the basis of chance. The level of over-representation of members of the same ethnic group among co-offenders varies somewhat between different ethnic groups depending on the whether the basis chosen for the comparison is the ethnic distribution of all co-offenders or of the population of Stockholm. The strongest tendencies to choose individuals from the same ethnic group, irrespective of the basis for comparison, are presented by actors with an African (excluding North Africa) or a South- and Central American background.

Having subjected the data to a closer examination, Pettersson identifies two clusters of ethnic groups who choose their co-offenders from among other groups in the same cluster more often than from groups outside this cluster. The first group is comprised of Swedes, Scandinavians and Europeans (excluding those from Turkey), whilst the other is made up of groups from the Middle East, Turkey and North Africa, Africa (excluding North Africa) and South- and Central America. This particular division of the ethnic groups is more noticeable in relation to such offences as assault and threatening behaviour and less so when it comes to mugging. The composition of the two clusters of groups corresponds in some ways with the residential segregation to be found in Sweden's metropolitan areas (SOU 1996: 156, Molina 1997).

9.4.2 Choices of victim

Pettersson also made the calculations described above in relation to the choice of victims (1998b: 47). Thirty-six per cent of the choices of victim produced a pair where the perpetrator and victim had the same ethnic background (in terms of the eight ethnic groups mentioned). Thus, as was the case with the choices of co-offender, the majority of choices of victims were ethnically heterogeneous. Nonetheless, the youths in most of the ethnic groups studied tended to choose victims from their own ethnic background

Table 9.3: *Individuals under 21 years suspected of violent offences in Stockholm 1995. The proportion of choices of victim from the same ethnic group as the perpetrator, divided by the proportion of such choices that would be expected if the choices had been made completely at random from the group containing all the studied victims, or from the whole of the population of Stockholm respectively*

Individuals with a background in:	In relation to all victims	In relation to the population of Stockholm	Total number of actual choices made
Sweden	0.9	0.7	859
Scandinavia excluding Sweden	0.7	1.1	224
Europe excluding Scandinavia and Turkey	1.6	2.0	265
The Middle East, Turkey and North Africa	1.3	2.0	355
Africa excluding North Africa	3.8	7.0	221
Asia excluding the Middle East	0.0	0.0	69
South- and Central America	1.5	2.5	170

Notes:
(Calculations based on Pettersson 1998: 34 and on table A9 in the appendix)

more often than would be expected if the choices had been made on a completely random basis.

Table 9.3 shows that individuals from Sweden and from Scandinavia excluding Sweden were chosen as victims by perpetrators from their own ethnic groups slightly (although insignificantly) less often than we would expect if the choices were made on a completely random basis. The reverse was true for all the other ethnic groups, with the exception of Asia (excluding the Middle East).[11] The probability of choosing a co-offender from the same ethnic group, as is shown in table 9.2, was somewhat greater. Thus with regard to the ethnic background of the perpetrator and the victim, the choice of victims seems to be somewhat more random than the choice of co-offenders.

We can also see from table 9.3 that the probability of choosing victims with one's own ethnic background varied between the different ethnic groups; for Swedes, other Scandinavians and for people from the Middle East, the measure assumed a value very close to one, indicating that such choices were more or less random, whilst for those from Africa (excluding North Africa) the choice of a victim from the same ethnic group was many times more probable than would be expected on the basis of chance alone. For individuals from South- and Central America and from Europe (excluding Scandinavia and Turkey), the probability of choosing a victim from one's own ethnic group was slightly higher than would be expected on the basis of chance.

Those ethnic groups who were most likely to choose co-offenders with a similar ethnic background were also more likely than the average to choose victims from within their own ethnic group. The two groups presenting the highest probabilities of a choice of co-offender and victim with a similar ethnic background, that is, those from Africa (excluding North Africa) and South- and Central America are among those ethnic minorities that in a study carried out by Lange (1995) stated more often than other minorities that they felt themselves to be the subject of various types of discrimination in Swedish society. The most likely explanation of these findings is that individuals from these groups tend more to associate with their fellow countrymen and less with others than do the members of the other ethnic groups studied. This relatively intense level of association among members of the same ethnic group increases the likelihood that both co-offenders and victims are chosen from among this group. The reasons for this phenomenon are probably to be found in the fact that individuals from these ethnic groups find themselves more isolated than others in Swedish society.

The results presented here can also be used to study whether any specific ethnic groups find themselves in conflict with other ethnic groups on a regular basis. Indicators of such conflicts, such as ethnic gang fights, for example, might manifest themselves by way of individuals from a certain ethnic group appearing as co-offenders to members of another group quite seldom, whilst they appeared relatively often as victims of offences committed by the other group. There is no evidence of any such pronounced ethnic conflicts in our material, however.

The classification of ethnic groups used here may of course conceal a number of internationally recognised ethnic conflicts. The bitterest enemies are often peoples who live as neighbours in geographical terms: Kurds and Turks, Iraqis and Iranians, Bosnians, Kosovo-Albanians and Serbs, and so on. This kind of conflict would be hidden by the classification of ethnic groups used in this study. A quick glance at the suspect–suspect and suspect–victim pairs shows, however, that such conflicts are uncommon among the youths studied here. Iraqi and Iranian youths are, for instance, found more often in the data as co-offenders than as perpetrator and victim of the same offence, and the same is true of youths from different parts of the former Yugoslavia.

9.5 Ethnicity and other variables

As has been indicated above, 41 per cent of the suspect–suspect pairs and 36 per cent of the suspect–victim pairs that appear in the data for 1995 are ethnically homogeneous. Table 9.4 presents the proportion of ethnically homogeneous pairs for co-offenders and suspects–victims on the basis of age, gender and various degrees of correspondence between postal codes.

Table 9.4 shows that the proportion of ethnically homogeneous pairs varies somewhat with age, gender and residential proximity among co-offenders or among perpetrators and victims. There seem to be a few common characteristics between variations in the proportion of ethnically homogeneous pairs across the suspect–suspect and suspect–victim pair types. The proportion of ethnically homogeneous pairs appears to be higher when the actors are younger, drops in the age range from 15 to 17 and then increases again for those aged 18 and over. This tendency is more visible for choices of co-offender than for choices of victim, but nonetheless can be identified to a certain degree even in the latter group. The proportion of ethnically homogeneous suspect–victim pairs is at its highest when the age difference between suspect and victim is greatest.

Taking a look at gender, we find that the proportion of ethnically homogeneous pairs was lowest for pairs comprised of two males (40 per cent of suspect–suspect pairs and 33 per cent of suspect–victim pairs). The largest proportion of ethnically homogeneous pairs (83 per cent) is to be found in suspect–suspect pairs where one of the suspects is a male aged twenty or less, and the other is a female. Examples of this type of combination are rare, however.

The proportion of ethnically homogeneous pairs declined with increasing geographical distance between co-offenders, measured here in terms of correspondence between postcodes. For individuals sharing the same postcode, 55 per cent of co-offender pairs were ethnically homogeneous, whilst the same was true of only 20 per cent of pairs comprised of individuals living in different counties. The suspect–victim pairs present a picture which is similar in some respects, but here the proportion of ethnically homogeneous pairs was somewhat higher among those living in different counties.

Not surprisingly, the delinquency of Swedish youths was more homogeneous in terms of its ethnicity than was the delinquency of youths from

Table 9.4: *Choice of co-offenders and victims for violent offences 1995. Proportion of ethnically homogeneous suspect–suspect and suspect–victim pairs (using the same eight ethnic groups as earlier) after age, gender and place of residence of the suspects and their victims*

	Suspect–suspect		Suspect–victim	
	%	N	%	N
Age				
≥14–≥14	58	72	30	47
≥14–15–17	36	56	9	4
≥14–18≥	–	–	45	27
15–17–≥14	35	22	25	19
15–17–15–17	31	177	26	87
15–17–18≥	50	54	34	358
18≥–≥14	–	–	60	12
18≥–15–17	47	44	32	37
18≥–18≥	47	122	44	264
Gender				
Female–female	44	38	41	39
Female–male	42	7	40	18
Male–female	83	5	42	106
Male–male	40	467	33	457
Residential proximity (number of postcode digits)				
All	55	133	45	76
3 digits	40	112	36	149
2 digits	47	90	36	92
1 digit	36	243	33	266
None	20	20	42	42

immigrant backgrounds. For Swedes, a little more than 60 per cent of co-offenders and victims had the same ethnic background (i.e. both individuals were Swedes), whilst for offences involving immigrant youths only around 30 per cent of co-offenders and 15 per cent of victims had the same ethnic background as the actor in question.

9.5.2 Corresponding proportions

To recap, tables 9.2 and 9.3 show that for youths suspected of violent offences, the probability of choosing a person from their own ethnic group as a co-offender was about three times as high would have been expected if the choices had been made completely at random, whilst the probability of choosing a victim with the same ethnic background was about 1.3 times as high. In order to have a basis for judging the significance of these results, the corresponding measures for gender, age and place of residence were also calculated.

These measures indicate that co-offenders were:

> of the same sex as the actor in question twice as often as would be expected if the choices had been random
>
> were the same age as the actor 4.8 times as often as would be expected
>
> lived in the same part of town (first three digits of postcode identical) 19.5 times as often as would be expected on the basis of chance alone

The corresponding measures for choices of victims indicate that these were:

> of the same sex as the perpetrator 1.4 times as often as would be expected if the choices were made at random
>
> of the same age three times as often as would be expected given random choices
>
> lived in the same area nine times as often as would be expected

On the basis of these calculations we can see that ethnic background is less significant for the choice of co-offenders and victims than age and above all residential location. The fact that ethnic background is more significant than gender may be a consequence of the fact that the study is so dominated by males. Females chose other females as co-offenders 12.1 times as often as would be dictated by chance, and as victims 3.5 times as often.

All calculations are carried out using the ethnic composition of the groups of suspects and victims included in the study as the basis for comparisons, that is, the calculation of the proportions expected given random choices are based on the ethnic composition of these two groups. If the comparisons had instead been based on the ethnic composition of the whole of the Stockholm population, the differences between the actual choices recorded and those expected on the basis of chance would have been greater. Residential location would still have shown itself to be a considerably more important factor in choices of co-offenders and victims than the other variables, however.

The finding that residence in the same part of town is of considerable significance in the choice not only of co-offenders but also of victims is not one that should surprise us. The criminological literature contains a great many references to the territorial nature of delinquency (Brantingham and Brantingham 1984; Wikström 1991), especially in relation to adolescent violence and gangs (Thrasher 1927; Loftin 1986; Klein 1995). What is surprising, however, is that ethnicity does not play a greater role in the choice of co-offenders than that indicated by our results. As was mentioned earlier, the American literature sees the ethnic homogeneity of gangs and other forms of co-offending as more or less axiomatic in the context of juvenile delinquency. It should be noted, however, that the relationship between place of residence and ethnic background is very different in the metropolitan areas of the USA as compared with the situation in Sweden. The residential segregation found in Stockholm, for example, is both less evident than that in America, and is also of a very different nature. In Sweden, different ethnic minorities are not found living in different parts of town, but, rather, many different minorities are dramatically over-represented in certain residential areas where they live side by side. The ethnic composition of the networks examined here indicates that they are to a large extent formed (at least to begin with) among youths living in the same area – especially in poorer areas where many immigrants tend to live. Co-offenders, and to a certain extent victims too, are often chosen from among others living in the same area. We could thus conclude that the 'ethnic dimension' of delinquency is actually governed in the first instance not by the ethnic background of the actors themselves, but rather by the type of residential segregation to be found in a society. The Swedish form of residential segregation, with many ethnic minorities and also certain underprivileged subgroups from within the ethnic majority population being driven by economic considerations to live in the same areas (Molina 1997), leads to the formation of delinquent networks with a certain form of ethnic structure specific to Sweden. In other societies, such as the USA, where residential segregation has a different character, this structure takes on another form.

The ethnic character of residential segregation found in Sweden and to some extent also in a number of other European countries is of course no accident, but is related to the view of immigration that holds sway in Swedish society in general, and it mirrors the division into 'Swedes' and 'immigrants' that is so characteristic of this discourse.

The type of ethnic and socio-economic residential segregation specific to Sweden has probably resulted in the evolution of a specific multi-cultural environment in certain parts of Swedish metropolitan areas. A number of Swedish academics (e.g. Ehn 1992, 1995; Ålund 1995, 1997) see two parallel tendencies in Swedish society, one towards a greater level of segregation and hostility towards immigrants (manifesting itself in, amongst other things, an increasingly marked residential segregation of immigrants and the majority population), the other towards a multi-cultural society (primarily in those residential areas where the various immigrant groups are found living together).

9.6 Summary and conclusions

Many of the theories employed by Swedish criminologists to understand the mechanisms underlying delinquent behaviour were produced in the USA and are based on conditions found in North American society. In most cases this probably does not constitute too serious a problem, since the mechanisms governing delinquency appear to be reasonably universal across the western world. When it comes to the role played in delinquency by racial/ethnic factors, however, the situation is somewhat different.

The results presented in this chapter indicate that a large proportion of the co-offending relations among the youths studied in Stockholm were formed across ethnic lines, at least with respect to violent offences. This is a very different picture from that given of the metropolitan areas of North America.

The choice of victims with a different ethnic background to that of the perpetrator also seems to be a lot more common in Stockholm than it is in the large cities of the USA. This does not mean that Stockholm plays host to a large number of conflicts among different ethnic groups, however. On the contrary, the mass media's contention that we are witnessing what amounts to a 'low intensity race war' finds no support in the data examined here. The ethnic mixture characteristic of the choice of both victims and co-offenders is quite simply the result of the way youths in Stockholm, particularly those with an immigrant background, and Swedish youths from families of low socio-economic status, who often live in the same residential areas as immigrants, reside in an ethnically mixed, or, to put it another way, multi-cultural environment. In this environment, the probability of meeting an individual from a different ethnic background, and becoming a friend and/or co-offender of this person appears to be about as great as the likelihood of meeting such an individual in a violent confrontation.

This is not to say that the ethnic aspects of the choice of co-offenders and victims are completely governed by chance. The probability of choosing a co-offender from one's own ethnic group was around three times as great as would be expected if such a co-offender was chosen at random from among the group of co-offenders registered by the police, and the probability of choosing a victim from the same ethnic group was around 1.3 times as great. This 'over-representation' of individuals from the same ethnic background in both suspect–suspect and to a lesser extent suspect–victim pairs was nonetheless smaller than the over-representation of individuals of the same age, or from the same residential area, in such pairs. In a context where most of the ethnic minorities are rather small, the majority of youths with an immigrant background committed most of their offences both with and against individuals from a different ethnic background.

The situation was somewhat different for Swedish youths for the simple reason that this was naturally the largest ethnic group in the material studied. Swedish youths most often committed offences together and against other Swedes, although even here a considerable proportion of their offences tied them to actors from different groups of immigrants.

Pettersson's study (1998b) shows that members of certain ethnic groups were more likely to commit offences with or against members of their own group than members of other ethnic groups. Individuals from these groups often came from countries that were both culturally and geographically more distant from Sweden. We know that these groups experience a higher level of discrimination in Swedish society. And it is also these groups who, together with other persons who have a low socio-economic status, and not uncommonly serious social problems of one kind or another, to a large degree populate the low-status suburbs of Stockholm from which a considerable proportion of actively delinquent youths are recruited.

We could perhaps go so far as to contend that the pictures presented of delinquency in America and Sweden generally correspond to the two countries' current conceptions of society's ethnic composition. American society is considered to consist of a number of different ethnic minorities, and the picture we see of crime in America is consistent with this. Swedish society, on the other hand, is comprised of a majority population and 'immigrants' who often find themselves among the underclass of society. The structure of the delinquent networks in Stockholm studied here confirms this image.

CHAPTER TEN

The 'Ängen gang'

As with many other quantitative studies, one of the problems with employing network analyses of this kind for the study of juvenile crime is that the picture produced lacks many of the nuances of social life. This chapter represents an attempt to redress the balance by combining network analysis with a 'softer' type of data. Comparing the results of the network analyses with information obtained from key informants and young people themselves (although in this instance these represent a rather small group) also provides a means of validating these methods.

This chapter builds primarily on a finals dissertation produced as a part of the network project by Anna William-Olsson (1998). William-Olsson's study focused on a group of delinquent youths, most of whom live in a suburb of Stockholm referred to by the pseudonym 'Ängen'. The study is based primarily on interviews with the following key informants:

specialist youth social workers in two social services districts, the one where the group resided, and a neighbouring district;
other youth workers from these two districts;
police who work with the investigation of juvenile offences in the area where the youths resided, as well as other officers from the police district which administrates this area, and also representatives from the Stockholm City police, where the youths occasionally spent time.

In addition, William-Olsson interviewed three of the youths concerned and was able to draw on her own experiences as a social worker who had worked with this group of young people herself. The interviews were carried out in the course of 1995.

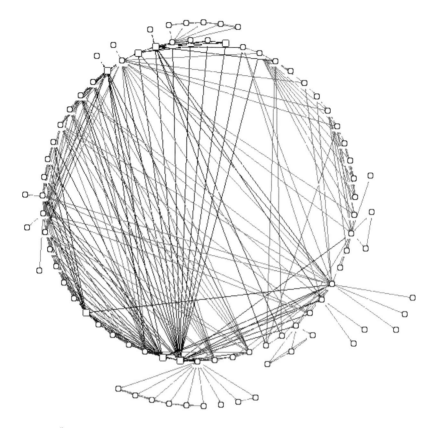

10.1 The 'Ängen Gang'. The seven individuals identified as members of the 'Ängen Gang' and their known co-offenders between 1991 and 1995 at one and two removes. The seven individuals originally identified are marked with squares, their personal networks marked in black, other individuals marked with circles, other links marked in grey. Scale 1:3

10.1 The network

Seven youths from the group in question were identified. These actors are marked with squares in figure 10.1. Co-offenders of these individuals (1991–1995) at one and two removes (network steps, that is, known co-offenders and co-offenders of co-offenders) have been identified in the network data. In total the network comprises fifty-eight individuals joined by 212 links. Of these links, 43 per cent go to/from the seven youths origi-nally identified (these links are marked in black in the figure). The network is linked into the Central Network as part of its largest cluster.

A brief glance at the network in figure 10.1 can quite easily give the impression that the graph is in large part similar to some of the graphs presented in the chapter on football hooligans. Here too we find a reasonably well-connected network with a large number of links joining an inner circle of actors. This impression is erroneous, however. This network is not comprised of links generated by a single event in which all the actors participated, but by a large number of events which took place over the course of a five-year period, successively linking together more and more of the youths in question. However, it is rare for more than two to four of these youths to have participated together in an offence.

A closer look thus shows that the network above is in fact less densely linked than most of the larger networks of football hooligans. The most important difference, however, is to be found in the average number of offence participations per individual. In the football hooligans' networks, this average lies close to one, whilst in figure 10.1 it lies at just over three offence participations per individual. This corresponds well with the findings of Warr's (1996) study based on the National Surveys of Youth from 1967 and 1972 (Gold 1970). Warr writes: 'Offenders typically commit offences with only a small number of co-offenders on any one occasion, but they have substantially larger networks of accomplices, the size of which is proportional to the offender's rate of offending' (1996: 33).

10.2 The group's size and composition

William-Olsson attempted to gauge the size of the group of delinquent youths in Ängen. She identified twenty-two individuals concerning whom at least three of the key informants interviewed were in agreement. If individuals named by one or two informants are also included, the group identified comprised forty-nine members. This result corresponds reasonably well with that of the network analysis, where it was deduced that a group comprised fifty-nine individuals by means of including those lying at a distance of two network steps or less from the seven youths originally identified. The results are further confirmed by the youths themselves, who said at interview that the group consisted of between twenty-five and fifty individuals. During the summer, the numbers involved increased, and the group might comprise anything up to 100 boys.

Both the key informants and the youths themselves reported that the group was made up of persons between the ages of 15 and 20. It was possible to distinguish an older and a younger subgroup, but with no clear dividing line between them. On occasion, the key informants also named a further group, consisting of somewhat younger youths from Ängen, but this group was not included in William-Olsson's study.

A large majority of the individuals included in the network were between the ages of 15 and 20 in 1995 when the interviews were carried out. Forty five per cent were aged between 14 and 17, and the same proportion were between the ages of 18 and 21. The remaining actors were older, the eldest two being 38 and 46 years of age respectively. These two individuals were positioned on the margins of the network, however, and both were included on the basis of drug-dealing offences. These two older men thus appear to be drug dealers who supplied a number of the network members.

According to the boys interviewed, all the members of the group were males. Girls were not included in group activities. If a group member had a girlfriend, then time spent with her was time spent away from the group.

One of the social workers interviewed stated that the boys in the group had an 'appalling view of women' which *inter alia* involved 'a great many sexist remarks, an extensive four letter word vocabulary' and so on. The boys worried about the view other group members would take of their girlfriends and thus 'they didn't dare take their girlfriends and show them to the group'. At the same time, however, at least one of the key informants said that besides 'girlfriends' who were often met with contempt and treated as 'sex objects', there were a few girls (with immigrant backgrounds) in the group who were treated with respect and were perceived almost as equals. In the network presented here, there are only three girls, constituting 5 per cent of the network membership.

One of these girls was suspected in connection with a single offence. At age 14, she was suspected of participating in a break-in at a department store together with ten other boys from the network. The remaining two girls were suspected of participating in an unlawful entry (probably to a party) when they were aged 15 and 16 respectively, together with seven other boys from the group.

The network analysis thus confirms that the positions occupied by the girls in the network in question were extremely marginal. In this particular section of the network data we find no trace of any girls taking part in the delinquency of the group on anything like an even footing with the boys.

In answer to questions regarding the group's ethnic composition, one of the three boys interviewed by William-Olsson claimed that he was the only Swede in the group. Such a conception is confirmed neither by the network analysis nor the statements made by key informants, however. The ethnic composition of the group was very mixed, and the key informants estimated that around one-third of the group members were of Swedish background. The statement made by the group member is interesting, however. It gives the impression that the Swedish characteristics of the group are 'played down' so that even if a considerable proportion of group members were in fact Swedes, the group nonetheless has an immigrant profile. It is likely that these youths were seen by outsiders as an 'immigrant gang'.

The non-Swedish members of the group came from a large number of countries. The boys joked that the only nationality not represented in the group were the Chinese. According to the key informants, the group contained representatives from Africa, South America, Asia and Southern Europe.

Within the network study, ethnicity data is available for only twenty-nine of the fifty-eight individuals in the network. The ethnicity of these twenty-nine individuals was distributed across the ethnic groupings used in the study (see chapter 9) in the following way:

ten individuals (34 per cent) were Swedes
one individual (3 per cent) came from one of the other Nordic countries
one individual (3 per cent) had a Southern European background
four individuals (14 per cent) were from the Middle East
two individuals (6 per cent) had South American backgrounds
one individual (3 per cent) was from Africa

The remaining ten individuals (34 per cent of the total) were from families where the one parent was Swedish whilst the other came from another country (three from Scandinavia, two from other European countries, two from Africa and one from South America).

The majority of the young people in the network were born in Sweden and had one or both parents also born there. This means that the ethnic composition of that part of the group for which ethnicity data were available contained a much more significant Swedish element than would be expected on the basis of the interviews with key informants and the youths themselves. One should be very wary of drawing conclusions on the basis of incomplete data such as this, but the picture presented may well be typical. A group of young people with social problems is seen and possibly even sees itself as containing a much stronger immigrant element than is in fact the case.

The interviews carried out by William-Olsson lend support to this interpretation. In the interviews, both the youngsters and the key informants speak of the importance of ethnic background for those individuals in the group who did come from immigrant homes. The youths speak of their backgrounds with pride ('except for the Swedish boy' writes William-Olsson, 1998: 57).

During the course of the interviews with the youths, a good deal is also said about racists and skinheads, whom the boys see as a threat. The conflict with racists is referred to in statements such as the following: 'Killing a skinhead who's enjoying the protection of the state is no crime . . .' (William-Olsson 1998: 34).

Both the youths and the key informants regard the boys' having grown up in the same part of town as being the most important factor contributing to the group's cohesiveness. They went to the same kindergartens, the same schools and often to the same after-school clubs. Data relating to contacts with youths from other parts of town are somewhat contradictory. A number of key informants say that the youths very rarely leave their own neighbourhood and that when they do so it is only to travel to neighbouring areas, whilst others suggest that the boys, especially those that are a little older, have contacts 'all over town'.

The network analysis shows that 71 per cent of the forty-nine individuals whose addresses were known lived in the 'Ängen' neighbourhood at the time of one of the offences for which they were suspected between 1991 and 1995. Some have moved away from the area, whilst others have moved into the neighbourhood, often from neighbouring areas. A further 8 per cent of the youths studied lived in parts of town directly bordering on the 'Ängen' area. The remaining individuals, with one exception, lived in neighbourhoods in the same part of Stockholm, for the most part a little further out from the city centre along the same underground line.

Thus for the network as it has been defined here (up to two steps from the seven individuals originally identified) there seems to be support for those suggesting only limited contacts with individuals outside the neighbourhood. It should nonetheless be remembered that the youths were members of the Central Network along with the most actively delinquent youths from the whole of the Greater Stockholm area. The boys themselves claimed to have friends from other parts of the city, including some who lived 'on the other side of town'. The boys said that contacts with youths from other parts of Stockholm usually resulted from meetings in and around the place where they went to do sports training and to meet one another in their own neighbourhood. The neighbourhoods from which these other youths came, like the 'Ängen' area itself, were typically populated by a high proportion of immigrants.

10.3 The group's activities

Delinquency was of course an important ingredient in the activities in which the youths took part together. This was also the ingredient that key informants, and especially those from the police, spent the most time talking about when the group was discussed. It is clear however that the youths also devoted themselves to a wide variety of other activities that cannot be identified using the kind of network representation employed here. Many of the youths were keen boxers or practised other martial arts, some with quite considerable success, whilst others played musical instruments and went to the cinema and so forth.

The most important factor however was quite simply to spend time together. According to one of the youth workers interviewed by William-Olsson, the boys could sit for hours 'drinking coke, smoking cigarettes, gossiping and trying to outdo one another' (1998: 51). They talked about girls, their own and others' successes in the boxing ring and in street fights, and other 'bloke stuff'. The language used in these conversations was often rough and the youths would wind one another up, using deprecatory remarks and occasionally resorting to pretend fighting. Real fights seldom broke out within the group, however.

This same source revealed that many of the boys were together for a large part of the day, particularly since some of them were neither at school or working. Contact between group members was also maintained by means of the mobile phones carried by several of the boys. These contacts involved keeping each other informed of what they were up to even when they were not together. The key informants and the boys themselves likened these relationships to those between siblings '. . . we're a bunch of mates who've known each other since we were little and who look out for one another', as one of the boys explained to William-Olsson (1998: 50). He went on to say: 'We're like a big family that keeps growing, and we love each other' (1998: 51). The social network was thus much tighter than can be seen by looking at their delinquent interactions alone. At the same time, William-Olsson points out that the feeling of community experienced by the boys ('we nearly always feel the same way') and the fact that everyone in the group knew everyone else, does not mean that they all spent time together at the same level of intensity (1998: 62).

According to the key informants, delinquency and other forms of deviant behaviour such as using drugs and alcohol did play an important part in the interactions between the youths in Ängen. That many of them had participated in criminal offences together (at least at some earlier juncture) was not denied by the youths who were interviewed. Their statements concerning their own (as they claim) essentially 'past' delinquency, as well as the key informants' descriptions of the youth's attitudes, contain what could be considered a model for all manner of what Sykes and Matza (1957) refer to as mechanisms of neutralisation, such as denial of responsibility, denial of injury, denial of the victim, condemnation of the condemners and not least appeals to higher loyalties. Thus the boys interviewed describe with some enthusiasm the way they and their older friends have 'taken care of' various deviants, such as a transvestite and another person who was interfering with children, for example, that the authorities have failed to deal with effectively. Other youths coming into the neighbourhood who failed to behave themselves were also 'dealt with' physically. Those who were assaulted in this way had simply been given what they deserved and thus had no right to turn to the authorities for help. The boys had little time for the authorities and claimed that frauds and thefts directed at the state were not in fact crimes, since 'the state is the biggest criminal of all' (William-Olsson 1998: 33).

It is difficult to judge the extent to which the accounts of the group's delinquency provided by the key informants and the youths themselves correspond to the reality of this delinquency. The boys boasted about some of their delinquent activities whilst denying participation in others, or at least reinterpreting their significance. The authority figures that were interviewed suspected the youths of a great deal more delinquency than that shown by the register data (on which the network analysis is based). These suspicions often built on similarities in *modus operandi* among unsolved offences and other offences to which the boys had already been linked, eye-witness descriptions of perpetrators, and anonymous tips to the police. Convictions for offences were even more rare. According to the statements of both the key informants and the boys who were interviewed, group members made a point of never admitting to offences for which they were suspected, and they hardly ever 'grassed' on one another.

The offences that the boys were thought to participate in varied a great deal:

Muggings and assaults both in the centre of Stockholm and in their own neighbourhood. In addition, the boys were said often to have threatened people in various ways. Such threats were directed not least at victims of the group's delinquency and at others who had witnessed their offences. The key informants talked of several cases of 'interference with witnesses'.

Unlawful entry – in connection with parties at which the members of the group were not welcome but where they wanted to get in anyway.

Thefts of various kinds, such as from shops and of cars.

Vandalism offences – broken windows and graffiti.

Buying and selling stolen goods – the group members, and in particular the older ones, were said to trade in stolen goods such as mobile phones, gold jewellery and computers.

The key informants asserted that alcohol and other substance abuse was common in the group. Home-distilled alcohol, hash, and pills were all used. There was also a suspicion that heroin was smoked.

One of the boys was suspected of drug dealing.

A few of the key informants made the point that not all the boys were delinquents.

When interviewed themselves, the boys directly or indirectly confirmed a

Table 10.1: *Offences for which members of the Ängen network were suspected between 1991 and 1995 according to the network data*

Offence type	%	N
Assault	25.6	45
Sex offences	0.0	0
Mugging	14.2	25
Other crimes against the person	15.9	28
Shoplifting	4.0	7
Other thefts including burglary	26.1	46
Criminal damage	4.0	7
Other crimes against property	0.0	0
Drug offences	2.3	4
Public-order disturbances, crimes against police officers/ public servants etc	5.1	9
Other offences	2.8	5
Total	100.0	176

good deal of what the key informants had said about the group's delinquency. Many smoked hash – 'some have got hooked on the stuff' (William-Olsson 1998: 37). Some used other drugs. Violence was common but 'often with good reason'. One of the boys said that the group had a bad reputation, which meant that they were not let in at private parties. It was this kind of thing that the key informants had claimed often led to unlawful entry and violence. The boys also said that youngsters from other parts of town did not dare to visit their neighbourhood, for fear of getting beaten up. On the one hand they were proud of their reputation and felt they had an obligation to maintain order in their own neighbourhood.

'Ängen is where we live, it's our home and when you're here you behave yourself. If you don't, then it kicks off and you've got nobody but yourself to blame' (William-Olsson 1998: 54). On the other hand the same boy claims that the reputation of the gang was exaggerated (William-Olsson 1998: 55).

On the matter of sources of income, the boys had this to say:

> There aren't many who rob people, five at most.... We do business, buy things that we then sell on for a bit more. You do deals with everyone you meet...you say hello and then one of you asks if the other wants to buy a phone for example. You can sell anything to anybody, maybe not completely legally, you don't pay tax and nobody cares where the thing came from to begin with . . . (William-Olsson 1998: 28).

The crimes for which the members of the network were suspected in the RAR register were distributed over the offence categories as set out in table 10.1. How well these data correspond to the picture of the group's activities is a matter for discussion. Table 10.1 clearly shows that the group's delinquency is of a very varied nature (as is usual for this kind of group). The level of violent offending is quite considerable, accounting for more than half of all offence participations. A significant proportion of these offence participations were assaults on males with whom the perpetrator was not acquainted. A number of these offences were judged by the police to be of a serious nature.

At interview, the boys claimed that they hit neither girls nor persons younger and weaker than themselves (although there was some discussion on this point). Among the registered offences, however, we find a number of cases of assaults both on females and children aged from 7 to 14.

The police data also contain a number of references to acts of violence committed by the boys against public servants, such as security officers. In spite of the fact that both the boys and the police revealed at interview that relations between the gang and the police were often bad, there were no registered cases of assaults on police officers.

Mugging (referred to in the RAR register as 'other robberies, out of doors') were relatively common in the data. The boys' contention that only a few and at most five of them committed such robberies is contradicted by the police data. Fifteen of the network members (i.e. just over a quarter of them) were suspected of at least one such offence, with twelve having been suspected of mugging in 1995, that is, in the year during which they were interviewed by William-Olsson.

Other offences for which the boys were registered frequently were miscellaneous thefts. These included both shoplifting offences (which were mentioned by the key informants), burglaries of various types, and other kinds of theft. Despite claims that the boys committed car thefts, such offences do not figure among the suspected offence participations. Similarly, none of the boys were suspected of selling or receiving stolen goods, nor of any type of fraud, despite the stories of the trading in stolen items told by and of the boys.

Although there is obviously a considerable level of drug use in the group, the police data contained only four registered drug offences. All four referred to relations between the older dealers, mentioned earlier, and members of the network.

Information portraying the group's delinquency as primarily limited to the youths' own neighbourhood corresponds well with the police data. Of all the links comprising the network, 66 per cent were produced by offences committed either in Ängen itself or in the surrounding areas. The remaining offences were distributed over a large part of Stockholm, but the majority took place in the city centre. Interestingly, perhaps, the majority of the street robberies committed (76 per cent of such links) and also of assaults on males not known to the perpetrator took place outside the Ängen neighbourhood.

10.4 Leaders and central figures

Neither the key informants nor the youths themselves felt that the group had any leaders. Decisions were arrived at democratically. 'Everyone has to agree', said the boys. At the same time it was conceded that certain individuals had more status within the group than others. It was felt that the older boys enjoyed a higher status, and had a bigger say in what went on. The boys interviewed by William-Olsson were in agreement that the 25-year-old brother of someone they knew was something of a role model (1998: 46).

The most central position in the network was occupied by two youths aged 18 in 1995. One of these had twenty-two known co-offenders (38 per cent of the network membership), the other twenty-eight (48 per cent of the network). One of them was born in Sweden to a Swedish mother and a father from another European country, whilst the other had a Swedish mother and an African father. They made their debut in the network data at ages 14 and 15 respectively, and both then turn up in several of the six-month study periods. Both lived either in Ängen itself or the neighbouring area, although they have apparently moved between different addresses. Neither has been placed in a secure care facility at any time.

These two individuals were the most actively delinquent in the network. The one had been suspected of fourteen offences, the other of twenty-four. The other individuals in the group had a significantly smaller number of known co-offenders (an average of 7.3) and were suspected of considerably fewer offences (3.2 on average). Both these figures nonetheless lie above the average for the individuals included in the network study as a whole, and the figure for the number of known co-offenders is a great deal higher here.

It has been shown (chapter 3) that for the network data in general, the number of known co-offenders and the number of suspected offence participations are related as a rule. There are exceptions to this general principle, as was seen for example in the section on football hooligans, but for the Ängen network, the rule holds up very well indeed. The most active delinquents were also those with the most central positions. But were they also leaders within the group?

The interviews carried out in the course of the Borlänge study (Sarnecki 1986) showed that the most active delinquents were also the most popular in their circle of friends and acquaintances and were those with the most prestige. The Borlänge study presented the hypothesis that this is the case where delinquency is the central activity of the group. If a certain type of activity dominates the interactions within the group, then those youths that are best at and most dedicated to this type of activity will have the most central positions. Interviews with key informants in Ängen suggest that delinquency played a fairly important role in the activities of the group. But was this role sufficiently central to make the most actively delinquent youths into leaders within the group?

The interviews suggest that the older boys had more of a say in the network than their younger counterparts. We find no confirmation of this in the results of the network analysis. Instead we find that it is those individuals born between 1978 and 1980 (i.e. the youngest group who were aged from 15 to 17 in 1995) who have the most central positions in the network. (In this sense the two 18-year-olds described above represent exceptions within their own age group, which makes them even more interesting). The average number of co-offenders for individuals born in different years was as follows. For individuals born in:

1949–1974   2.1 co-offenders (SD = 1.6; N = 10)
1975–1977   7.6 co-offenders (SD = 7.3; N = 22)
1978–1981   9.2 co-offenders (SD = 5.7; N = 25)

It is far from certain, however, that the data from the network study are sufficient to provide a reliable foundation for making judgements as to which individuals assumed the most central roles in the Ängen network. The definition used to identify the principal population excludes the delinquency of persons aged 21 and over to the extent that they are not suspected of committing the offence in question together with someone younger than themselves. We would therefore find it difficult to identify older individuals in the Ängen gang who whilst they might be highly delinquent, did not commit offences together with younger co-offenders but nonetheless played an important role in the group. The network analysis employed here is clearly subject to some fairly important limitations.

10.5 A gang?

During the time spent working on this study, the question of whether there are 'gangs' in Sweden, particularly in the larger metropolitan areas, has been brought to the fore. Here the word 'gang' is used in the American sense of the term, the corresponding Swedish concept having a slightly different application. In the course of the debate surrounding this issue, claims have been made that cohesive groups of highly delinquent and violent youths are becoming increasingly common in cities such as Stockholm. Two reports from the police authority in Stockholm (Länskriminalens Integrationsgrupp 1997; 1998) have focused on this question, for example, the first of them reporting that Stockholm plays host to between sixty and seventy local gangs of delinquent youths. The second puts the number of such gangs at around a hundred.

At first glance, these claims may seem to be confirmed by the network analysis presented here. As has been shown above, it was possible to identify a sizeable number of both large and smaller networks in the data for 1995, for example. Many networks showed signs of a high degree of attachment to a particular area and could thus be used as illustrative of the local gangs mentioned in the police reports. As has also been shown, a similar study six months or a year earlier would identify more or less the same number of networks. A closer look at the data has shown, however, that the composition of these two sets of networks in terms of individual membership would be very different. It has also been shown that when the analysis is expanded to cover a 5-year period, most of the larger networks, comprised of more actively delinquent youths, become instead a single large, central network with members from all over the county. If the term 'gang' is used to refer to separate groups, which are durable and also often in conflict with one another (compare Klein 1971, 1995; Huff 1991; Decker and Van Winkle 1996), the picture produced by the network analysis does not support the thesis that we have gangs here in Stockholm of the kind found in North America.

Results from other research also indicate that (at least up to the present time) this type of gang structure is not to be found in Stockholm. An interview study was carried out in 1995 where representatives of local police and social welfare authorities in Stockholm were asked about the occurrence of gangs of young delinquents in their districts (Fondén and Sarnecki 1996). A large number of groups of actively delinquent youths were reported. Among these groups, though, very few were seen by the respondents as possessing a significant degree of durability, and virtually none of them had their own gang names, symbols and uniforms. It was also very uncommon for the respondents to report the existence of conflicts of a more persistent nature between different 'gangs'.

The question of whether there are gangs to be found in Stockholm is complicated by the fact that, as was pointed out in the opening chapter of this book, there is still no generally accepted definition of the term 'gang'. Several researchers (e.g. Klein 1995; Decker and Van Winkle 1996) think that the single most important criteria for defining a group of delinquent youths as a gang is perhaps the youths identifying themselves as members of a gang. The data collected in the course of interviews with the informants named above shows that durable networks of delinquent youths who see themselves as members of 'gangs' are more or less non-existent in Stockholm.

According to the boys interviewed by William-Olsson, 'The Ängen gang doesn't exist.' Information provided by key informants within the police force and social services backs up this view.

In the course of her interviews, William-Olsson also attempted to identify various external signs of the kind that function as unifying symbols in a typical American gang and which are mentioned by many of the writers of the literature on American gangs (e.g. Klein 1995; Decker and Van Winkle 1996). She found no evidence of uniforms, tattoos or secret signals, however. 'Of course the youngsters have tattoos,' remarked one of the key informants; 'but tattoos are all the rage just now, and getting tattoos has nothing to do with gang membership' (William-Olsson 1998: 23). On the matter of clothing, it was once again a question of culture and not of group behaviour. The boys took care of their appearance and dressed in designer labels. They affect one another's choice of clothing so that they may well dress in very similar clothes, but once again this does not seem to constitute an explicit statement of group identity.

The key informants did indicate on the other hand that the youngest members of the group, those not included in William-Olsson's study, 'played' at being part of an American gang. This was felt to be no more than a game, however – a result of 'the influence of American films'.

In other respects, characteristics of American gangs are more easily identified in the descriptions of the Ängen youths. Several of the American gang researchers (e.g. Moore 1991: 78) write of the territoriality of gangs. Moore has studied gangs in Los Angeles and writes of three distinct characteristics of gangs: they are territorially based, internally structured into age-based cliques, and their principal activity was fighting.[1] The territorial base is obviously present among the Ängen youths, even those who now and then committed offences with individuals from other parts of Stockholm and often spent time in the city centre. But what of the other two gang characteristics named by Moore?

As far as age-based divisions are concerned, the existence of such divisions was intimated by both the youths themselves and the key informants. They spoke of three groups: the oldest, a middle group, and the youngest. The network analysis provides no confirmation of this information in relation to joint participation in criminal offences, however. The cluster analysis produced only a single cluster. A closer study of the choices of co-offenders made by the youths in the network (516 in total), shows a tendency similar to that in the rest of the material to choose individuals who are of roughly the same age as oneself. When the youths are divided into three age groups, we find that the youngest group, with an average age of 13.3 years, chose co-offenders with an average age of 14.0 years. The middle group was on average 15.9 years old, and chose individuals with an average age of 16.1 years as co-offenders. The oldest group, on average 18.5 years old, chose co-offenders aged 18.0 years. If we exclude all those youths who do not actually live in the Ängen area (146 choices), the age difference between co-offenders becomes somewhat smaller whilst the general tendency remains much the same. Whether or not this is sufficient to speak of the network as showing signs of an obvious age structure is unclear.

And finally to the question of fighting. As has been demonstrated, violence constitutes a considerable part of the activities of the Ängen network. But is this enough to make the claim that the group's activity is centred on violence? Once again the answer is unclear. According to the data from the police register, the youths committed more thefts than they did assaults, besides which the group spent time on a great many other activities which were not necessarily criminal and thus would not be represented in the police data. Nor did the interviews with the youths themselves suggest that violence played so central a role in their lives.

William-Olsson's interviews indicate that the boys for the most part spent a good deal of time together doing 'nothing in particular'. This factor would weigh against the notion that we are dealing with a gang in Moore's (1991) sense of the term. But there are, as mentioned above, a number of writers who contend that this kind of 'hanging around' is the most common form of activity for a gang. Among these writers we find Klein (1971), Short and Strodtbeck (1974), and also Moore (1991). Thus the fact that only a lesser proportion of the group's activity takes the form of violence and that simply spending time together is more important would not in itself prevent us from seeing the group as a gang.

All the writers mentioned above (as well as, for example, Thrasher 1927) suggest that conflict both with mainstream society, and perhaps above all with other gangs, is vital to the gang's existence and for the non-delinquent solidarity which this demands of the gang members. Even in this respect, our findings are rather diffuse. Whilst both key informants and the youths themselves do indeed speak of the existence of conflict between the group and the representatives of mainstream society, perhaps primarily the police, and also with youths from other parts of Stockholm, it is difficult on the basis of William-Olsson's interviews to draw the conclusion that the Ängen youths are engaged in some form of acute conflict with their environment.

The interviews produced a consensus view that the solidarity of the Ängen group is very strong and that betraying a friend is considered unthinkable. If a group member is attacked in some way, everyone else will go to his defence irrespective of whether the 'assailant' is a public authority or a private individual. In addition to this apparent solidarity, the key informants said they saw evidence of the group members showing a considerable degree of tolerance for one another. An occasion was mentioned, for example, when one of the group members, having been arrested, told the police a great deal about his own and his friends' offending. There was a fear that in the traditional manner of the gang, the group would exact its revenge, but nothing happened. Following his release, the youth, at least for a time, was able once again to spend time with his friends in the absence of any visible reprisals.

10.6 Summary and conclusions

A number of individuals from the Central Network were identified as members of a network based in one of Stockholm's more central suburbs, here referred to as 'Ängen'. The known co-offenders of these individuals at a distance of one and two network steps were identified, producing a group of fifty-eight individuals in total. This network is here assumed to be identical with a particular group of delinquent youths that has been the focus of considerable media attention in Sweden, and that is referred to here as the 'Ängen gang'.

Within the framework of the network project, William-Olsson (1998) carried out a number of interviews with key informants from the police and social services who in the course of their work had come into contact with the youths in question, as well as with a few of the youths themselves. The information collected in these interviews has been employed in this chapter partly to supplement the network data and partly to validate them.

In general there appears to be a large degree of correspondence between the information volunteered by the key informants and the youths at interview, and the results from the network analysis. Thus the network analysis could confirm that there really was a group of interrelated, highly delinquent youths based in the suburb in question. Information from the interviews concerning the size and composition of the group, and also the pattern of the members' delinquent activity, presented a fairly high level of consonance with the data from the network analysis.

The level of correspondence was far from perfect, however. It was thus possible with the help of the register data to falsify a number of the claims made by the youths about their delinquent activities, claims that presented the group's activities in a somewhat more positive light than they deserved. This type of glorification of one's own delinquency is related to various types of neutralisation mechanism and is common among delinquent youths. It is also common for adults and professionals to accept the truth of such claims.

The register data have also helped to correct the picture presented both by the youths themselves, and also by a number of the key informants, of the group's ethnic composition.

At the same time the exercise has made it very clear that a network analysis based on register data of this kind gives only a partial picture of the networks under study. Important data concerning non-delinquent relations within the group for example is missed when a network analysis based only on data from the police register is employed. In other respects too, the picture produced by this kind of network analysis is somewhat cursory. What this chapter shows is that data triangulation is clearly desirable when it comes to researching delinquent networks or gangs, just as is the case with research in other fields. Network analysis of the kind employed here can provide a valuable structural base for the study of individual networks. It can also provide an illuminating overview of the larger system of interconnecting relations which provides the context for such individual networks. Various types of interview can then be used to flesh out this structure with important detail. Preferably, there should be more interviews with the youths themselves than was the case in the study presented in this chapter, since it is they who constitute the focus of the research.

In the course of her interviews with the youths and key informants, William-Olsson attempted to provide an answer as to whether the Ängen youths, who had been depicted by the police and in the media as a gang of the kind found among youths in North America, could in fact be considered members of such a gang. When asked directly whether Ängen played host to a gang of delinquent youths, both the key informants and the youths who were interviewed answered that this was not the case. The gang literature identifies youths' self-perception as gang members as an important indicator of the existence of a gang, as well as the perceptions of the immediate environment regarding whether or not the youths in question are to be considered members of a gang. The network also lacks many of the other characteristics typical of the 'traditional' North American gang. Over recent years in the USA, however, the gang concept has begun to be applied to a much broader youth phenomenon than the traditional studies of Bloods or Crips or other similar groups that had previously dominated the literature. If we take the typology of gangs presented by Klein *et al.* (2001), for example, then the Ängen network, with its limited number of members, relatively loose structure, vague leadership, and relatively short history might very well be considered an example of the 'compressed gang' type. This particular type of gang, which according to Klein *et al.* appears to be the most common in American society, has very little in common, however, with the cohesive and well-organised specialist gangs or traditional gangs that are often referred to in the mass media, and that have been described in traditional gang literature.

As was described in chapter 1, the research is rather confused regarding the content of the gang concept. It is not possible in the context of this book to attempt to bring a semblance of order to the ways in which the concept is employed. I will therefore content myself with saying that the character of the 'Ängen Gang' (and the character of several other delinquent youth networks described in this study) is consistent with the gang definition employed by certain authors (e.g. Klein *et al.* 2001 – compressed gang or Thrasher 1927 – gang of stage 1), whilst it deviates dramatically from that used by others (e.g. Sanchez–Jankowski 1991 but also Decker and Van Winkle 1996). One important conclusion which I think can be drawn from the results presented in this chapter, however, is that network analysis, in combination with other methods that are well established in this area of research, constitutes a useful means of studying the group character of youth delinquency irrespective of the label applied to these groups.

CHAPTER ELEVEN

Conclusions

11.1 Anything new?

The research presented in this book constitutes the second study where I have employed network analysis in the examination of juvenile delinquency. As has been pointed out, analyses of this kind have become fairly common within the social and behavioural sciences more generally, whilst they remain rare in the field of criminology.

Traditional, quantitative analyses in the social sciences often work on the implicit assumption that individuals are not related to one another, an assumption which is at odds with the majority of social scientific[1] theories. Network analysis, on the other hand, makes the assumption that actors are related to one another and thus provides a more nuanced picture of the social phenomena being studied by taking these relations into consideration (and often focusing on them quite specifically).

Even though network analysis is still rarely used in criminological studies, many criminological theories on the causes of crime (i.e. those of a sociological nature) are grounded in the assumption that delinquency is affected (or quite simply caused) by interactions or relations between various actors. Such theories are therefore highly compatible with the network perspective.

At the same time the various theories are based on a number of different views of both society and the individual. They thus have different things to say about the way individuals influence one another, and about the effects of this influence. Certain theories view delinquency as a behaviour learned in the course of interactions between actors, for example, whilst others talk instead of the transference of different elements of cultures/subcultures such as norms and values. Still others describe such influences in terms of the transmission of control.

Irrespective of the theoretical position chosen, network analysis provides us with the opportunity to study patterns in the relationships between different actors, that is, the interpersonal channels through which influence is transmitted. This is not to say that network analysis will automatically provide answers about the nature of such influences or their effects, however, which means that network analysis is unlikely to provide a simple means of testing different criminological theories in order to decide which of them best describes a posited criminological reality.

This study focuses on a specific type of relationship from among the many and various relationships which may be of interest to criminology, namely co-offending. Research on co-offending is also fairly rare in the field of criminology. Naturally enough, the research on co-offending that has been carried out contains elements of a network perspective, even if this is not always expressly noted by the writers concerned. The usual means of conducting research into co-offending however, has been to employ traditional survey methods and/or to examine samples of individuals who are unrelated to one another, or perhaps rather who are related to one another but in an unknown way (Reiss and Farrington 1991; Warr 1996; Conwey and McCord 1997). This type of research design can examine only the personal networks of the individuals included in the sample. In addition, the information obtained concerning relations within these personal networks remains one-sided, since it is based only on statements made by the principal person in each network.

By way of contrast, the type of analysis carried out in the current study provides an overview of the whole co-offending structure within a specific geographical area. This means that we have information relating to the choices of co-offenders made by all the actors[2] involved and can study both direct and indirect links between actors. This type of study examines all the members of a network. Since it is difficult to know in advance which individuals comprise a network, all relevant individuals must be looked at. When the research covers a large geographical area, this will involve the examination of a very large population, which in turn necessitates the use of register data as the only practicable alternative.

The disadvantage with employing this method (a disadvantage which is typical for studies relying on register data in general) is that the data is inevitably rather limited and lacking in detail, unless it is complemented with data from other sources.

The methods used in this study also provide a rather unique opportunity to study changes in network structure over time, and thus to gain insights into the temporal stability of co-offending relationships.

11.2 An 'underworld' – or gangs?

Probably the most important finding from this study is the discovery in Stockholm of a Central Network comprising individuals related to one another either directly or indirectly by means of the joint commission of offences, a network which drew together the vast majority of the most delinquent youths in the city and which also included those with serious social problems. The discovery of this structure was only possible as a result of the employment of network analysis. But how is the finding to be interpreted? Does the discovery of the Central Network mean that we now have scientific evidence for the existence of some kind of underworld of delinquent relationships among juveniles in Stockholm?

The idea of a criminal underworld is fairly widespread within the police and among crime journalists. Even if the term is rarely defined, it is often spoken of as a substantive social phenomenon. A typical way of referring to this phenomenon is to say that a person has obtained information, personal favours, weapons etc. through 'contacts in the underworld'. We might describe this 'underworld' as a network of hard-core criminals – and the Central Network described in this study might provide a graphic illustration of the relations (or some of them at least) within the 'youngsters section' of this criminal underworld.

As has been seen repeatedly throughout the course of this book, however, the relations of which the Central Network is comprised are almost exclusively short-lived. In this sense, the structure of the Central Network does not correspond well with established conceptions of the character of the criminal underworld. The Central Network certainly does not represent a rationally functional structure of organised or semi-organised crime.

One possible alternative to the picture that emerges from this study would involve a structure consisting of a number of durable network structures that were unrelated to one another through co-offending. Such structures might well be linked to one another by means of several links of the suspect–victim type, on the other hand. This type of structure is not to be found in Stockholm, which leads to the conclusion that the type of gang formations often described as typical for the metropolitan areas of the USA do not exist here.[3] The question of whether this finding should be interpreted as indicating that there are no gangs in Stockholm is entirely dependant on which of the gang definitions available in the literature one chooses to apply, however. A number of the delinquent youth networks studied here, as was the case with the 'Ängen Gang' presented in the previous chapter, and particularly those linked into the Central Network, could be defined as 'compressed gangs' on the basis of the typology developed by Klein *et al.* (2001) but not if other definitions are used.

In Borlänge too a large central network was found which accounted for a large part of the visible juvenile offending One question that needs to be addressed in this context is whether the discovery of these central networks is anything more than a method-specific finding. It is conceivable that one will always identify a large central network if one studies the co-offending patterns of juveniles in a certain geographical area over a reasonably long period. This interpretation would constitute a legitimate alternative to that presented earlier in this book, that is, that a co-offending pattern character-ised by a large central network of this kind is in fact typical for Sweden (and possibly for western Europe more generally).

The method commonly used to collect data on the presence and struc-ture of gangs in a certain area involves interviewing key informants. Such key informants are often representatives of the police and other authorities who work with problems of this kind in the area concerned. Klein (1995), for example, employed this method to collect the majority of the data used to describe the current gang situation in the USA. Similar studies, as men-tioned in chapter 10, have also been carried out by the Police Authority in Stockholm (1997 and 1998). These reports received a great deal of atten-tion in the media and the perception that criminal gangs similar to tradi-tional American gangs were also to be found in Stockholm soon gained currency among the general public and politicians alike.

Whilst the reports from the Police Authority refer to a period of one to three years after the time covered by the study presented in this book, it seems highly unlikely that the gang situation in Stockholm would have changed so dramatically within so short a space of time. Instead we might consider the possibility that the results produced by the police are them-selves a function of the methods used to collect the data. The police study was carried out by means of asking the local police districts in Stockholm County whether there were currently any gangs in their area. No defini-tion of what was meant by the term 'gang' was specified. If there were gangs, the respondents were asked to provide a number of details. The various police districts were not very well informed as to the contacts among the delinquent networks to be found in their own areas and other such networks. Nor were the police representatives questioned about how the juvenile groups they were being asked to describe changed over time.

It is thus perhaps not all that surprising that the findings produced took the form they did.

It is also possible that the co-offending structures found may vary both with the methods used to study such structures and the time-frame employed. Different methods might also emphasise different aspects of offending patterns. Even in the USA, the majority of juvenile crime is not gang-related[4] (Reiss 1986, 1988). Studying juvenile crime using the kind of all-inclusive analysis of co-offending employed here may well produce a more complete picture than that which results from the study of gangs alone. At the same time, it is possible that the methods of analysis used here might miss certain substructures within the co-offending networks that might constitute graphical representations of gangs. In order to identify such substructures, the network data would probably need to be complemented with information from other sources, such as that employed here in chapters 7, 8 and 9, for example. We will only know whether gangs and other delinquent structures can easily be discovered using the methods of network analysis and whether extensive co-offending structures of the kind found in the two Swedish network studies (Borlänge and Stockholm) exist elsewhere once similar studies have been carried out in other countries.

Chapter 9, which takes up the question of the ethnic composition of co-offending networks, shows that there are in fact a number of differences between the co-offending patterns found in Stockholm and those described in the North American literature. The networks studied in Stockholm were strikingly multiracial, a factor which probably owes a great deal to the patterns of residential segregation found in Sweden which are signally different from those of the USA. In Sweden we find members of the many, and often small, ethnic minority groups living in the same areas (these areas commonly being suburbs of the large cities). The population of such suburbs thus comprises individuals from a large variety of ethnic backgrounds. The delinquent networks formed in these areas comprise youths from the various ethnic minorities and also a small proportion of Swedes (often from underclass families which also live in these suburbs).

The members of the networks commit offences not only in their own residential areas, but also often in the city centre. Some of the delinquent networks (for example several of those committing muggings against youths of the same age) comprise youngsters from a variety of suburbs who have probably met in and around the city centre. These too are most commonly multiracial in their composition. It is also relatively common for the youths in these multiracial networks to themselves have a mixed-race background (often having one Swedish and one immigrant parent). These *de facto*

Swedish youths are often perceived by outsiders (and sometimes by themselves) as immigrants, which adds to the impression that a considerable proportion of delinquent networks in Stockholm are comprised of immigrants.

The delinquent networks which form in middle-class suburbs, where the population is primarily comprised of families with a Swedish background, are made up of Swedish youths. According to Pettersson's findings (1998), confrontations among networks where the majority of members are Swedes, and those where the majority are immigrant youths (or youths from mixed ethnic backgrounds) are rare, however (even if the Swedish media has occasionally claimed otherwise).

Of course it is interesting that we find different societies' perceptions of the ethnic composition of their respective populations being reproduced in discussions of the crime structure. In Sweden, where society is perceived as comprising 'Swedes' and 'immigrants', delinquent networks are also perceived as being made up of these two groupings. In North America, where society is commonly perceived as comprising a number of different ethnic minorities, this perception is also reproduced in the composition of the juvenile networks.

To return to the question at hand, however, the most reasonable conclusion that can be drawn from the findings presented here is that Stockholm has neither an 'underworld' of delinquent juveniles (at least if we use this term to signify a pattern of well-organised and cohesive relations among delinquent youths) nor any cohesive and organised violent gangs of the kind commonly perceived to characterise North American society. What we do find, on the other hand, is a structure of delinquent relationships among young people which is durable in the sense that it extends over a long period of time, but which at the same time does not normally contain any durable ties among the actors of which it is comprised. It requires no great leap of faith to regard this structure as being of some significance for the extent and character of juvenile crime in Stockholm both at the local and the individual level. The exact significance of this structure can only be partly illustrated, however, if we restrict ourselves to the use of a network analysis of the kind presented here.

11.3 The character of delinquent relations

The findings produced by this study regarding the low durability and highly changeable nature of co-offender relationships have some interesting theoretical implications. Several of the criminological theories discussed here assume that the influence exerted between individuals is greatest where relations between such individuals are intensive, deep and long-lasting. This is true irrespective of whether, like Sutherland (1939, 1947), one is looking at the learning of various aspects of delinquent (or conformist) behaviour, or at control by means of attachments to significant others, as with Hirschi (1969). Our problem is that the co-offending relationships examined here have proved to be extremely unstable. The suggestion that this finding might also be a function of the methods employed and a result of the low clear-up rates associated with juvenile offending can be rejected with reference to similar findings produced by both Reiss and Farrington (1991) and Warr (1996) on the basis of self-report data.

When these findings were discussed earlier in the book, I presented the hypothesis that the relations within these delinquent networks can be likened to the weak ties which Granovetter (1974) identified as having been used by well-educated men in Boston in their search for new job opportunities. As was mentioned in the introduction, the study by Lee (1969) of women using their friends as a means of finding someone to carry out an illegal abortion represents another example of the way weak ties can function in practice. This example is possibly of additional interest since, given the circumstances at the time, it represents a study of criminal behaviour. What we find in both these examples is that weak ties become significant in those situations where actors make the effort to actively exploit the potential offered by such ties. In both instances the actors concerned were highly motivated to achieve a specific objective. The question then becomes whether the circumstances surrounding the co-offending links studied here are similar to those just described. For example, are juvenile delinquents motivated actors focused on a specific objective and looking for information on suitable targets for crime, or for ways to neutralise their delinquent activities, or for co-offenders with whom to commit planned offences?

In some instances seeking co-offenders might be the case. An individual who seeks out a person who is considerably older and who neither lives nor spends time in the same place as the actor himself, in order to buy drugs for example, or to sell stolen goods, or to procure a weapon for use in a crime he is planning to commit, is unquestionably acting in a focused and rational way (see Tremblay, 1993). If someone wants to buy drugs, the weak ties of the friendship group will very likely provide a means of finding a suitable dealer.

Most of the choices of co-offender described in this book are not of this kind, however. It seems clear that these choices are made more or less spontaneously from among the group of individuals with whom the actor in question has contact on a more or less everyday basis, who live in the same area and/or are in the same class at school. In this instance it seems misleading to talk about conscious, active choices made in a network of weak ties (links). On the basis of the findings from the Borlänge study (Sarnecki 1996) I concluded that most of the delinquent activities studied were spontaneous in character and were to a large degree the result of a number of coincidences. The nature of these activities does not correspond at all well with the idea of a focused goal-conscious choice of co-offenders and offences. Such offending patterns are much more reminiscent of the concepts associated with a drift into delinquency as presented by Matza (1964).

Another finding produced by the Borlänge study was that many of the delinquent youths, particularly those presenting higher levels of delinquency, often committed offences together with their best friends. How does this finding fit with the lack of durability displayed by these delinquent relations? One reasonable explanation would be that the friendship relations of the youths studied are also fairly short-lived and changeable. Switching friends in this way is fairly typical among boys in their early teenage years and can in addition be regarded as a common characteristic of youths with adjustment difficulties. These boys often seem to find it easy to establish new friendships and commonly have a large and shifting circle of friends (Sarnecki 1978 and 1983a). The instability of delinquent relations might also to some extent be the result of an instability typical of the social relations of delinquent youths in general. These findings support Hirschi's conception of delinquency-prone individuals as somewhat defective when it comes to forming relationships with others in their social environment, including members of the peer group. This does not mean that Hirschi is correct to assume that the delinquent influences which such relations may involve do not affect the criminal behaviour of the youths concerned in any significant way, however. The fact that such friendships are brief and changeable does not necessarily mean that they lack intensity while they last (cf. Ring 1999). This being so, such relations cannot really be regarded as examples of the weak ties discussed above. Instead, what we are looking at may well be contacts that despite being short-lived are both intense and frequent during their relatively brief duration. A mutual learning process would appear to be rather likely in the context of such relationships.

The youths studied also have friendships that are considerably more durable, of course. In the interviews carried out by William-Olsson, and presented in chapter 10 above, the boys talked of very close friendships with youths of the same age that they had known since 'nursery school days'. It is probable, however, that the intensity of contacts among such friends varies over time and that different individuals are chosen from this circle as co-offenders on different occasions.

Certain of the analyses presented in chapter 6 may also serve to illustrate the content of the co-offending relationships described in this study. One of the issues touched on in this chapter was the question of the offending patterns presented by co-offenders of youths with specific problem profiles. Even here, the picture presented by the data is not unequivocal. To begin with, the youths often presented a complex of problem profiles rather than a single profile. It was not possible to identify many 'specialists' in the data who concentrated on crimes or other deviant behaviours of a specific type. Nonetheless, it was possible to establish that in those parts of the Central Network where many of the profiled individuals who presented high levels of violent offending were to be found, there were also other individuals who presented higher than average levels of violent offending. The situation in those parts of the Central Network where the substance-abuse profile individuals were to be found was similar in that here there were a number of other individuals presenting higher than average levels of drug-related offending. A closer examination showed, however, that these individuals were in fact to be found in the same high-intensity delinquency areas of the network. Belonging to these parts of the Central Network seemed to involve being more highly delinquent in general, and there does not seem to be any notable degree of correspondence between the types of offence committed by the profiled actors and those committed by their co-offenders.

The conclusions presented here coincide with those drawn by Shannon (1998) on the basis of his study of certain subsections of the network data, namely that the behavioural expressions of an individual's problems are more closely related to characteristics at the level of the individual him or herself than to the network affiliations of the individual in question. The extent of such problems on the other hand may well be a function of such network affiliations. In addition, the shifting structure of delinquent relations would provide support for antisocial behaviour at a more general level, rather than influencing individuals towards a specialisation in certain types of antisocial (delinquent) activities.

The discussion presented above indicates that the content of both the co-offending links examined and of the more complex relations which underlie these links can vary considerably. Network analysis of the type carried out here can only provide us with an intimation of the character of the relations between delinquent actors.

11.4 The effect of interventions

Chapter 6 presented findings relating to the delinquent networks formed around youths placed in secure care facilities. The results of these particular analyses lead to unexpectedly positive conclusions regarding the effects of this particular type of intervention. Among other things, the chapter examined the hypothesis that placement in this type of secure institution is related to increased levels of delinquency on the part of those admitted. It is clearly not possible for us to say whether socialising with other youths placed in these institutions leads to the actors learning new types of offence and other forms of deviant behaviour. We can however contend that a stay in one of these institutions does not lead to the establishment of new contacts with other delinquent individuals which are then maintained in the form of co-offending once the youths are released. In general, the youths admitted to secure care facilities were more delinquent and also had more social problems of other kinds than the rest of the youths included in the study, and they were commonly affiliated to a network of highly delinquent individuals. The study shows, however, that the links in such a network were not established during the time spent in secure care.

It should be noted, nevertheless, that stays in secure care facilities are seldom prolonged. It would therefore be interesting to examine the effects of stays in prison, and particularly those of a more sustained nature undergone by younger inmates. A network analysis of co-offending patterns, possibly complemented by interviews, would be an extremely useful tool in a study of this kind.

Another interesting finding produced in this part of the study had to do with the effect that placement in a secure care facility appeared to have on the co-offenders of the individuals admitted. Our results suggest that the level of offending among the co-offenders of those placed in secure care facilities decreased once the placements had occurred. At this stage this finding must be regarded as provisional, and the finding requires further research. Among other things, the criminal careers of the co-offenders of those placed in secure care should be examined a good deal more closely than has been possible here.

This discovery is interesting nonetheless (theoretically speaking), since it suggests quite strongly that the exertion of influence among members of a network, which constitutes one of the fundamental assumptions of this study, does in fact take place. In addition, the findings suggest that evaluations of the effects of incapacitation and other forms of individual prevention should also take into consideration the indirect effects of these interventions (a factor which may have a great deal of practical significance – compare Reiss 1986, 1988). It is quite possible that such evaluations will lead to misleading conclusions as long as there is no consideration of the network effects of the interventions being examined.

11.5 Studying specific groups

The network analysis method is perhaps most suited to the study of relations in specific groups of delinquents, groups where we would like to know more about the composition of the membership, about how the members are linked to one another, about persons who may play a central role and so forth. Analyses of this type were presented in chapters 7, 8 and 10, and were based on data relating to a number of individuals (sometimes just a few) who were known to be members of a specific group (right- and left-wing extremists, members of various groups of football hooligans, and members of a local delinquent 'juvenile gang'). By means of a network analysis which describes the co-offender ties of these individuals and examines the co-offenders themselves, it is possible to build a more complete picture of these groups and their activities. Using the network method to identify other (previously unknown) members of a specific group is in fact simply another way of drawing a snowball sample of the kind often used in social scientific research.

The network method also provided information on the level of cohesion within the groups examined, as well as on their contacts with other groups and with other delinquent networks. The analysis of the football hooligans showed that whilst the members of different groups often had contact with each other in the context of violent confrontations of one kind or another, those who also committed offences more generally did so occasionally with members of other hooligan groups unaffected by the presence of these football-related antagonisms.

Another interesting finding concerns the differences between groups of right- and left-wing extremists, where the former seemed to comprise loose-knit networks of delinquent individuals, often linked into the Central Network, and who occasionally 'spiced up' their delinquency with the occasional politically or racially motivated offence. By contrast, the latter group comprised considerably more cohesive networks with no links to other delinquent groupings, and who did not appear to commit any offences other than those with a political motivation.

Network analysis, particularly when based on register data, also provides the opportunity to study the way a network changes over time. This type of study can probably provide better answers than have been possible up to now with regard to questions concerning the relationships among the criminal careers of specific network members and the career of the networks as a whole. This type of study would also profit from the use of supplemental data from alternative sources.

The kind of analysis that limits itself to one or a few networks is particularly suitable for a data triangulation, where a network analysis of co-offending is combined with a number of the other data collection methods common in social science, such as interviews with key informants, interviews with the study objects themselves, and observation studies. There is nothing to prevent the use of network methods to analyse the data from sources other than the police register in such a study. Nor would such an analysis have to confine itself to an examination of data relating to co-offending, but might profit by focusing in addition on other friendship relations. The method can also be usefully employed to examine a combination of co-offending and suspect–victim, or other kinds of conflict-based relationships.

11.6 Network analysis as a criminological method

Since network analysis is a reasonably neutral methodological tool from the perspective of criminological theory, it can be applied to the study of empirical data in association with a variety of different sociologically based theoretical perspectives. It is quite possibly an unusually suitable method for the study of certain types of criminological questions (not least those concerned with co-offending). But, as has been shown above, the fact that network analysis is a theoretically neutral methodological tool does not of course mean that criminological analyses carried out with the help of network methods lack theoretical implications.

It has been repeated on a number of occasions in the course of this chapter that network analyses, particularly where they are based on register data, should be supplemented with other analytical methods. A network analysis can profit from being complemented by interviews with strategically chosen members of the network, or other informants who are familiar with the network in question. Various types of observational method can also be used in conjunction with network analysis. In studies of this kind, the network analysis can provide a framework of 'hard data' to guide the focus of the other methods. Network analysis can then be employed to study the pattern of relations within a network, whilst the other methods provide the more nuanced and detailed information on the content of such relations.

It is also quite possible to complement the register data relating to the structure of the network with data from other sources. In the context of research into co-offending, for example, one could by means of interviews or observation collect data on more links than those to be found in the police register. In addition, to use Sutherland's (1939, 1947) terminology, such methods could be used to collect data not only on links binding an individual to models for deviant behaviour, but also those binding him or her to models of conformist behaviour.

Appendix

Table A1: *Age difference between youths suspected of offences in Stockholm 1991–1995 and their co-offenders. Pairs*

Age of principal population	Average age of co-offenders	SD	N
10 or lower	+4.0	10.0	353
11	+0.9	2.6	264
12	+1.3	4.7	543
13	+0.9	2.6	1,347
14	+0.9	2.9	3,384
15	+1.1	3.3	5,074
16	+1.5	3.6	8,600
17	+1.3	4.4	7,608
18	+1.0	4.3	6,968
19	+1.6	5.2	5,072
20	+1.4	5.7	4,941
21[1]	+1.8	6.7	2,432
Total	+1.3	4.5	46,576

Notes:

[1] Age reckoned on the basis of year of birth. Individuals shown as 21 years of age will turn 21 at some point during the year in question.

Table A2: *Proportion of co-offenders of same gender chosen by boys and girls suspected of offences in Stockholm 1991–1995. Per cent*

Age[1]	Female/Female	Male/Male
10	83	92
11	70	96
12	92	96
13	93	98
14	88	97
15	71	96
16	51	94
17	50	93
18	48	92
19	35	92
20	36	93
21	28	93
Total	56	94

Notes:
[1] Age reckoned on the basis of year of birth.

Table A3: *Correspondence between residential postcodes for youths suspected of offences in Stockholm 1991–1995 and their co-offenders, after offender's age. Pairs. Per cent*

| Age[1] | Number of identical digits in postcode | | | | | | |
	All	First 3	First 2	First	None	Sum	N
10 or younger	53.8	39.6	2.2	4.4	0.0	100.0	159
11	32.7	41.3	9.6	16.3	0.0	100.0	178
12	43.5	36.7	10.2	8.8	0.7	100.0	248
13	23.4	53.7	15.7	7.1	0.0	100.0	888
14	20.0	54.6	16.2	8.2	1.0	100.0	2,183
15	17.5	48.2	17.9	12.3	4.1	100.0	2,165
16	13.0	51.1	12.8	21.0	2.2	100.0	2,315
17	12.4	34.2	17.7	30.3	5.3	100.0	2,101
18	11.5	26.6	13.5	42.7	5.7	100.0	2,118
19	7.4	19.9	15.6	46.5	10.6	100.0	1,852
20	8.9	18.7	16.1	42.4	13.9	100.0	1,648
21	8.0	18.4	17.1	45.9	10.6	100.0	900
Total	14.5	37.3	15.4	27.3	5.5	100.0	16,755

Notes:
[1] Age reckoned on the basis of year of birth.

Table A4: *Correspondence in residential postcode between youths suspected of offences in Stockholm 1991–1995 and their co-offenders, after offender's gender. Pairs. Per cent*

		Number of identical digits in postcode					
Gender	All	First 3	First 2	First	None	Sum	N
Female	17.4	33.9	13.5	29.5	5.7	100.0	2,451
Male	14.0	37.8	15.7	27.0	5.5	100.0	14,305
Total	14.5	37.3	15.4	27.3	5.5	100.0	16,756

Table A5: *Choices of co-offenders. Proportion of co-offenders of the same age as, younger and older than youths suspected of offences in Stockholm 1991–1995. Average age difference, and standard deviation, after offence type. Pairs*

Offence type	Younger %	Same age %	Older %	Sum %	Average age diff.	SD	N
Assault, attempted murder, murder	28.5	31.2	40.4	100.0	+.9	4.5	4,109
Sex offences	17.6	44.0	38.5	100.0	+1.4	3.8	91
Mugging	26.9	34.4	38.7	100.0	+.8	3.3	2,057
Other crimes against the person	28.8	27.7	43.5	100.0	+1.1	3.9	4,923
Shoplifting	27.8	36.9	35.4	100.0	+.7	3.9	4,142
Other thefts including burglary	29.7	27.5	42.8	100.0	+.9	4.0	9,818
Criminal damage	30.7	33.1	36.2	100.0	+.4	3.0	4,453
Other crimes against property	18.6	20.7	60.7	100.0	+4.6	7.9	1,549
Drug offences	12.9	14.0	73.1	100.0	+5.9	7.3	852
Public order offences	31.8	16.0	52.2	100.0	+1.3	3.8	11,653
Other offences	22.2	22.4	55.5	100.0	+3.2	6.8	2,918
Total	28.7	25.9	45.5	100.0	+1.3	4.5	45,565

Table A6: *Choices of co-offenders. Gender of youths suspected of offences in Stockholm 1991–1995 and their co-offenders. After offence type. Per cent*

Offence type	Male/ male	Male/ female	Female/ male	Female/ female	Total	N
Assault, attempted murder, murder	88.5	1.7	2.1	7.7	100.0	4,109
Sex offences	100.0	0.0	0.0	0.0	100.0	91
Mugging	90.7	2.1	2.7	4.5	100.0	2,057
Other crimes against the person	56.9	14.0	16.8	12.2	100.0	4,923
Shoplifting	41.4	2.9	4.1	51.6	100.0	4,142
Other thefts including burglary	92.2	2.6	3.1	2.1	100.0	9,761
Criminal damage	86.7	4.9	5.0	3.4	100.0	4,441
Other crimes against property	67.9	4.7	14.6	12.7	100.0	1,530
Drug offences	80.4	5.3	11.0	3.3	100.0	848
Public-order offences	86.0	6.4	6.8	0.8	100.0	11,637
Other offences	69.2	5.8	14.2	10.6	100.0	2,894
Total	79.1	5.2	6.9	8.9	100.0	46,399

Table A7: *Choices of co-offenders. Correspondence in residential postcodes among youths suspected of offences in Stockholm 1991–1995 and their suspected co-offenders, after offence type. Per cent*

Offence type	None	First digit	First two digits	First three digits	All digits	Sum	N
Assault, attempted murder, murder	5.0	17.4	17.3	45.9	14.4	100.0	1,888
Sex offences	0.0	10.5	42.1	42.1	5.3	100.0	66
Mugging	7.0	37.1	15.2	32.0	8.6	100.0	884
Other crimes against the person	5.9	46.4	16.4	22.1	9.3	100.0	2,292
Shoplifting	1.5	12.3	14.5	48.3	23.4	100.0	2,064
Other thefts including burglary	2.9	19.3	17.3	42.5	18.0	100.0	4,849
Criminal damage	3.1	23.4	12.8	46.0	17.7	100.0	1,943
Other crimes against property	6.3	29.8	14.0	38.9	10.9	100.0	492
Drug offences	14.5	47.0	12.0	19.3	7.2	100.0	143
Public-order offences	29.9	50.4	7.1	11.4	1.4	100.0	971
Other offences	4.5	44.2	15.3	22.9	13.0	100.0	1,114

Table A8: *Level of delinquent experience (offence participations) 1991–1995 after offence type for the youths in the various problem profile groups and their co-offenders, and for the study population as a whole. Per cent*

Crime	Crime profile	Substance-abuse profile	Psych-problem profile	Sexual disturbance profile	Profile 0	All suspects
			Actors			
Assault, attempted murder, murder	17.9	11.3	14.8	13.9	14.4	13.7
Sex offences	0.3	0.0	0.0	0.0	0.5	0.3
Mugging	6.8	12.0	5.7	5.9	6.9	2.9
Other crimes against the person	8.0	5.1	6.8	7.9	7.5	6.7
Shoplifting	8.0	13.4	9.9	15.8	8.5	23.4
Other thefts including burglary	28.9	21.3	25.8	21.8	31.1	18.2
Criminal damage	4.9	5.8	7.6	3.0	4.2	9.9
Other crimes against property	3.8	7.6	9.9	6.9	5.0	8.3
Drug offences	8.0	4.4	6.0	5.9	7.6	7.0
Public-order offences	6.0	12.2	5.7	8.9	5.9	3.4
Other offences	7.4	6.9	7.8	10.0	8.5	6.2
Sum	100.0	100.0	100.0	100.0	100.0	100.0
N – number of offence participations	1,038	600	329	93	740	33,896

Table A8 (*cont.*)

Crime	Crime profile	Substance-abuse profile	Psych-problem profile	Sexual disturbance profile	Profile 0	All suspects
			Co-offenders			
Assault, attempted murder, murder	13.6	10.2	11.8	17.4	13.7	15.3
Sex offences	0.4	0.2	0.0	0.0	0.5	0.3
Other crimes against the person	7.0	7.3	5.5	6.9	7.6	7.8
Shoplifting	6.3	8.0	6.8	9.9	6.3	16.2
Mugging	8.5	8.4	8.9	18.6	8.3	3.4
Other thefts including burglary	33.4	30.9	32.6	29.1	34.9	23.4
Criminal damage	5.9	8.1	6.1	2.3	5.4	9.6
Other crimes against property	3.7	2.8	6.4	3.4	4.9	6.7
Drug offences	7.9	5.8	6.2	3.5	7.1	6.0
Public-order offences	7.6	11.7	8.7	2.3	7.0	4.1
Other offences	5.7	6.7	7.0	6.6	4.3	7.2
Sum	100.0	100.0	100.0	100.0	100.0	100.0
N – number of offence participations	1,969	843	888	172	1,736	26,496

Table A9: *Ethnicity of co-offenders to youths suspected of violent offences in Stockholm 1995, victims of these offences, and of the entire population of Stockholm. Per cent*

Individuals with a background in:	Co-offenders	Victims	Population of Stockholm
Sweden	43	62	73
Scandinavia excluding Sweden	10	11	7
Europe excluding Scandinavia and Turkey	13	10	8
The Middle East, Turkey and North Africa	16	8	5
Africa excluding North Africa	8	4	2
Asia excluding the Middle East	2	1	2
South- and Central America	7	3	2
Others	1	1	1
Total	100	100	100
N	1,192	1,838	771,119

Notes

1 For an overview of the more recent research in this area see Wasserman and Galaskiewicz 1994, Wasserman and Faust 1997 (and in Swedish, Borell and Johansson 1994).

2 A number of such studies have nonetheless been published. Baron and Tindall (1993), for example, published a study entitled 'Network Structure and Delinquent Attitudes within a Juvenile Gang.' In 1994, Waring published a doctoral thesis entitled 'Co-offending in White-Collar Crimes: A Network Approach.' Network analysis has also been employed in areas closely related to the field of criminology. There are a number of network studies of drug abuse, for example Jansson (1997), and examples of the network method are also to be found in treatment research (e.g. Borell and Johansson 1994) and research into the spread of HIV (e.g. Miller 1999). In addition, networks appear in criminological research in the sense that the network is used as an analytical concept, but without any network analyses as such being carried out (Loftin 1986: 554; Johansen 1996; Decker 1996: A46).

3 Questions asking whether young people commit offences together or on their own are relatively common in self-report studies. A question of this type was included in a self-report study covering all boys in year 9 (approximately 16 years old) in Örebro, a town lying to the west of Stockholm (Olofsson 1967 and 1971; Dunér and Haglund 1974). The study was repeated in 1996 with a comparable population and with identical measuring instruments (Ward 1998). Despite the 25-year difference between the two studies, the results were in many respects very similar. Of the youths who reported having committed offences, a majority said they had done so 'sometimes with friends and sometimes alone' or 'always with friends'. Only a small group reported having always committed offences by themselves.

4 The same self-report studies mentioned in note 3 (Olofsson 1967; 1971; Duneur and Haglund 1974; Ward 1998) show that the individuals with whom the young offenders committed the offences were the same friends with whom they spent time in a more general sense. Sarnecki's findings (1986), based on a comparison

of police data concerning juveniles suspected of co-offending and reports from the juveniles themselves concerning their friendship ties, support this.

5 This failure to give an account of the transmission process is in fact seen as one of the major shortcomings of cultural deviance theorists (Costello 1997).

6 However there are researchers who feel that the existence of relationships among criminal individuals is the result of a tendency for individuals with similar problems to gravitate to one another (e.g. Glueck and Glueck 1950).

7 An increase which seems incidentally to have levelled off over the last two decades (Estrada 1999).

8 Certain authors (Scott 1991, Pettersson 1998b) instead split the network analytical tradition into three different approaches, of which two originate in different parts of social psychology.

9 This research tradition is still very much alive. Hedström (1997) and others, for example, have studied the diffusion of the social-democratic ideology espoused by the labour movement in Swedish society.

10 The method is known as 'snowball sampling' and works by using the social networks of subjects with specific characteristics to make contact with new subjects with similar characteristics.

11 Although it can be seen in the work of representatives of the Chicago School (Short 1998b).

12 The following discussion of the situation of the underclass is also applicable to ethnic minorities or immigrants. In a recently published article, von Hofer *et al.* (1997) use strain theory to explain the overrepresentation of immigrants among persons convicted of criminal offences in Sweden.

13 Innovation, ritualism, retreatism and rebellion (Merton 1938).

14 Gustav Jonsson (1971: 49), for example, claims that these theories owe more to time spent in libraries than to direct fieldwork.

15 The authors point out that they are aware that the symbol is also a form of communication. They have nonetheless made a conscious decision to differentiate between these two elements (Curry and Decker 1998: 3)

16 Klein *et al.* (2001): refers to gangs of this type as 'speciality gangs'.

17 The term 'gang' is actually even older. Yablonsky (1962) states that the first scientific use of the gang concept must be ascribed to Sheldon (1898).

18 Perhaps one of the most fervent adherents of social bonding theory, Ruth Kornhauser (1978) claims that the group character of juvenile offending lacks criminological relevance, since group behaviour is a characteristic of more or less all forms of activity among young people.

19 According to Short (1998: 14), Shaw and McKay and their colleagues contended in their earlier work that lone offenders were also influenced by delinquent peers.

20 For these crimes he was sentenced to twenty years in prison.

21 This contention is in line with Hirschi's (1969) view that delinquency does not constitute a learned behaviour.

22 A Swedish municipality of around 50,000 inhabitants lying about 250 km from Stockholm.

23 The word 'network' is used here to refer to groupings that graph-theoretical terminology would more precisely describe as connected components. See the discussion in chapter 2.

2 THE AIMS AND METHODS OF THE STUDY

1 Warr himself employs such a study, namely the National Survey of Youth (NSY) from 1967: Gold (1970).
2 A might be B's boss, for example, while B is A's subordinate.
3 In one of the analyses (graph 4) the actors are criminal networks and the relation studied is the movement of individuals between these networks over time.
4 In certain contexts, the relation between perpetrator and victim will also be examined.
5 One way of viewing a network is to see it as a social organisation comprised of links between members. Frank (1999: 2) suggests that an important element of the social capacity of organisations is the ability of members to receive support from one another. One aspect of this ability is found in the degree to which the members of the organisation can reach one another. The greater the level of reachability, the greater the capacity for support (p. 4).
6 In some instances we will be presented with an opportunity to compare the RAR data with other sources of data on the delinquency of the individuals being studied. These occasions will give us the chance to examine the validity of the RAR data.

3 ACTORS AND LINKS

1 All Swedish residents have a unique identity number consisting of their date of birth and four additional digits.
2 Individuals as young as this are extremely rare in the data. Children under 10 years of age comprise around one per cent of those studied.
3 In practise the principal population is defined on the basis of the year of birth. The eldest individuals included in the principal population for 1991 were born in 1971. Those included in 1992 were born 1972 or later and so on. This means that some individuals were included in the study even though they would very soon be turning 21.
4 Official crime statistics in Sweden count offences in more than one way. The 'offence participation' count takes into consideration the number of co-offenders present at an incident. A single burglary committed by five co-offenders would be counted as five offence participations, for example. If two of these actors are then suspected of together committing a further offence, the number of offence participations increases to seven while the number of offences increases to two.
5 Two factors are significant in connection with the missing postcode data. One is that these data are more often missing for offences committed during 1991 and 1992 than for those committed during the remaining three years. The other factor is that postcode information is missing for individuals living outside the county of Stockholm somewhat more often than for those living within the county.
6 This proportion may well be somewhat higher given the patterns observed in the missing data.

7 This figure relates to offence participations for members of the principal population *and* their co-offenders aged 21 years and older. For those individuals aged 21 and over, only those offences are counted for which they were suspected together with members of the principal population.

8 Unlike links between perpetrators and victims which are regarded in the context of the present study as unidirectional, from perpetrator to victim (see chapter 9, p. 130).

9 During the course of the five-year study period, the members of the principal population made a total of 46,576 choices of co-offender. These 46,576 choices (or 'pairs' as they are referred to in chapter 4 of this book) constitute the basis for the production of the networks. This was the form the data were in when they came to us from the police's RAR register.

10 Curvilinear models do not represent this relationship any more effectively.

11 It is as well to emphasise once again the fact that registered criminality constitutes only a fraction of the actual level of offending, which means that the actual number of pairs committing offences together on several occasions will be considerably higher than that indicated by our results. This does not mean that the *proportion* of durable co-offending relationships is necessarily higher in reality than that presented in our results, however.

12 All those individuals aged 21 or over included in the study are by definition co-offenders.

13 A further problem involved in interpreting the results presented here consists in the possibility referred to earlier that the risk of detection is lower for individuals who commit offences alone than for those committing offences in a group.

14 In this context the word 'debut' is used to indicate the time when these individuals first appear in the data.

15 PBR and RAR differ too in the following respect: having been suspected of an offence is sufficient for an individual to remain connected with that offence in the RAR offence report register, while these offences are not listed against the person in the PBR offender register unless the individual is actually convicted, formally cautioned or fined by the prosecutor for the offence.

4 THE CHOICE OF CO-OFFENDERS

1 Note that the method of calculation means that the majority of individuals (if under 21 years of age) are counted both as actor and as co-offender in connection with the same offence.

2 As was mentioned earlier, such young individuals are very rare among those suspected of offences.

3 For males from the principal population suspected of co-offending with females, the age difference was on average 1.3 years (SD 6.4).

4 The county of Stockholm has about 1,600,000 inhabitants.

5 The city of Stockholm has about 800,000 inhabitants.

6 The wards are numbered between 10 and 19, where 10 and 11 refer to the centre, 15 is missing, and 17 refers to two different areas of the metropolitan area. The calculations above take these factors into account.

7 The problems faced by all studies which rely on registered delinquency are very clear in this context. As a result of the low clearance rates, it is very likely that many individuals who have never been registered as committing offences do in fact have some delinquent experience. A high level of delinquency will however increase the risk of being registered as an offender.

8 Data concerning members of the principal population is, as has been mentioned, limited to offences committed in Stockholm between 1991 and 1995.

5 THE NETWORK

1 As was pointed out earlier, the term 'network' is here used in place of the connected component concept found in graph theory.

2 i.e. the graph had to be reduced by a factor of 50 in order to fit it on to the page.

6 THE NETWORK CONNECTIONS OF JUVENILES ADMITTED TO SECURE CARE FACILITIES

1 A change to the law in 1999 means that persons under the age of 18 are to all intents and purposes never sentenced to a prison term. This change came into effect after the data employed in the study had been collected, however.

2 A further, follow-up study, focusing on these same individuals, now as adults, is at present under way (Bergström 2000).

3 The length of stay for the majority of the young people studied was under two months.

4 Further studies are needed which focus on youths kept in such institutions for longer periods, and on institutions with large numbers of inmates. It is possible that a similar study of adult prison inmates might produce quite different findings.

5 There is little point studying the effects of incapacitation in the context of this study, since placements in secure care facilities are often brief, lasting no longer than two months in the majority of cases. Possible deterrent effects on co-offenders, on the other hand, are highly relevant.

6 The following eighteen variables were included in the factor analysis: theft and shoplifting, mugging, vandalism, assault, alcohol abuse, illicit drug abuse, abuse of prescription drugs, solvent abuse, running away from the facility, psychosis, brain damage, emotional disturbances, suicide attempts, school problems, truancy, sexual assault (victim), promiscuity, prostitution and bad physical health.

7 Assault, attempted murder, murder, sex offences, mugging and assaults on police officers/public servants, as well as other crimes against the person such as threatening behaviour, coercion and the like.

8 Thefts including burglaries and shoplifting, fraud, criminal damage etc.

9 Primarily possession and the purchase/sale of drugs.

10 This difference in the level of delinquency cannot be completely explained by the fact that we find among the co-offenders a number of individuals aged 21 and over whose offence data is therefore incomplete. A calculation based only on those individuals under 21 years of age produced the same difference in

delinquency levels. On the other hand, whilst it is possible that that the older co-offenders were more delinquent than the members of the different profile groups (who were on average younger) and whilst this would lead to a reduction in the difference in the levels of delinquency presented by the profile group members and their co-offenders respectively, such a reduction would not be particularly large, since the older co-offenders were relatively few in number. Thus the conclusion is that the co-offenders present levels of delinquency that are on average lower than those of the youths placed in secure care facilities, even when we take the co-offenders higher average age into consideration.

11 As we know, links can cover several crimes and offence types if two individuals are suspected of jointly participating in a number of offences.

12 In some cases, both these offences were present in the same link.

13 In total there were up to twelve such steps in the networks of the crime profile individuals, but the last four of these comprised a very small number of links (not quite 1 per cent of the total) and were excluded for this reason. The calculations are reckoned from each of the individuals in the profile group irrespective of whether the others to whom they are linked are themselves members of the same profile group or not.

14 See table 6.1.

15 See the discussion concerning football hooligans and political extremists in the following chapter, however.

7 FOOTBALL HOOLIGANS IN THE NETWORKS

1 And other groups of individuals too, such as the politically active youths to whom I shall return in the following chapter.

8 POLITICALLY AND IDEOLOGICALLY MOTIVATED OFFENCES

1 The crimes for which these individuals were suspected were anti-immigrant/racist offences (72 persons), anti-Semitic offences (5 persons), homophobic offences (2 persons) and other extreme right-wing offences (4 persons).

2 The crimes for which these individuals were suspected were often motivated by a concern for the environment and were directed against a number of motorway construction projects in the Stockholm area. Other offences falling under this rubric were directed against members of extreme right-wing groups or against police officers in connection with animal rights demonstrations (State security police 1996, 1997, 1998).

3 Expressed in terms of sampling, this constitutes a two-wave snowball.

4 Postcode information is available for seventeen of the group's members.

9 ETHNICITY

1 Kontos (2000) contends, however, that a number of researchers have exaggerated the level of ethnic homogeneity in American gangs, and Thrasher had

pointed out, as early as 1925, that a number of the gangs he studied were of multi-ethnic composition.

2 Non-white youths constitute a very small group in this particular study, however (12 of 411 youths).

3 The violent offences included were murder, manslaughter, assault, threatening behaviour, muggings, and assaults on and threats against public servants.

4 The categorisation into ethnic groups was based on the individual's and the parents' citizenship and country of birth.

5 Pettersson's results are confirmed by an as yet unpublished study by Tom Ageby. Ageby examined the ethnic backgrounds of the individuals in a large network formed by Stockholm youths suspected of offences (not only violent offences) in 1990. Thirty-six per cent of these youths came from Swedish backgrounds whilst the remainder were first or second generation immigrant youths from a variety of different European and non-European backgrounds.

6 See the discussion presented in chapter 4 on the use of the choice concept in this study.

7 I am fully aware that this is a somewhat complex question. There are many offences, not least violent offences, where the victim also plays an active role (Wolfgang 1958, Fattah 1991). The most logical approach in the context of the present study, however, is to work on the assumption that the choice of victim is one made solely by the perpetrator.

8 Data on the ethnicity of one or both actors is missing for 7 per cent of suspect–suspect pairs and for 9 per cent of suspect–victim pairs. There is no reason to believe that the ethnic distribution differs substantially between the pairs for which ethnicity data is available, and those for which it is not.

9 The parents counted here are the biological parents, which means that children adopted from abroad are reckoned to have the ethnic background of their country of origin. This creates problems of its own of course.

10 In some instances this is likely to produce unreasonable classifications since it means that a number of youths who think of themselves as completely Swedish would in fact be classified as immigrants. However, this is precisely the classification used in a number of official publications in Sweden (Regionalplane- och trafikkontoret 1991).

11 Pettersson (1998b) elucidates the same questions as those discussed here. She compares the proportion of co-offenders chosen from the same ethnic background with the proportion of choices made of co-offenders from other ethnic backgrounds, however. Whilst our calculations are based on different methods, Pettersson's results and my own are very similar, and our conclusions are identical.

12 Proportion measures of choices of victims were fairly similar irrespective of whether they were reckoned in relation to victims or in relation to the population of Stockholm. This shows that the ethnic composition of the group of victims is to a large extent similar to that of the population of Stockholm.

10 THE 'ÄNGEN GANG'

1 Moore's view on what constitute typical gang characteristics is not shared by all gang researchers however (compare Klein *et al.* 2001)

11 CONCLUSIONS

1 As early as 1843, John Stuart Mill wrote in his 'System of Logic' of two currents within the 'moral sciences', the one concerned with the study of individuals in isolation (psychology), the other concerned with relations between individuals (general social science, later to become known as sociology) (Mill 1997)

2 At least inasmuch as the actors are in the relevant age group, and make their choices of co-offender (i.e. are suspected of offences) within the relevant geographical area.

3 The presence of suspect–victim links between members of co-offender networks has not been examined in those parts of the study presented in this book. A study was made of the presence of such links by Pettersson (1998) in the context of her examination of Stockholm youths suspected of violent offences.

4 Once again, though, the proportion of crime that is gang related can vary substantially depending on the gang definition employed.

References

Agnew, R. (1985): 'A revised strain theory of delinquency.' *Social Factors* 64: 151–167.

Ahlberg, J. (1985): *Vilka står för läktarvåldet?* (Who is responsible for the violence on the terraces?) Kansli PM. Stockholm: Brottsförebyggande rådet (BRÅ).

Ahlberg, J. (1996): *Invandrares och invandrares barns brottslighet. En statistisk analys.* (The criminality of immigrants and their children. A statistical analysis.) BRÅ – report 1996: 2. Stockholm: Brottsförebyggande rådet.

Akers, R. L. (1998): *Social Learning and Social Structure. A General Theory of Crime and Deviance.* Boston: Northeastern University Press.

Aksamit, U. and Krzyzanowska, B. (1999): *Hur ungdomsbrottligheten utvecklas med respektive utan medbrottslingar.* (The development of juvenile delinquency with and without co-offenders.) Stockholm University.

Alsterholt, U. (1997): *Geografisk rörlighet hos brottsaktiva ungdomar i Stockholm.* (Geographical mobility among delinquent youths in Stockholm.) Stockholm University.

Ålund, A (1995): *Ungdomar, gränser och nya rörelser.* (Youths, borders and new movements.) Norrköping: Statens Invandrarverk.

Ålund, A (1997): *Multikultiungdom – kön, etnicitet, identitet.* (Multicultural youth – gender, ethnicity, identity.) Lund: Studentlitteratur.

Armstrong, G. (1998): *Football Hooligans: Knowing the Score.* Leamington Spa: Berg

Barnes, J. A. (1954): 'Class and committees in a Norwegian island parish.' *Human Relations* 7, 39–59.

Baron, S. and Tindall, B. (1993): 'Network structure and delinquent attitudes within a juvenile gang.' *Social Networks* 15, 255–273.

Bauman, Z. (1992): *Intimations of Postmodernity.* London: Routledge.

Bergström, U. (2000): *Upplevelse av ett ungdomshem. En intervjuundersökning.* (Experiences from a reformatory.) Stockholm University.

Bergström, U. and Sarnecki, J. (1996): 'Invandrarungdomar på särskilda ungdomshem i Stockholms län.' (Immigrant youths in secure care facilities in the county of Stockholm.) Armelius B.-Å., *et al.* (ed.), *Vård av ungdomar med sociala problem – en forskningsöversikt.* (The care of youths with social difficulties, a review of the research.) Falköping. Statens Institutionsstyrelse/Liber Utbildning AB.

Bondeson, U. (1977): Kriminalvård i frihet. (Dealing with offenders without institutionalising them.) Stockholm: Liber Förlag

Borell, K. and Johansson, R. (1996): *Samhället som nätverk.* (Society as a network.) Lund: Studentlitteratur.

Börjesson, B. (1968): *Om påföljdens verkningar.* (On the effects of sentences.) Stockholm: Almqvist and Wiksell.

Bott, E. (1955): 'Urban families: conjugal roles and social networks.' *Human Relations* 8, 345–383.

Brantingham, P. J. and Brantingham, P. L. (1984): *Patterns in Crime.* New York: Macmillan Publishing Company.

Box, S. (1983): *Power, Crime and Mystification.* London: Tavistock.

Breckinridge, S. P. and Abbot, E. (1917): *The Delinquent Child and the Home.* New York: Russell Sage.

Brottsförebyggande rådet (1986): *Läktarvåld, orsaker och åtgärder.* (Violence on the terraces, causes and responses.) Utredningsrapport. 1986: 3. Stockholm: Brottsförebyggande rådet.

Brottsförebyggande rådet (1998): *Kriminal Statistik 1997.* (Criminal Statistics. Official Statistics of Sweden.) BRÅ-rapport 1998: 3. Stockholm: Brottsförebyggande rådet.

Burgess, R. L. and Akers, R. L. (1966): 'A differential association-reinforcement theory of criminal behavior.' *Social Problems* 14: 128–147.

Bureau of Justice Statistics. (1984): *Criminal Victimization in the United States, 1982.* National Crime Survey Report no. NCJ-92820. Washington, DC: US Government Printing Office.

Carlsson, G. (1972): *Unga lagöverträdare II. Familj, skola och samhälle i belysning av officiella data.* (Young offenders II. Family, school and society in the light of official data.) Statens offentliga utredningar 1972: 75. Stockholm Justice Department.

Cartwright, D. (1959): *Studies in Social Power.* Ann Arbor, Mich.: Institute for Social Research

Cartwright, D. and Harary, F. (1956): 'Structural balance: A generalization of Haider's theory.' *Psychological Review.* 63, 277–292.

Chin, K.-L. (1991): 'Chinese gangs and extortion.' In Huff, R. C. (ed.), *Gangs in America.* Newbury Park: Sage Publications

Clark, R. V. and Cornish, D. B. (eds.) (1983): *Crime Control in Britain.* Albany, NY: State University of New York Press.

Cloward, R. A. and Ohlin, L. E. (1960): *Delinquency and Opportunity.* Glencoe, Ill.: Free Press.

Cohen, A. K. (1955): *Delinquent Boys: The Culture of the Gang.* Glencoe, Ill.: Free Press.

Cohen, L. E. and Felson, M. (1979): Social change and crime rate trends: A routine activity approach. *American Sociological Review,* 44, 588–608.

Coleman, J. S., Katz, E. and Menzel, H. (1957): The diffusion of an innovation among physicians. *Sociometry,* 20, 253 -270.

Coleman, J. S., Katz, E. and Menzel, H. (1966): *Medical Innovation.* Indianapolis: Bobbs-Merrill.

Conwey, K. P. and McCord, J. (1997): 'Co-offender influence on juvenile violence: A longitudinal study.' Paper given at The American Society of Criminology 49th Annual Meeting. San Diego November 1997.

Costello, B. (1997): 'On the logical adequacy of cultural deviance theories.' *Theoretical Criminology.* Vol 1. No 4: 403–428.

Curry, G. D. and Decker, S. H. (1998*): Confronting Gangs. Crime and Community.* Los Angeles: Roxbury Publishing Company.

Decker, S. (1996): 'Deviant homicide: A new look at the role of motives in victim–offender relationships.' *Journal of Research in Crime and Delinquency.* 33: 427–449.

Decker, S. H. and Van Winkle, B. (1996): *Life in the Gang. Family, Friends, and Violence.* Cambridge University Press.

Dishion, T. J., Capaldi, D., Spracklen, K. M. and Li, F. (1995): 'Peer ecology of male adolescent drug use.' *Development and Psychopathology.* 7: 803–824.

Dunér, A. and Haglund, B. (1974): *Tonårspojkar och brott.* (Teenage boys and crime.) Utbildningsforskning. SÖ rapport 8. Stockholm: Skolstyrelsen.

Ehn, B. (1992): 'Youth and multiculturalism.' In Palmgren, C., Lövgren, K. and Bolin, G. (eds.), *Ethnicity and Youth Culture.* Stockholm: Akademitryck.

Ehn, B. (1995): *Öppenhet och slutenhet.*(Open and closed.) Norrköping: Statens Invandrarverk.

Einstadter, W. and Henry, S. (1995): *Criminological Theory: An Analysis of its Underlying Assumptions.* Fort Worth, Texas: Harcourt Brace College Publishers.

Elliott, D., Huizinga, D. and Ageton, S. (1985*): Explaining Delinquency and Drug Use.* Beverley Hills, Calif.: Sage Publications.

Empey, LM. T. and Stafford, M. C. (1991): *American Delinqency.* Belmont, Calif.: Sage.

Estrada, F. (1999): Ungdomsbrottlighet som samhällsproblem. Utveckling uppmärksamhet och reaktion. (Juvenile delinquency as social problem. Evolution, media attention and societal response.) Stockholm University.

Fattah, E. A. (1991*): Understanding Criminal Victimization. An Introduction to Theoretical Victimology.* Scarborough, Ontario: Prentice-Hall.

Ferrell, J. and Sanders, C. R. (1995): *Cultural Criminology.* Boston: Northeastern University Press.

Fondén, C. and Sarnecki, J. (1996): *Brottsliga ungdomsnätverk i Stockholm 1995* (Delinquent youth networks in Stockholm in 1995.) Samordningskansliet för brottsförebyggande åtgärder. Stockholm: Stockholms Stad.

Frank, O. (1991): Statistical analysis of change in networks. *Statistica Neerlandica.* Vol. 45, no. 3.

Frank, O. (1999): *Measuring Social Capital by Network Capacity Indices.* Research Report 1999: 9. Stockholm University.

Frank, O. and Nowicki, K. (1993): 'Exploratory statistical analysis of networks' in J. Gimbel, J. W. Kennedy and L. V. Quintas (eds.). *Quo Vadis, Graph Theory? Annals of Discrete Mathematics,* 55, 349–366.

Freeman, L. (1979): 'Centrality in social networks, conceptual classification'. *Social Networks.* 1, 215–239.

Glueck, S. and Glueck, E. T. (1940): *Juvenile Delinquents Grown Up.* New York: Commonwealth Fund.

Glueck, S. and Glueck, E. T. (1950): *Unraveling Juvenile Delinquency.* New York: Commonwealth Fund.

Gold, M. (1970): *Delinquent Behavior in an American City.* Belmont, Calif.: Brooks/Cole.

Gottfredson, M. and Hirschi, T. (1990): *A General Theory of Crime*. Stanford, Calif.: Stanford University Press.

Government of Japan (1988): *Summary of the White Paper on Crime* 1998. Tokyo: Research and Training Institute, Ministry of Justice.

Granovetter, M. (1974): *Getting a Job*. Cambridge, Mass.: Harvard University Press.

Hagedorn, J. and Macon, P. (1988): *People and Folks: Gangs, Crime, and the Underclass in a Rustbelt City*. Chicago: Lake View Press.

Hamm, M (1994): *Hate Crime: International Perspectives on Causes and Control*. Northern Highland Heights, Ky: Academy of Criminal Justice Sciences, Northern Kentucky University.

Hedenbro, G. (1977): *Att informera om avvikande grupper. En genomgång av några olika samhällsområden*. (How to provide information on deviant groups.) Brottsförebyggande rådet 1977: 2. Stockholm: Liber.

Hedström, P., Sandell, R. and Stern, L. (1997): *Spatial Diffusion and Agitation: Multi-Level Networks and the Growth of the Swedish Social Democratic Party*. Stockholm University.

Hedström, P. and Swedberg, R. (1998): *Social Mechanisms. An Analytical Approach to Social Theory. Studies in Rationality and Social Change*. Cambridge University Press.

Hindelang, M. J. (1973): 'Causes of delinquency: a detailed replication and extension.' *Social Problems*. 20: 471–487.

Hindelang, M, J. (1976): 'With a little help from their friends: group participation in reported delinquency.' *British Journal of Criminology* 16: 109–125.

Hirschi, T. (1969): *Causes of Delinquency*. Berkeley: University of California Press.

Hofer, H. von (1985): *Brott och straff i Sverige*. (Crime and punishment in Sweden) Urval nr 18. Stockholm Statistiska Centralbyrån.

Hofer, H. von, Sarnecki, J.and Tham, H. (1997): 'Minorities, crime, and criminal justice in Sweden.' Marshall, I. H. (ed.). *Minorities, Migrants and Crime. Diversity and Similarity Across Europe and the United States*, Thousand Oaks, Calif.: Sage Publications.

Hofer, H. von and Tham, H. (2000): 'Stöld i Sverige' 1831–1998. (Theft in Sweden.) ed. T. Goldberg, *Samhällsproblem*. Lund: Studentlitteratur.

Hood, R. and Sparks, R. (1970): *Key Issues in Criminology*. London: Word University Library.

Horowitz, R. (1991): 'Sociological perspectives on gangs: conflicting definitions and concepts.' In Huff, R. C. (ed.). *Gangs in America*. Newbury Park: Sage Publications.

Huff, R. C. (ed.) (1991; 1996): *Gangs in America*. Newbury Park: Sage Publications.

Ianni, F. (1975): *Black Mafia: Ethnic Succession in Organized Crime*. New York: Pocket Books.

Jansson, I. (1997): *On Statistical Modeling of Social Networks*. Stockholm: Stockholm University.

Johansen, P. O. (1996): *Nettverk i gråsonen: et perspektiv på organisert kriminalitet* (Networks in the grey zone. A perspective on organized crime) Oslo: Ad Botam Gyldendal

Johnson, R. E. (1979): *Juvenile Delinquency and Its Origins*. Cambridge University Press.

Jonsson, G. (1971): Den teoretiska bakgrunden. (The theoretical background.) *1956 års klientelundersökning rörande ungdomsbrottslingar*. Unga lagöverträdare Undersökningsmetodik. Brottsdebut och återfall. Stockholm: Statens offentliga utredningar; 1971: 49.

Junger, M. (1990): *Delinquency and Ethnicity*. Boston: Klower.

Kerr, J. H. (1994): *Understanding Soccer Hooliganism*. Buckingham: Open University Press.

Killias, M (1989): 'Criminality among second-generation immigrants in western Europe: A review of the evidence'. *Criminal Justice Review* 14 (1), 13–42.

Klein, M. W. (1971): *Street Gangs and Street Workers*. Englewood Cliffs, New Jersey. Prentice-Hall.

Klein, M. W. (1995): *The American Street Gang. Its Nature, Prevalence, and Control*. New York: Oxford University Press.

Klein, M. W. and Crawford, L. Y. (1967): 'Groups, gangs and cohesiveness'. *Journal of Research in Crime and Delinquency* 4: 142: 65.

Klein, M. W., Kerner, H.-J., Maxson, C. L. and Weitekamp, E. G. M. (eds.) (2001): *The Eurogangs Paradox: Street Gangs and Youth Groups in the U.S. and Europe*. Dordrecht: Klower.

Knox, G. W. (1991): *An Introduction to Gangs*. Berrien Springs, MI: Vande Vere Publishing.

Kontos, L. (2000): 'Scientific Overstatement on the Literature of Gangs'. A paper presented to the 52nd Annual Meeting of the American Society of Criminology. San Francisco, 15–18 November. Session 37.

Kornhauser, R. (1978): *Social Sources of Delinquency: An Appraisal of Analytic Models*. University of Chicago Press.

Krohn, M. D. and Massey, J. L. (1980): 'Social Control and Delinquent Behavior: An Examination of the Elements of the Social Bond.' *The Sociological Quarterly* 21 (Autumn 1980): 529–43.

Lange, A. (1995): *Invandrarna om diskriminering. En enkät- och en intervjuundersökning om etnisk diskriminering på uppdrag av Diskriminerings ombudsmannen. (DO).* (Immigrants on discrimination.) Stockholm: Centrum för Invandrarforskning (CEIFO)/Statistiska Centralbyrån.

Länskriminalpolisens Integrationsgrupp (1997): *Rapport om kriminella gäng, rasism och främlingsfientlighet*. (Report on delinquent gangs, racism and anti-immigrant hostility) Stockholm: Länspolismyndighet.

Länskriminalpolisens Integrationsgrupp (1998): *Rapport om kriminella gäng, rasism och främlingsfientlighet*. (Report on delinquent gangs, racism and anti-immigrant hostility) Stockholm: Länspolismyndighet.

Le Blanc, M. and Caplan, A (1993): 'Theoretical Formalization, a Necessity: The Example of Hirschi's Bonding Theory.' In Adler, F. and Laufer, W. (eds.). *New Directions in Criminological Theory*. New Brunswick: Transaction Publishers.

Lee, N. H. (1969): *The Search for an Abortionist*. University of Chicago Press.

The Link Notebook. User's Guide. (1995): Version 4.00. Cambridge: i2 Limited.

Loeber, R. and Farrington, D. P. (Eds.) (1998): *Serious and Violent Juvenile Offenders. Risk Factors and Successful Interventions*. Thousand Oaks, Calif.: Sage Publications.

Loftin, C. (1986): 'Assaultive violence as contagious process.' *Bulletin of the New York Academy of Medicine* 62: 550–555.

McLeode, J. (1987): *Ain't No Making' It: Leveled Aspirations in a Low-Income Neighborhood*. Boulder, Colo.: Westview.

Marshall, I. H. (ed.) (1997): *Minorities, Migrants, and Crime. Diversity and Similarity Across Europe and the United States*. Thousand Oaks, Calif.: Sage Publications.

Marsden, P. V. and Friedkin, N. E. (1994): 'Network studies of social influence.' In Wasserman, S. and Galaskiewicz, J. (eds.): *Advances in Social Network Analysis. Research in the Social and Behavioral Sciences.* Thousand Oaks. Sage Publications.

Martens, P. L. (1992): 'Criminal and other antisocial behavior among persons with immigrant and Swedish background – a research note.' In B. Åkerman *et al.* (eds.), *Studies of Stockholm's Cohort* (pp. 83–108), Project Metropolitan, Research Report No. 39. Stockholm University.

Martens, P. L. (1998): *Brottslighet och utsatthet för brott bland personer födda i Sverige och i utlandet: resultat från en intervjuundersökning.* (Crime and exposure to crime among individuals born in Sweden and abroad: results from an interview study.) Stockholm: Brottsförebyggande rådet (BRÅ): Fritzes

Matza, D. (1964): *Delinquency and Drift.* New York: Wiley.

Merton, R. K. (1938): 'Social structure and anomie.' *American Sociological Review,* 3: 672–682.

Merton, R. K. [1948] (1968): 'The self-fulfilling prophecy.' *Social Theory and Social Structure,* pp. 475–90. New York: The Free Press.

Mill, J. S. (1997): *Mill/Texts, Commentaries Selected and Edited by Alan Ryan.* New York. Norton.

Miller, M. (1999): 'A model to explain the relationship between sexual abuse and HIV risk among women.' *AIDS Care* 1999 Feb. 11(1): 3–20

Miller, W. B. (1958): 'Lower class culture as a generating milieu of gang delinquency.' *Journal of Social Issues* 14: 5–19.

Mitchell, J. C. (1969): 'The concept and use of social networks.' Mitchell, J. C. (ed.). *Social Networks in Urban Situations.* Manchester University Press.

Molina, I. (1997): *Stadens Rasifering. Etnisk boendesegregation i folkhemmet.* (The racialisation of the city. Ethnic residential segregation in the context of the Swedish welfare state.) Uppsala University.

Moore, J. W. (1991): *Going Down to the Barrio: Homeboys and Homegirls in Change.* Philadelphia: Temple University.

Morash, M (1983): 'Gangs, groups and delinquency.' *British Journal of Criminology* 23: 309–331.

Moreno, J. L. (1934): *Who Shall Survive?: Foundations of Sociometry, Group Psychotherapy, and Sociodrama*: Washington, DC: Nervous and Mental Disease Publishing Co.

Morris, M. (1994): 'Epidemiology and social networks. modeling structured diffusion.' Wasserman, S. and Galaskiewicz, J. (eds.): *Advances in Social Network Analysis. Research in the Social and Behavioral Sciences.* Thousand Oaks, Calif.: Sage Publications

Murray, C. and Cox, L. A. (1979): *Beyond Probation: Juvenile Corrections and the Chronic Delinquent.* Beverley Hills, CA: Sage.

Ohlsson, L. B. (1997): *Bilden av den 'Hotfulla ungdomen'. Om ungdomsproblem och om fastställandet och upprätthållandet av samhällets moraliska gränser.* (The image of the 'Youth threat'. On youth problems and the setting and maintenance of moral limits in society.) Lund: Värpinge Ord and Text.

Olofsson, B. (1967): *Brottslighet bland skolbarn i Örebro.* (Criminality among schoolchildren in Örebro.) Stockholm: Örebroprojektet.

Olofsson, B. (1971): *Vad var det vi sa! Om kriminellt och konformt beteende bland skolpojkar.* (What did we tell you! On criminal and conformist behavior among schoolboys.) Stockholm: Utbildningsförlaget.

Padilla, F. M. (1992): *The Gang as American Enterprise*. New Brunswick, NY: Rutgers University Press.

Pettersson, T. (1998a): 'Registrerad brottslighet hos individer som bedömdes vara de mest våldsbenägna supportrarna i Stockholm.' (The registered delinquency of individuals judged to be the most violence-prone football supporters in Stockholm.) *Trygghet och trivsel vid idrottsevenemang – om insatser mot idrotts anknutet våld*. Ds 1998: 38. Bilaga 2. Inrikesdepartementet. Stockholm

Pettersson, T. (1998b): *Etnicitet och brottsliga nätverk bland ungdomar i Stockholm som misstänks för våldsbrott*. (Ethnic background and criminal networks among youths suspected of violent offences in Stockholm.) Barn – och ungdomsdelegationen. Stockholm: Regeringskansliet.

Rées Nordenstad, H. du (1998): 'Våld och oroligheten i samband med idrottsevenemang, polisens roll.' (Violence and disturbances at sporting events, the role of the police.) *Trygghet och trivsel vid idrottsevenemang – om insatser mot idrotts anknutet våld*. Ds 1998: 38. Bilaga 1. Inrikesdepartementet. Stockholm.

Regionalplane- och trafikkontoret (The Office of Regional Planning and Urban Transportation). (1991): 'Invandare 1990 12 31 i Stockholms län.' (Immigrants in the county of Stockholm on 31/12/1990.) *Statistik över Stockholms län no. 8 1991*. Stockholm: Stockholms läns landsting.

Reiss, A. J. Jr. (1980): 'Understanding changes in crime rates.' In Fienberg, S. E., Reiss, A. J. Jr. (eds.), *Indicators of Crime and Criminal Justice: Quantitative Studies*. Washington, DC: Bureau of Justice Statistics.

Reiss, A. J. Jr. (1986): 'Co-offending and criminal careers.' Blumstein, A., *et al.* (eds.), *Criminal Careers and 'Career Criminals'*. Washington, DC: National Academy Press

Reiss, A. J. Jr. (1988): 'Co-offending and Criminal Careers.' Tonry, M. and Morris, N. (eds.), *Crime and Justice: An Annual Review of Research*. University of Chicago Press.

Reiss, A. J. Jr. and Farrington, D. P. (1991): 'Advancing knowledge about co-offending: results from a prospective longitudinal survey of London males.' *Journal of Criminal Law and Criminology*, 82: 360–395.

Ring, J (1999): *Hem och skola, kamrater och brott*. (Home and school, peers and delinquency.) Stockholm University.

Roethlisberger, F. J. and Dickson, W. J. (1934): *Management and the Worker: Technical vs. Social Organization in an Industrial City*. Boston, MA: Publication of the Graduate School of Business and Administration, Harvard University

Säkerhetspolisen (State security police) (1996): *Brottslighet kopplad till rikets säkerhet. 1994/95*. (Crimes linked to national security issues 1994/95.) Stockholm. Rikspolisstyrelsen

Säkerhetspolisen (State security police) (1997): *Brottslighet kopplad till rikets säkerhet. 1995/96*. (Crimes linked to national security issues 1995/96.) Stockholm. Rikspolisstyrelsen

Säkerhetspolisen (State security police) (1998): *Brottslighet kopplad till rikets säkerhet. 1997*. (Crimes linked to national security issues 1997.) Stockholm. Rikspolisstyrelsen

Sampson, R. J. and Groves, B. W. (1989): 'Community structure and crime. Testing social disorganization theory.' *American Journal of Sociology*. 94: 774–802.

Sanchez Jankowski, M. (1991): *Islands in the Street. Gangs and American Urban Society*. Berkeley: University of California Press

Sarnecki, J. (1978): *Ungdomsgårdarna i Stockholm.* (Juvenile care facilities in Stockholm.) Sociologiska Institutionen. Stockholms Universitet

Sarnecki, J. (1982): Brottslighet och kamratrelationer. Studie av ungdomsbrottsligheten i en svensk kommun. (Delinquency and peer relations. a study of juvenile crime in a Swedish municipality.) Rapport 1982: 5. Stockholm: Brottsförebyggande rådet.

Sarnecki, J. (1983a): Fritid och brottsligheten. (Leisure time and crime.) Brottsförebyggande rådet. Rapport 1993: 7. Stockholm. Liber, Allmänna Förlaget.

Sarnecki, J. (1983b): *Brottsliga ungdomsgäng.* (Delinquent Juvenile Gangs.) Stockholm. Brottsförebyggande rådet. Rapport 1983: 2.

Sarnecki, J. (1985): *Predicting Social Maladjustment.* Stockholm: The National Council for Crime Prevention. Sweden: Allmänna Förlaget.

Sarnecki, J. (1986): *Delinquent Networks.* Stockholm The National Council for Crime Prevention. Sweden: Allmänna Förlaget.

Sarnecki, J. (1987): *Skolan och brottligheten.* (School and Crime.) Stockholm: Carlsson Bokförlag.

Sarnecki, J. (1990a): 'Delinquent networks in Sweden.' *Journal of Quantitative Criminology,* vol. 6, No 1: 31–51

Sarnecki, J. (1990b): *Socialanpassning och samhällssyn.* (Social adjustment and social perspective.) BRÅ-rapport 1990: 4. Stockholm: Allmänna Förlaget.

Sarnecki, J. (1995): 'Peter Pan och Hans moderna vänner i landet Aldrig – Aldrig.' (Peter Pan and his modern friends in Never Never Land.) *LOCUS Tidskrift för barn- och ungdomsvetenskap* Nr 2 1995: 5–19

Sarnecki, J. (1996): 'Problemprofiler hos ungdomar inskrivna på särskilda ungdomshem i Stockholms län åren 1990–1994.' (Problem-profiles among youths admitted to secure care facilities in the county of Stockholm 1990–1994.) Armelius B-Å., m.fl. (ed.). *Vård av ungdomar med sociala problem – en forskningsöversikt.* (The care of youths with social difficulties, a review of the research.) Falköping. Statens Institutionsstyrelse/Liber Utbildning AB.

Sarnecki, J. (1997): 'The dilemma of control, western perspectives.' In Raska, E. and Saar, J. (eds.), *Crime and Criminology at the End of the Century.* Tallinn: Publishing Office of Estonian National Defense and Public Service Academy. pp. 36–49.

Scott, J. (1991): *Social Network Analysis. A Handbook.* London: Sage Publications

SFS 1990: *52 Lag med särskilda bestämelser om vård ar unga.* (Special Youth Treatment Act.) Sveriges Lagar Göteborg: Fakta Info Direkt.

Shannon, D. (1998): *Karriärprofilskillnader hos ett urval av problembelastade ungdomar i Stockholm.* (Career profile variations in a sample of problem youths in Stockholm.) Stockholm: Stockholm University.

Shaw, C. R. and McKay, H. D. (1931): *Male Juvenile Delinquency as Group Behavior. Report on the Causes of Crime.* No 13. National Commission on Law Observance and the Administration of Justice. Washington, DC: Government Printing Office.

Shaw, C. R. and McKay, H. D. (1942): *Juvenile Delinquency and Urban Areas.* University of Chicago Press.

Sheldon, H. D. (1898): 'The institutional activities of American children'. *The American Journal of Psychology,* vol. 9, No. 4: 425–448.

Sherif, M. and Sherif, C. M. (1964): *Reference Groups: Exploration into Conformity and Deviation of Adolescents.* New York: Harper and Row.

Shikita, M. and Tsuchiya, S. (1990): *Crime and Criminal Policy in Japan from 1926 to 1988. Analysis and Evaluation of the Showa Era.* Kasumigaseki, Japan: Criminal Policy Society.

Short, J. F. Jr. (1990): *Delinquency and Society.* Englewood Cliffs, NJ: Prentice-Hall.

Short, J. F. Jr. (1996): *Gangs and Adolescent Violence.* Boulder, Colo.: Center for the Study and Prevention of Violence.

Short, J. F. Jr. (1998a): *Poverty, Ethnicity and Violent Crime.* Boulder, Colo.: Westview Press.

Short, J. F. Jr. (1998b): 'The level of explanation problem revised. The American Society of Criminology 1997 Presidential Address. *Criminology'.* Vol. 36. No. 1, 1998: 3–36.

Short, J. F. Jr. and Strodtbeck, F. L. (1965*): Group Process and Gang Delinquency.* The University of Chicago Press.

Skogan, W. (1990*): Disorder and Decline: Crime and the Spiral of Decay in American Neighborhoods.* New York: Free Press.

SOU 1996: 156: *Bostadspolitik 2000 – från produktions- till boendepolitik. Slutbetänkande av bostadspolitiska utredningen.* (Housing policy 2000 – from production to housing policy. Report from the Inquiry into Housing Policy.) Stockholm: Fritzes Förlaget

Spergel, I. A. (1966): *Street Gang Work: Theory and Practice.* Reading, Mass.: Addison-Wesley.

Spergel, I. A. (1995): *The Youth Gang Problem: a Community Approach.* New York: Oxford University Press.

Sullivan, M. (1989): *'Getting Paid': Youth Crime and Work in the Inner City.* Ithaca: Cornell University Press

Sutherland, E. H. (1939): *Principals of Criminology,* 3rd edn. Philadelphia. Lippincott.

Sutherland, E. H. (1947): *Principals of Criminology,* 4th edn. Philadelphia. Lippincott.

Sutherland, E. H., Cressey, D. R. and Luckenbill, D. F. (1992): *Principals of Criminology,* eleventh edn. Dix Hills, New York. Deneral Hall.

Svedhem, L. (ed.) (1985): *Nätverksterapi, teori och praktik.* (Network therapy, theory and practice.) Malmö: Carlssons.

Svedhem, L. (1991): *Social nätverk och beteendeproblem i skolan hos 11–13-åringar. En teoretisk och empirisk grund för nätverksterapi.* (Social networks and behavioral problems of eleven- to thirteen-year-olds in school. A theoretical and empirical basis for network therapy.) Stockholm: Carlssons.

Sveri, B. (1980): *Utlänningars brottslighet: en jämförelse mellan om för grövre brott övertygade personer 1967 och 1977.* (Aliens' crime: A comparison of persons convicted of serious offences in 1967 and 1977.) Stockholm: Kriminalvetenskapliga institutet. Stockholm University.

Sveri, K. (1960): *Kriminalitet og alder.* (Criminality and age.) Stockholm: Almqvist and Wiksell.

Sykes, G. M. and Matza, D. (1957): 'Techniques of neutralization. A theory of delinquency.' *American Sociological Review,* 22: 664–70.

Thornberry, T. P., Lizotte, A. J., Krohn, M. D., Farnworth, M., and Jang, S. J. (1991): 'Testing interactional theory: An examination of reciprocal causal relationships among family, school, and delinquency.' *Journal of Criminal Law and Criminology,* 82: 3–33.

Thrasher, F. (1927): *The Gang.* University of Chicago Press.

Tonry, M. (ed.) (1997): *Ethnicity, Crime and Immigration. Comparative and Cross-national Perspectives. Crime and Justice. A Review of Research. Year 21.* The University of Chicago Press.

Tremblay, P. (1993): 'Searching for suitable co-offenders.'. In Clarke, R. V. and Felson, M. (eds.), *Routine Activity and Rational Choice Advances in Criminological Theory,* vol. 5. New Brunswick, NJ: Transaction Publishers.

Ward, M. (1998): *Barn and Brott av vår tid? Självdeklarerad ungdomsbrottslighet 1991–1996.* (Children and Crimes of Our Time? Self-Reported Juvenile Delinquency 1991–1996.) Stockholm University.

Waring, E. J. (1994): 'Co-offending in White Collar Crimes: A Network Approach'. Unpublished dissertation presented to the Faculty of the Graduate School, Yale University. Ann Arbor, MI: University Microfilms International.

Warr, M. (1996): 'Organization and Instigation in Delinquent Groups.' *Criminology,* vol. 34, No. 1.

Wasserman, S. and Faust, K. (1994): *Social Network Analysis: Methods and Applications.* Cambridge University Press

Wasserman, S. and Galaskiewicz, J. (eds.) (1994): *Advances in Social Network Analysis. Research in the Social and Behavioral Sciences.* Thousand Oaks: Sage Publications.

West, W. G. (1977): 'Serious Thieves: Lower-Class Adolescent Males in a Short-term Deviant Occupation.' In Vaz, E. and Lodhi, A. (eds.), *Crime and Delinquency in Canada.* Toronto: Prentice-Hall.

Westin, C. and Dingu-Kyrklund, E. (1998): *Widening Gaps. The Swedish RIMET Report* for 1997. Stockholm: CEIFO.

Wikström, P-O. H. (1991): *Urban Crime, Criminals and Victims. The Swedish Experience in an Anglo-American Perspective.* New York. Springer-Verlag.

Wilson, W. J. (1987): *The Truly Disadvantaged.* University of Chicago Press

William-Olsson, A. (1998): *Ängengänget. En studie av brottsligt aktivit nätverk av unga män.* (The Ängen gang. A study of an actively delinquent network of young men.) Stockholm: Kriminologiska institutionen, Stockholm University.

Wolfgang, M. E. (1958): *Patterns in Criminal Homicide.* Philadelphia: University of Pennsylvania Press.

Yablonsky, L (1962): *The Violent Gang.* Baltimore: Penguin Books.

Index